Allegany to Appomattox

Allegany to Appomattox

THE LIFE AND LETTERS OF
PRIVATE WILLIAM WHITLOCK
OF THE 188TH NEW YORK VOLUNTEERS

Valgene Dunham

FOREWORD BY BILL POTTER

SYRACUSE UNIVERSITY PRESS

For a listing of books published and distributed by Syracuse University Press,
visit our website at SyracuseUniversityPress.syr.edu.

ISBN: 978-0-8156-1011-3

Library of Congress Cataloging-in-Publication Data

Dunham, Valgene L., 1940–

Allegany to Appomattox : the life and letters of Private William Whitlock of the
188th New York Volunteers / Valgene Dunham ; foreword by Bill Potter. — First edition.

pages cm

Includes bibliographical references and index.

ISBN 978-0-8156-1011-3 (cloth : alk. paper) 1. Whitlock, William, 1829–1865—
Correspondence. 2. United States. Army. New York Infantry Regiment, 188th (1864–1865)
3. New York—History—Civil War, 1861–1865—Regimental histories. 4. United States—
History—Civil War, 1861–1865—Personal narratives. 5. Soldiers—New York (State)—
Correspondence. 6. Appomattox Campaign, 1865. 7. Virginia—History—Civil War,
1861–1865—Campaigns. 8. Allegany (N.Y.)—Biography. 9. Whitlock family. I. Title.

E523.5188th .D86 2013

973.7'38—dc23   2012050460

Manufactured in the United States of America

*To Betty Anne, who helped navigate
the back roads of Virginia and fifty years of life,*

and to Howard Mark Whitney, the family "Collector"

People will not look forward to posterity, who never look backward to their ancestors.

—Edmund Burke, "On the Causes
of the Present Discontents"

I can never turn their tiny leaves, or even take one in my hand, without the actual army sights and hot emotions of the time rushing like a river in full tide through me. Each line, each scrawl, each memorandum, has its history. Some pang of anguish—some tragedy, profounder than ever poet wrote. Out of them arise active and breathing forms. They summon up, even in this silent and vacant room as I write, not only the sinewy regiments and brigades, marching or in camp, but the countless phantoms of those who fell and were hastily buried by wholesale in the battle-pits, or whose dust and bones have been since removed to the National Cemeteries of the land, especially through Virginia and Tennessee.

—Walt Whitman,
"Memoranda, &c."

War is the sum total of its individual stories, from comedy to romance to drama to tragedy.

—Joseph T. Glatthaar,
General Lee's Army

VALGENE DUNHAM is a native of Jamestown, New York, was raised in Cherry Creek and Westfield, New York, and finished grades 1 through 12 in Lorain, Ohio. Following a degree from Houghton College, Houghton, New York, and graduate degrees from Syracuse University, he pursued a career in plant biochemistry with research/teaching positions at Purdue University, State University of New York at Fredonia, and Western Kentucky University. After a tenure of thirteen years in administrative positions at Coastal Carolina University, Dr. Dunham retired and currently holds the position of Distinguished Professor Emeritus at Coastal Carolina University. *Allegany to Appomattox* is his first major publication outside of the sciences.

Contents

Illustrations

Maps and Tables

Foreword

Many years ago my grandfather gave me an old photograph taken in the first decade of the twentieth century. Twenty-one dark-uniformed old men from western New York sit or stand in front of a tall granite war memorial flanked by a large cannon and surrounded by thousands of graves. Each face is resolute, though the presence of many walking sticks and canes testifies to the irretrievable past when their resolution was translated into ardor for their cause and when instead of the peacefulness of a Memorial Day graveyard they experienced the roar and flash of combat. Looking at the old, bearded warriors always reminds me of the African adage that when a man dies, a thousand stories die with him.

Not every experience that engulfs young men at war goes untold. No doubt some of the men in the picture regaled their sons and grandsons with the stories of the remembered past, incidents that changed their lives forever. Perhaps some of them wrote impassioned letters to their parents or wives from distant fields, describing landscapes and people they would otherwise have never seen had not the hand of Providence brought them to unknown places to kill or be killed by other unknown young men.

Around the same time that my grandfather identified those old veterans in the picture and in the same beautiful Allegheny River valley where I grew up, a cousin of mine showed me a cache of letters written by his great-great-grandfather during the Civil War. My direct ancestor of the same generation was seated in that photograph taken some forty years after the war, but his was not.

Killed in Virginia in 1865 in an anonymous woodlot during an attack in freezing weather, Will Whitlock, a thirty-five-year-old farmer with a wife and four children, was silenced forever and buried in a soldier's grave. I held in my hands the cherished letters that a loving family had received from Will and had kept on a shelf or in a drawer since 1865.

When I hold such artifacts from the past, I feel a connection to that generation; they hardly seem gone and may be just around the corner, telling their stories. Those accounts resonate with soldiers and families of every generation. The letter writers speak of sacrifice and loss; they ask questions of their family regarding the children's health and the state of the crops. They wonder about the meaning of the war they are in, and they assure their loved ones or at least express the hope that they will do their duty, stand in the day of battle, and come out alright.

The letters of the life and times of Will Whitlock are a distant echo of the many thousands of men who flocked to the colors, North and South, learned to march thousands of miles, coped with the vicissitudes of camp life, sprang to arms when the bugle called, and marched to the sound of the guns. Valgene Dunham, who descends from Will and other settlers of the Allegheny's picturesque valley who sent many sons to war in the early 1860s, has interpreted these soldier letters in their social and historical environments. He senses the disruption of the timeless rhythms of the agrarian life by the call to war to preserve the Union. He seeks to know what these men knew and unintentionally preserved for posterity in their letters. The men and women of that bygone era were under no illusions regarding the shortness of life. Although most of them passed in the vapors arising from the rivers and creeks of home, a few were called upon to vanish in the smoke of gunfire.

Bill Potter
Historian and Curator
American History Guild
Roswell, Georgia, 2011

Preface

The large Victorian brick farmhouse constructed in 1895 and the associated barns, milk house, and sawmill were once the pride and joy of the Whitlock and Whitney families. In 1897, William Whitlock's oldest son, Stanley, moved his family into the large house at the corner of Five Mile Road and Morgan Hollow Road outside of Allegany, New York. The former Elmwood Farm was characterized by huge American elm trees and numerous barns. Today, the statuesque elms and barns are gone, and the house is slowly being destroyed by the elements. Sparked by a new interest in family history, Howard Mark Whitney began to search the old house for items telling that history when he moved into the house in 1978. While looking through the old and dusty attic a year later, he discovered a box between the rafters. The hinged letter box contained documents, pictures, and letters of the Whitlock and Whitney families. Among these documents were thirty-nine letters written by William Whitlock to his wife, Mary Eliza Trowbridge Whitlock, during the Civil War. William Whitlock was Mark's and my great-great-grandfather. In addition to the letters, the box contained William Whitlock's military and other family historical documents. With increasing interest, Mark read through the letters and the other documents, and in anticipation of finding additional items of family history he revisited the attic about six months later. He was attracted to a single paper he spotted between the dusty rafters of the old house. Mark had found another letter that was written by a friend of William's in the 188th New York Volunteers to William's brother. This letter detailed how and when William was killed in the Battle of Hatcher's Run II, February

6, 1865. This amazing find tied the Whitlock letters together and pointed Mark toward a clearer understanding of William Whitlock's life and furthered Mark's quest for knowledge of the family over the decades. In the early 1980s, Mark's cousin Bill Potter, a former resident of Allegany and the author of the foreword to this book, transcribed the letters. Mark gave a copy of the Potter transcripts to my mother, Viola Whitlock Dunham. In 2005, while my sister, Vaughn Dunham Estep, and I were talking about family documents and pictures left by our mother, she asked me if I had seen the letters left by William Whitlock, our great-great-grandfather. She left the table and returned with the Potter transcripts, which immediately sparked my interest.

In this book, which is based on these forty letters, I tell the story of a thirty-five-year-old farmer-lumberman, husband, and father of four children who enlisted in the 188th New York in Allegany, New York. His enlistment was late in the war, September 1864, and he was killed just two months before General Robert E. Lee surrendered, hence the title *Allegany to Appomattox*. In Will's letters, I have seen his love for his family, his God, and the United States of America. I have also seen his loneliness; his fear of battle, which he admitted to his wife, "Lide"; and his concern for the welfare of his children.

In general, the story is correlated as to the time the letters were written and describes the conditions of life at the battle front and back on the farm. Some of the letters that are not used at the beginning of chapters but are frequently referred to in the text can be found in appendix C. I have intended to write the story as a "travelogue" so that the reader may see what Will saw or could have seen during his service to the country. My life in the southern United States for more than a quarter of a century has influenced discussions that include both the Union and the Confederate sides of the conflict. Contextual information, added to give the reader background for William's comments and experiences, certainly reflect my "southern exposure," my being raised in a minister's home, and my career in plant molecular biology. I conclude with an epilogue about the future of some of Will's friends during the war and the legacies he left to the Whitlock/Whitney family: faith, a desire for education, and the importance of family.

Valgene Dunham
Conway, SC
August 25, 2012

Acknowledgments

I thank a number of friends and colleagues in Conway, South Carolina, for their encouragement during the writing of the manuscript. I was also encouraged by colleagues at Coastal Carolina University, including Ben Burroughs, regional historian and research specialist, and Aron Goff, computer technologist, who rescued me several times. Rod Gragg, director of the Center for Military and Veterans Studies and adjunct professor of history, has been a valued colleague, adviser, and friend. The staff of the Horry County Memorial Library in Conway was helpful and encouraging. The library staffs at Olean and Allegany, New York, also assisted in research, and Sharon Fellows, historian of Cattaraugus County, New York, assisted in research of members of the 188th New York.

I greatly appreciate the support provided by Donald Housley, emeritus professor of history at Susquehanna University and my former undergraduate roommate at Houghton College. When I informed him that I was writing outside of the sciences, he immediately gave me *A Pocket Guide to Writing in History* by Mary Lynn Rampolla. Other individuals associated with Houghton College, past and present, who have been sources of encouragement and information include President Shirley Mullen and Dr. and Mrs. Richard Troutman. I was also aided by Chris Calkins, historian at Sailor's Creek Historical Battlefield, who assisted in the confirmation of William Whitlock's burial site, and staff members at Five Forks and Poplar Grove National Cemetery. Gary Williams, clerk of the Circuit Court at Sussex Court House in 2009, took time out of his schedule to help me get historical background on the Weldon Railroad. Hal Jespersen provided the excellent maps for the three battles reported in the book. Peter Whitlock of the Whitlock Family Association was personally helpful with Whitlock genealogy. Steve Wiezbicki, historian for the 169th New York Volunteers, assisted me in outlining an organized plan of research on the history of the 188th. My sister, Vaughn Dunham Estep, and my cousin and his wife, Tony and Joyce Nudd, provided places for me to stay while I was doing research in New York and Pennsylvania. Special appreciation is also extended to Bill Potter and Howard Mark Whitney for their transcription and handling of the Whitlock letters. Both of these men were of great assistance in providing access to the letters and family documents and helpful comments during the writing of the book. Will's letters are currently held by Howard Mark Whitney in Allegany, New York.

I appreciate the staff of Syracuse University Press for the patience and expertise they have displayed in bringing this project to completion.

My thanks are also extended to Annie Barva, manuscript copy editor who specializes in bringing order out of chaos.

Allegany to Appomattox

I

Allegany Atmospheres

Upon entering the United States in the late eighteenth and early nineteenth centuries, many families were attracted to central and western New York. The heavily forested rolling hills and green river valleys, accompanied by the deep Finger Lakes carved out by glaciers long ago, provided a beautiful setting in which to raise a family. The region offered many opportunities to establish employment to support these pioneering families, including various products of agriculture for family and commercial use, forestry, and fishing. The mountains, streams, buildings, and people along this "Southern Tier," extending into western New York along the present Route 17 (Interstate 86), speak of the region's past to the tuned-in listener.

John Whitlock, one of three sons of Reuben and Christina Whitlock of Monmouth, New Jersey (see the family tree in appendix A), apparently heard the call of central New York. After he married Mary Morris on December 26, 1793,[1] they moved to a town at the tip of one of the Finger Lakes, Cayuga Lake, an area that would be named "Tompkins County" in 1817. Records indicate that the couple had five children when they moved, including twin boys, Thomas and Morris, who were born April 24, 1801, in New Jersey (Census Office 1810). This move was quite adventuresome because the area had been under the control of the Saponi and Tutelo tribes of the Cayuga Indians as

---

1. US Census 1810; "John Whitlock Household, Genoa Township" 1810. Series M252, roll 31, p. 80, *National Archives Micropublication Series*, National Archives, Washington, DC.

late as 1789 (Swanton 2003, 74). By an act of early Congress on September 16, 1776, the federal government offered bounty land warrants for veterans of the Revolutionary War. A veteran, if awarded a warrant, had to apply for a land patent, which granted ownership. These land warrants could be transferred to other individuals or sold (K. Powell 2012). Each state also offered land warrants for veterans but also to induce enlistments. In 1781, for example, New York's legislature passed an act that would allow warrants for individuals who enlisted for three years. After restricting the warrants to any of five New York regiments in 1782, a "new military tract of land" was opened in central New York that included the area of what would be Ithaca, New York (Kammen 2004; K. Powell 2012). These land warrants served not only to reward veterans for their service to the new country, but to expand settlements farther west, where new natural resources could be found. It should be noted that these early land warrants were controlled by the wealthy, those connected to power and the newly formed federal government. In addition, early land warrants were confusing because the Native American tribes—the Iroquois in particular—sold land to other tribes that did not belong to them (Jortner 2012, 23). In 1784, the State of New York's delegation to discuss land ownership with the Six Nations brought alcoholic beverages to give to the Iroquois. Federal agents seized the gifts but were themselves seized by the New York sheriffs (Jortner 2012, 52).

Ithaca was a lively frontier town at the southern tip of Cayuga Lake and was known by various names, including "Cayuga City," "Flats," "Markle's Flats," "Sodom," and "Sin City" (Dieckmann 2004). The latter two names arose owing to the town's reputation for horse racing, gambling, Sabbath breaking, profanity, and the use of alcoholic beverages. This new tract, opened in 1782, was surveyed by the state surveyor General Simeon DeWitt. General DeWitt employed a clerk, Robert Harpur, who had a great knowledge of and fascination for Greek and Roman history. Mr. Harpur used this knowledge in advising his employer concerning possible county and town names. The Commission of Lands of New York State, chaired by Governor George Clinton, approved these suggestions, and as a consequence in

1804 the town was named "Ithaca" after the Island of Ithaki, where the Greek hero Ulysses lived ("The Military Tract" 2012). This Greek theme was also used in the naming of a county to the north of Ithaca along the western side of Cayuga Lake, Ulysses County, and of the town Ulysses, also on the west side of the lake.

John and Mary Whitlock established a large family of thirteen children and joined the First Presbyterian Church in Ithaca on June 9, 1816.[2] At this time, the area around the town of Ithaca had densely forested rolling hills, approximately eight hundred feet in elevation, with streams that could be used for grist and lumber mills. Families of European descent began to move to the area and use the natural resources in occupations that they and their ancestors had before arriving in Tompkins County. Owing to this rapid influx of people and the increase in lumbering, tanning, and agriculture, the county was reported as having "improved" three-fourths of its surface before the beginning of the Civil War (Selkreg [1927] 2012).

Both Thomas, one of John and Mary's twin boys, and one of his sons, William, the focus of this book, married women from Rice, New York (renamed Ischua in 1855). At the age of nineteen in 1820, Thomas married Jane Norton, who was two years younger. Between 1830 and 1835, Thomas moved his wife and their six children (see appendix A) to Rice, Jane's hometown. Not only was the town Jane's birthplace and where her family lived, but it was also significantly far enough away from the activity and reputation of Ithaca. More important, the rapidly depleted forests of Tompkins County may have pointed the family to the less developed area around Rice. Rice's topography is characterized by dense forests on rolling hills that reach six hundred feet above the valley of Ischua Creek, which runs through the center of town. By 1861, the town produced the following major commodities: 640 pounds of butter; 33,749 bushels of oats; 19,188 pounds of

2. Jean D. Worden, "Records from the First Presbyterian Church of Ithaca, New York," 1983, Tompkins County New York Church Records, Manuscript no. 4045, Box 27, Cornell Univ. Archives, Ithaca, NY.

maple sugar; and 8,078 bushels of potatoes (F. Ellis [1879] 2004). The census returns of 1855 (Census Office 1855) also indicated that these and other products were produced from improved land, which represented only 37 percent of the land within the town. Thomas and Jane Whitlock lived in Rice (Ischua) for twenty years. I remember trips in the early 1950s from Allegany to Ischua's regional cattle sales with my grandfather, Wesley Dunham, and my cousin Anthony Nudd. While Grandfather was taking care of cattle sales, we boys sold cow dog puppies for fifty cents.

The Thomas Whitlock family grew along with the town, as evidenced by the addition of eight more children, making a total of fourteen (appendix A; Census Office 1850). By the time the Thomas Whitlock family was complete (with Jane's birth in 1841), the family was well established in the region. It is apparent from friendships and resulting marriages that members of the Whitlock family found their way around Cattaraugus County, including the towns of Hinsdale, Humphrey, and Allegany. For example, in the 1830 census of Ithaca, Thomas was mentioned as head of the household at age twenty-nine. Five years later, the 1835 census in Hinsdale listed Thomas as head of a household of four males and five females. Five years later in the 1840 census at Hinsdale, Thomas was listed as head of the household, with all of his children except the two oldest, Freeman (nineteen) and Amanda (seventeen), and the three youngest, two of whom were not yet born (appendix A; see also Census Office 1830, 1835, 1840).

For the Whitlock family, involved in farming and lumbering, this area of western New York held quite a few advantages. The area's vegetation included a variety of maples—the sugar maple conspicuous among them—oaks of several species, the American elm (before Dutch Elm disease), and rich, large cherry amid the green pines and hemlock. I remember playing on and cutting the lawn under huge elm trees in the yard of the Whitlock/Whitney Farm on Five Mile Road in Allegany during the late 1940s and early 1950s.

Because of these trees, the farm's original name was "Elmwood Farm." Down the road at the Dunham Farm, I froze my young hands on chains while "helping" or getting in the way of my grandfather,

1. Whitlock/Whitney Farm, 1955. William Whitlock's oldest son, Stanley, and his wife, Medora Linderman Whitlock, moved their family into Elmwood Farm, as the farm was known in 1897. Will Whitlock's letters were found in the attic. Several of the barns were added at a later date. Courtesy of Mark Whitney, Allegany, New York.

who used a team of horses in the dead of winter to harvest large beautiful pine and hemlock trees. One of the most picturesque places in all of western New York is the Five Mile Creek valley seen from Chapel Hill, a steep hill that separates the valley from Humphrey on the other side. From the hill, it is possible to see the house that used to be the Five Mile Baptist Church, where numerous members of the extended Whitlock family gathered to worship, and the Five Mile Cemetery, where they rest. Meandering through this former area of dairy farms is the Five Mile Creek, which flows toward the town of Allegany, where the creek meets the Allegheny River.

A significant advantage of the area for early settlers was the Allegheny River, which originates near Raymond (Potter County) in north-central Pennsylvania. The river meanders into western New York for approximately thirty miles before returning to Pennsylvania, where it joins the Monongahela River in Pittsburgh to form the Ohio River. In the Treaty of Paris of 1763, the British gained control of the area but

2. Five Mile Valley, Allegany, New York, 2009. Seen from Chapel Hill, Five Mile Creek flows through this valley of former dairy farms and sawmills to join the Allegheny River. Photograph by the author.

refused to open the land for white settlements in part to mend relationships with the Native Americans. This restriction on settlement is considered one of the causes of the American Revolutionary War ("The Kings Proclamation" [1892] 2012; "Proclamation of 1763—October 7, 1763" 2012). With the defeat of the British, settlements quickly arose along the river, including Allegany and Olean, New York. The river provided transportation of people and products such as lumber as well as the power to run grist and sawmills. During the thirty-year period from 1830 to 1860, lumber production from the town of Allegany was estimated to be 3,750,000 feet annually, totaling 112,500,000 feet for the entire thirty years ("History of the Town of Allegany" 1893, 418; McKay [1879] 2004). Lumbering and associated occupations brought people from New England and directly from foreign countries to settle along the river. For example, numerous heads of households that settled in the Allegany area were born in various foreign countries, including

Germany, Belgium, and countries of the present United Kingdom.[3] These individuals brought their own cultures and skills to the area, resulting in occupational opportunities usually related to agriculture and lumbering, especially tanneries, grist mills and sawmills, wood working, and construction.

William Whitlock was a shingle maker and farmer. He was born on May 3, 1829, in Tompkins County, New York, the sixth child of Thomas and Jane Norton Whitlock (Census Office 1830). At age eleven, William was listed in the 1840 census as living with his parents in Hinsdale in Cattaraugus County, New York. By the 1850 census, at age twenty-one, he was listed as living in Rice (Ischua), New York, and had moved out of his parents home and was employed working with wood as a shingle maker. On September 9, 1850, William was married to Mary Eliza Trowbridge in a double-ring ceremony in Humphrey, New York. Mary Eliza was a special lady who had four children with William and was the recipient of William's letters from the war. "Lide," as William affectionately addresses her in his letters, was the eighth of ten children born to Dr. James and Olive Sackett Trowbridge on October 30, 1831 (Census Office 1850). Dr. Trowbridge was one of the first medical doctors to settle and practice in the Allegany area. He was raised on a farm in Trowbridgeville, Worcester, Massachusetts, and served as surgeon's mate in the 2nd Regiment of Light Troops in the Massachusetts Militia from September 20 to November 1, 1814. Two years later, on March 3, 1816, he married Olive Sackett and moved to New York. After practicing medicine in Hinsdale, New York, he moved his family to Pennsylvania in approximately 1839, then to Ohio, and in 1842 to Spring Prairie, Walworth County, Wisconsin.[4] Upon Dr. Trowbridge's death on July 25, 1846, Olive and her children moved back to the Allegany area, where she eventually remarried (Kleman 2001).

---

3. Census Office 1830; country of birthplace as indicated in the census is used as place of origin.

4. Kleman 2001; Evelyn Penman to Ginni Morey, May 16, 2002, Cattaraugus County Historian, at http://freepages.genealogy.rootsweb.ancestry.com/~reinwald/p331.htm#i3366.

TABLE I.I
DOUBLE-RING WEDDING CEREMONY, 1850

Date of Wedding	Names as Given in Transcription	Town of Origin
September 9, 1850	A. M. Trowbridge and Elizabeth Whitclock (Whittock?)	Humphrey and Rice, New York
September 9, 1850	Wm Whittlock and Mary Ellen Trowbridge	Rice and Humphrey, New York

Source: Transcribed by K. and E. Steward, USGenWeb Project.

The double-ring ceremony in September 1850 certainly brought the two families closer together because William's younger sister Elizabeth and Mary Eliza's brother Marshall Trowbridge were married that same day.

This was not the first time that the two families were tied together by marriage: just two years earlier in another double-ring ceremony, William's sister Cristina Whitlock had married William Henry Trowbridge. In 1855, five years after their wedding, and again in the 1860 census, the Whitlocks and the Trowbridges are listed as neighbors in Allegany.

While living in Rice/Ischua, William and Mary Eliza were blessed with two children, beginning with a daughter, Frances Euzetta Whitlock, on July 18, 1851, and a son, Stanley Meade Whitlock, two years later on December 13, 1853. After moving his family to Allegany, another daughter, Clara Hulda Whitlock, was born on August 10, 1856. The couple's youngest child, Henry C., arrived on July 6, 1860.[5] As William's letters from the war to Mary Eliza and their children show, William cared greatly for the family's welfare and the children's education and missed them terribly while he was away. How things would change for this family in the next five years.

5. *Population Schedule, Cattaraugus County, N.Y., June 18, 1870*, M593, roll 908, p. 34, *National Archives Micropublication Series.*

2

Failed Compromises

By 1850, most citizens realized that the United States of America had serious problems that, if not successfully negotiated, could lead to civil war. As the country expanded westward and new states sought to join the Union, political battles might evolve into military battles if compromises could not be reached. As early as 1828, when Vice President John C. Calhoun "anonymously" published *The South Carolina Exposition and Protest*, it was apparent that regionalism—brought on by federal taxes, land sales, and tariffs—had resulted in an emphasis on states' rights, especially in the West and the South (Bartlett 1993, 149–52). Calhoun did not recognize the United States as a nation but saw it as an agreement among states, each of which had the power to rule on the constitutionality of a federal law (a power referred to as the "doctrine of nullification"; see Bartlett 1993, 180–81). Making matters worse in some people's eyes, on May 19, 1828, President John Quincy Adams signed the Tariff of Abominations, which raised tariff duties from 30 to 50 percent (Dangerfield 1952, 405–9). Calhoun wanted a country in which states had reserved powers and the federal government had delegated powers.

In December 1845, John Calhoun returned to the Senate after a brief retirement and became a "peace" senator who did not support war with England over land in Oregon or pending conflicts with Mexico. He wished for nations to reach and hold compromises. Calhoun said that "war may make us great, but let it never be forgotten that peace only can make us both great and free" (quoted in Bartlett 1993, 333). As he approached the end of his days, he actively wrote and spoke in the Senate for states' rights and anti-abolitionism as much as his health would permit.

Sectionalism, abolitionists, and open talk of secession made the forming of a functional Congress very difficult in the fall of November 1849. It took sixty-three ballots and heated discussions over a three-week period just to elect a Speaker of the House (Bartlett 1993, 369). On January 29, 1850, Henry Clay introduced the Compromise of 1850 to the Senate.[1] The compromise involved California's application for statehood as a "free state"—in other words, a nonslave state. New Mexico was expected to follow the California example. Southerners supported making Texas a new slave state (Bartlett 1993, 369–70). Owing to deteriorating health, Calhoun was carried to the Senate on March 4, 1850, because he could no longer stand for any period of time. He had to sit and hear his words on how to save the Union being read by James Mason of Virginia. Saving the Union, Calhoun had written, required the opening of the West for slavery, silencing the abolitionists, enforcing the Fugitive Slave Law, and allowing for states' rights (Bartlett 1993, 372). Six days later Daniel Webster gave his response on how to save the Union. At his political peril, he agreed with Calhoun on enforcing the Fugitive Slave Law and spoke against abolitionists but did not go as far as Calhoun wished.[2] In spite of the abilities of the Great Triumvirate—John Calhoun, Henry Clay, and Daniel Webster—some Southern politicians still considered secession a solution to the nationwide problems.

By the time Will Whitlock's family was complete in 1860, the United States of America was in turmoil. On October 16, 1859, just weeks before national elections, John Brown of Kansas led a terrorist group to steal guns and ammunition from the federal arsenal at Harpers Ferry, Virginia, to start and supply slave uprisings. The US

1. For further discussion of the Compromise of 1850, see Heidler and Heidler 2010, 227–35; McPherson 1988, 69–71.

2. John C. Calhoun to Thomas Clemson, Mar. 10, 1850, in Jameson 1900, 783.

Marines, led by Colonel Robert E. Lee and Lieutenant J. E. B. Stuart, captured Brown and seven of his men (McPherson 1988, 206). Antagonistic feelings in both the North and the South were deepened when the source of Brown's funds was revealed to be a group of New England intellectual abolitionists, the "Secret Six" (McPherson 1988, 204).[3] Although Brown was praised in poetry by Louisa May Alcott (Alcott 1860, 3) and in speeches by Ralph Waldo Emerson (McPherson 1988, 209), Republicans no less important to the future as Abraham Lincoln and William Seward thought far less of Brown and said so (see, for instance, Lincoln 1860). Northern opposition to Brown's raid had little impact, however, on the fervor of southern politicians such as Edmund Ruffin, a Virginian agronomist and entomologist who had moved from Virginia to accept employment as a surveyor in South Carolina. Ruffin's response to the John Brown incident was that the pikes (modified spears) that John Brown and his group had brought to Harper's Ferry were "devised and directed by Northern Conspirators, made in Northern Factories, paid for by Northern funds, and designed to slaughter sleeping Southern men and their awakened wives and children" (quoted in Walther 1992, 258–59). Ruffin later joined the Palmetto Guards, fired one of the first shots at Fort Sumter, and walked into the surrendered fort carrying the Palmetto Guard flag (Walther 1992, 266–67). After the war and the Northern victory, his hatred for Yankees resulted in suicide: he wrapped the Confederate flag around his shoulders and penned in his diary before killing himself, "I would rather be dead than live in a country subjugated by the Yankee race" (quoted in Walther 1992, 228–29). It is interesting to note that the entomologist Mr. Ruffin helped start a war in which insects were to play a major role in the spreading of several major diseases.

3. The Secret Six included: Gerrit Smith, vice president of the American Peace Society; Thomas Higginson, clergyman and writer; Theodore Parker, leading Unitarian; Samual Howe, physician; George Stearns, manufacturer; and Franklin Sanborn, educator and protégé of Ralph Waldo Emerson.

3. Edmund Ruffin, 1864. Ruffin, a Virginian agronomist and entomologist, moved to South Carolina because he was disappointed that Virginia delayed in voting for secession. He joined the Palmetto Guards and enthusiastically participated in the shelling of Fort Sumter. Courtesy of the Library of Congress, Washington, DC.

It should be pointed out that people were not of one accord in the North or in the South, and major political differences existed among the residents of each region. For example, Will Whitlock mentioned in his letters home the Copperheads of the North, who did not agree with Lincoln on many issues.[4] Charles Biddlecom of Company A, 147th New York, an educated soldier from Monroe County, had a hatred for Copperheads. His letters to his wife, Esther, contained numerous examples of his negative feelings for Copperheads and his support of President Lincoln (Aldridge 2012, 120, 245–47). The future-named "Scalawags" in the South were against secession before the war and played a major role in reconstruction after the war (Baggett 2003, 7–10).

With the election of Abraham Lincoln, who received only 40 percent of the popular vote but a large majority in the Electoral College, South Carolina headed toward secession. Governor Gist asked

4. William Whitlock to Mary Eliza Whitlock, letter 12, Nov. 1, 1864, in Mark Whitney's collection, Allegany, New York; E. Ellis 1966, 297.

other Southern governors to join South Carolina in considering secession (Channing 1974, 245; Klein 1997, 9). On December 18, 1860, the
secession convention in Charleston voted secession, with five other
Deep Southern states joining South Carolina. Delegates to the convention remain heroes in South Carolina to the present time. On February 4, 1861, delegations from the seceded states of the Deep South
met in Montgomery, Alabama, to form the government, adopt a con-
stitution, devise the procedures to raise 100,000 volunteer soldiers to
serve for one year, and issue instructions to take over all federal forts
("Organization" 1904). Other more northern states such as Virginia
and North Carolina had many citizens who were not so eager for
secession. North Carolina, for example, sent two separate delegations,
one to Washington, DC, and the other to Montgomery, Alabama.
Judge Thomas Ruffin of the delegation to Washington gave an excellent speech in favor of the Union. The delegation to Montgomery, also
favoring conciliation with the Northern states, arrived late in Montgomery and found that the states farther south were already in control
(Spencer [1866] 1993, 15–16). At the community and family levels in
the more northern states of the South, sharp disagreements about the
war were evident. Rufus H. Peck, of Fincastle, Virginia, Company C
of the 2nd Virginia Cavalry, fought the entire war through some of
the most dangerous battles. Yet before the war he tried to convince his
father that slavery was morally wrong and that secession was not the
way to solve the country's problems (Peck 1913, 73).

Five days after the meeting on February 10, 1861, the Confederate
Congress chose Jefferson Davis as president and Alexander Stephens
as vice president, to be inaugurated in Montgomery on February 18,
1861. That same day, following the election of Abraham Lincoln, a
newspaper editorial in the *Philadelphia Morning Pennsylvanian* characterized the two presidents as follows: "The President of the Southern
Confederation is a gentleman, a scholar, a soldier, and a statesman. . . .
The President Elect of the United States is neither a scholar, a soldier,
nor a statesman. . . . [W]ithout the polished elegance of the well bred
man he has all the rough manners and coarse sayings of the clown"
("Two Inaugurations" 1891, quoted in Klein 1997, 248).

On the way to give his inaugural speech on March 4, 1861, Lincoln traveled by train to many stops between Indiana and Washington, DC. These stops included western New York, specifically at Westfield and Dunkirk. At Westfield, he gave a presidential kiss to a girl who had written him requesting that he let his whiskers grow (Klein 1997, 264–65). In Dunkirk, he took hold of the staff of the American flag and said, "Standing as I do, with my hand upon this staff, and under the folds of the American flag, I ask you to stand by me so long as I stand by it" (quoted in Klein 1997, 265). In his Inaugural Address, the newly elected president of the United States indicated that the government would protect and defend all federal property, including coastal forts (Lincoln [1861] 1939, 1:129). The newly formed Confederate States of America (CSA) sent a delegation to Washington, DC, that offered to pay for coastal forts and to sign a peace treaty. Compromise was not reached again when the federal government refused any offers because it did not recognize the Confederate States as a separate government (Sandburg 1939, 1:85–90).

By the early spring of 1861, South Carolina already had 5,000 armed men, mostly focused on Fort Sumter ("Fort Sumter" 2012; Griffin 2004, 4; McPherson 1988, 317). Compromise failed again when the Union commander of Fort Sumter, Major Robert Anderson, and the CSA commander General Pierre G. T. Beauregard met to decide who would control the fort. Major Anderson, who was hampered by changes in the administration and their indecision, said the supplies were running low and that the Union would leave the fort within forty-eight hours (Sandburg 1939, 1:207–10). Beauregard did not wait for them to do so, however, and opened fire twelve hours later on April 12. Beauregard ironically had been one of Major Anderson's best students at West Point (Detzer 2001, 208; Griffin 2004, 6). The new CSA flag, the Stars and Bars, was soon seen flying over the fort.

The author of *A Pictorial History of the Confederacy,* John Chandler Griffin, a person "dedicated to the South and the Confederacy" and great-grandson of Private John Thomas Stone, Company H, 5th South Carolina Cavalry Regiment, suggests that the "South's opening fire on Fort Sumter must go down in history as one of the most irresponsible moves ever taken by any government in the western world" (quoted in Detzer 2001, 208; Griffin 2004, 41). A new nation, with little if any military force, might well have left Fort Sumter to the Union because it posed no great danger to South Carolina or the harbor in Charleston. The South was lacking more than military force. After the upper four Southern states joined the Confederacy in 1860, the South had only 3 percent of the country's manufacturers of firearms, 6 percent of cloth, 7 percent of pig iron, and 10 percent of boots and shoes (Griffin 2004, 6). The two nations were now just three months away from the first Battle of Bull Run.

The war was brought to the people in both the North and the South by a call to arms. President Abraham Lincoln ordered Simon Cameron, US secretary of war, to send a call to arms on April 15, 1861, asking for a national fighting force of 75,000 men for a term of three months (McPherson 1988, 318). A letter and telegram were sent to the governor of New York, Edwin C. Morgan, asking for 13,280 officers and men from New York. The next day the New York legislature authorized the governor to call up 30,000 men and set aside $3 million for their support. The state eventually contributed 13,906 men from this first call (Phisterer 1890, 7). Telegrams were immediately sent back to Washington from "border states"—Kentucky, Missouri, North Carolina, and Tennessee—refusing to call up troops for the Union. CSA president Jefferson Davis quickly followed on April 17, 1861, with a call for 32,000 men, 5,000 from each Confederate state, except for Florida, which initially was asked to supply the Confederacy with 2,000 troops (Keegan 2009, 49).

It is difficult to determine just how many of these events the lumberman-farmer Will Whitlock knew about and how he received the news. His letters that include knowledge about newspapers and education in general indicate that his family was well aware of current events. Will did not answer this first call to arms in April 1861 or a later call in 1862. Based on recruitment practices, however, it is quite certain that he was cognizant of the developing war. Local prominent officials and individuals who were interested in being officers in the military would visit surrounding villages and ask for men to enlist.

These individuals attended specially arranged recruitment meetings as well as other regularly scheduled town and church meetings. Posters were in place announcing the meetings as well as giving details on who was in charge of developing the company and into which regiment the company would report.

When it was realized that the war was not going to be over in three months and the Union was not going to win battles quickly, President Lincoln called for 300,000 volunteers to join the army's decreasing ranks. Governor Edwin D. Morgan of New York responded and on July 7, 1862, asked for units to be formed as quickly as possible (Griffin 2004, 4). In New York, the state was divided into thirty-two senatorial districts so that each district could handle individually the US War Department's order to raise twenty-eight new regiments. Each district developed a Military Committee that represented the counties in the district (W. Hyde 1866, 1, 2). For the adjoining Cattaraugus and Chautauqua counties, this committee was headed by the Honorable Augustus F. Allen of Jamestown (my own birthplace) and was composed of the "most energetic and respected men" to organize and operate the recruitment efforts (W. Hyde 1866, 10–11). In Cattaraugus County, the committee consisted of H. C. Young, J. P. Darling, Addison G. Rice (named the first colonel of the 154th Regiment, New York Volunteers), D. E. Still, and J. C. Devereaux. In Chautauqua County, the committee was made up of George W. Patterson, John G. Hinckley, Milton Smith, John F. Phelps, and Charles Kennedy (W. Hyde 1866, 11–12). In both counties, the committees posted announcements of war meetings to rally the citizens in support of the war efforts as well as to recruit future soldiers. Perhaps this two-county committee reminded the citizens of Lincoln's earlier successful visit to both Westfield and Dunkirk.

The Cattaraugus and Chautauqua Military Committee assisted in the development of the 112th and the 154th Regiments. Leadership of the 112th, as was the custom, was to be given to Augustus Allen, the committee's chair, but he was not physically able to accept the responsibility and had pressing business concerns. The committee interviewed several candidates but rejected them because of lack of military experience, or the candidates turned down the offer because of other military commitments. The *Jamestown Post Journal* published an article in August 1862 stating, "We have raised a splendid Regiment, and now let us have men worthy to command them. And of all curses do keep out political favorites and party hacks" ("Commander for the 112th" 1862). On August 14, the committee elected Captain Jeremiah Drake of the 49th New York Regiment to lead the 112th and provide an influence that would "save these young men from the inevitable demoralizing influences of army life." He was commissioned, with his promotion to colonel, on September 2, 1862 (W. Hyde 1866, 13).

Colonel Drake had left the ministry at the Baptist Church in Westfield to join the military. Approximately eighty years later, this same church hired my father, Reverend Verne L. Dunham, as pastor. Colonel Drake was severely wounded on June 1, 1864, at Cold Harbor and died the next day (W. Hyde 1866, 135–38).

In 1862, with each state being given a quota for recruitment, the process was more directly controlled by the military (Billings 1888, chap. 2). Soldiers were promised bonuses for enlisting, such as $100 or more, with the federal government, the state, and even local committees adding to the incentive (Billings 1888, chap. 2). The end of the summer of 1862 was a bad time to recruit farmers. With harvest time arriving, the oats, corn, and fruit crops were ripening and would require the usual manpower. It is quite possible that Will Whitlock felt the pressures of farming and supporting his family of four children as well as the additional pressures that might have come from the Allegany community. In this relatively small community, in addition to the Military Committee's overt recruiting efforts, people were talking about the war. It is quite possible that Will heard about the war from recruiting soldiers in uniform and from returning soldiers who either had finished the required three-month service time or had survived disease, injury, or the medical treatment of a wound. As is often the case in any war, young men enlisted for a wide range of reasons, including the general excitement among their friends, the lure of far places, the desire for a change in one's life, economic need, opportunity to be involved in freeing the slaves, sense of duty, and the love of country and hatred for those who were perceived as destroying it.

The problem facing both nations related to the development of a strong military force was how to enlist many soldiers of quality in a short period of time. The choices were to develop a volunteer military or to use conscription or both. Both nations did both, especially when early battles resulted in a tremendous loss of life and volunteers began to decrease or desert. In addition, on both sides one could "volunteer" another person by paying them. The list of exemptions from military service, both volunteer and conscription, owing to employment and other factors was long and varied. On April 16, 1862, the Confederacy passed the first of three conscription acts (Manning 2007, 55–56; A. Moore 1924), and the Union did the same a year later, in March 1863 (Bernstein 1990, 288). These conscription acts were to provide additional troops, but it was also hoped that they would also encourage more volunteers. The public in both nations were not prepared for conscription or for some of the accompanying loopholes, such as substitutes, bounty-jumping, and desertion. If one was of means and a property holder, one could pay a substitute. Some members of the medical profession declared healthy men unfit for service or would send physically or mentally unfit individuals into the service.[5] Following a fifteen-month investigation of the effectiveness of medical examinations of recruits, Frederick Olmsted reported to President Lincoln in July 1862, "The careless and superficial medical inspection of recruits made at least 25% of the volunteer army raised last year not only utterly useless, but a positive incumbrance and embarrassment."[6] Enforcement of the conscription laws resulted in mayhem. In the South, a landowner with more than twenty slaves was not drafted, thus

5. Frederick L. Olmstead (New York Sanitary Commission) to Abraham Lincoln, July 21, 1862, Library of Congress, Abraham Lincoln Papers, available at http://memory,loc.gov/cgi-bin/ampage; Rutkow 2005, 260–64; "Instructions for Physical Examinations," 1899, *Official Records of the Union and Confederate Armies in the War of the Rebellion (OR)*, series III, chap. 2, pp. 139–40.

6. Olmstead to Lincoln, July 21, 1862.

allowing the wealthier men to stay at home (Manning 2007, 102–3). In the North, the laws touched off riots in New York City in July 1863. Blacks, who were not considered citizens, were not subject to the draft. Immigrants and the poor especially disliked the draft because they sensed that it would place free blacks on an equal par with them to compete for positions within the military and at home. Additional pressure was placed on immigrants who had not as yet become citizens in that they were given sixty days to leave the country, or they would be subject to the draft. Within a short time after the first names were announced on July 12, 1863, groups of rioters, eventually numbering up to 50,000, began to attack people and buildings in New York City. One black man was attacked by 400 rioters, hung from a tree, and burned. Because a large portion of the New York State Militia was in the battle at Gettysburg, Pennsylvania, at the time, rioters ran wild; at least 120 civilians were killed, and 2,000 were injured (Bernstein 1990, 288; Pennington 2010; Simmons and Thomas 2010, 189). Approximately fifty buildings were burned, with total damages estimated at more than $1.5 million. Some regiments of the New York State Militia had to be recalled to assist police in keeping the peace. Colonel William F. Berens of the 65th Regiment of the New York State Militia reported saving the lives of two black individuals by placing them in the middle of his troops.[7]

Because of ineffective leadership by several Union generals that resulted in a severe loss of men, President Lincoln continued his calls for more volunteers during the spring and summer of 1864. Will Whitlock apparently considered military service. His later letters home indicate that before he went into the service, he was concerned about the dissolution of the country and no doubt had known of the terrible losses being suffered by the regiments organized in western New York. The news from the front was spread by various means. For example, James W. Phelps from Great Valley found eight wounded

7. William Berens, *New York State National Guard*, 1899, OR, series I, chap. 27, part 2, p. 253; Harris 2003.

men from the 154th in an 11th Corps hospital tent following the Battle of Gettysburg. Upon returning home, Phelps not only wrote letters to the relatives of the eight men but compiled a list of the wounded and dead in the entire regiment (Dunkelman 2004, 148). The return of the wounded and the news of the death of soldiers of the 112th and 154th New York Volunteers certainly influenced the enlistment of men in Chautauqua and Cattaraugus counties.

Will and Mary Eliza Whitlock most likely heard the story about a family in nearby Portville, New York. Sergeant Amos Humiston had left his wife, Philinda, and three children to join Company C of the 154th New York ("Hardtack Regiment"). He was killed at Kuhn's Brickyard during the Battle of Gettysburg on the first day (Dunkelman 2004, 33). Dr. John Bourns of Philadelphia, who was assisting wounded soldiers and the collection of the deceased, found the body of the unidentified soldier later that week at a secluded spot near York and Stratton streets in Gettysburg, holding an ambrotype of three children in his hand. Dr. Bourns had copies of the picture made, and a written description of the children was printed in the *Philadelphia Inquirer* on October 19, 1863, under the title "Whose Father Was He?" This description was published nationally, including in the *American Presbyterian*, a church magazine. Philinda read the description and four months later finally saw the picture and knew that her husband had been lost. To assist the family, many contributions were made, including a nationally recognized song by James C. Clark, "The Children of the Battle Field" (Clark [1863] 1977).[8]

By the summer of 1864, people in western New York were well aware of the war's progress. Not only were the wounded and recently released soldiers coming home, but news of the battles was being published in area papers such as *The Republican*, *The Freeman*, and *The Union* and in town and city newspapers such as the *Fredonia Censor*, the *Olean Morning Times*, the *Jamestown Journal*, and *The Westfield Republican* (Dunkelman 2004, 132, 133).

8. For a detailed description of Amos Humiston's life, see Dunkelman 2004.

At this point, Will and Mary Eliza may have thought that their children were old enough (Euzetta, Stanley, Clara, and Henry were now thirteen, eleven, eight, and four years old, respectively) to be of assistance to Mary Eliza in holding the farm together. With the expected assistance of other family members, including Mary Eliza's family, the Trowbridges, Will may have thought it was his time to support his country. This enthusiasm for service was certainly shared by numbers of Allegany men who later became comrades in the Army of the Potomac (see letter 1, chapter 3).

In this third year of the war, recruitment had been altered somewhat so that the military had more control of the establishment of leadership for new regiments. This change was needed because the organization of some of the new regiments was not nearly as efficient as it had been earlier in the war. Will Whitlock was involved in some of this confusion when the 183rd and 188th New York Volunteer Regiments were being formed. The 183rd Regiment had a very difficult time attracting men. Colonel George A. Buckingham received authority to recruit the 183rd, but that authority was revoked on August 3, 1864 (Phisterer 1890, 513–14). The few men recruited (Company C) were transferred to the 188th Regiment as Company A (Phisterer 1890, 513–14). Company A of the 188th Regiment (men recruited from Cattaraugus and Chautauqua counties by Captain James M. Curtis) was the first company of the 188th Regiment to arrive for training in Elmira (Phisterer 1890, 513–14; see also chap. 3). So Will must have left Allegany, his family, and his friends with a soldier's enthusiasm for the cause but with apprehension about military life, his family's well-being, and the dangers involved.

3

Elmira Excitement

Elmira, Sept. 14 64

Dear Wife

i am well and stuf. We got here last night. i am in the barax. There is lots of soldiers here and it is all excitement. The greatest objection i have is there is to much noys.

we have not got our clothes yet and dont know when we will; it may be two or three days. First when we do i will get a box, put my clothes and Sam Roes in it and send it to you and you can get same to Allegany some how. Now lid i am well and doing well enough so dont worry about me but take cair of yourself and children and i will try and take care of my self.

Now lide, i dont know as you can write to me yet for i don't know how you would have to direct yet.

but when i find out i will write again and then you may write as often as you are a mind to if it is every day.

i have not much to write today only dont worry about me. i dont know as you can read this for there is about 150 men dancing jumping and they make the old bilding farely shake. i will write agan in a few days.

no more from
Will

Letter 2

Elmira, September 17 64

Dear Wife and Children

I take the present oppetunity to write a few lines to you to let you know that I am well and doing well and hope this will find you the same.

we have not got our clothes yet and dont think we will get them today. we have no officers yet and dont know when our captin will get here. we have nothing to do but to eat and lay around. plenty of time to write if there was not so much confusian. there is three or four thousand people in the Barrix now and plenty of excitement I tell you.

lide I cant get lonesome and it would do me no good if I should for I would not try to run the gards for all the money I got. there is six or eight runs the gards every night. Some gets away and more gets shot; the most of them wounded. they say there was one shot ded last night. I did not se him. those that runs are subs.

nowlide for our fair—we have plenty of good bread and coffe for brecfast and bread and been soupp for dinner and that is good and bread and coffee for supper. also fresh beef twice a day. so you se we have plenty to eat.

Sept. 18—well lide I will try and finish this letter if they dont set me crazy. I want you to dress yourself and children comfortable. the first thing you do. and take care of your helth for lide I tell you I dont want to hear of eny of you being sick until my return. dont be concerned about me, I will take cair of myself.

give my respects to Mr. Kratts folks. tell them all to write to me and not wate for me for I have a good meny others to write to our folks today.

I suppose you are moved and all settled by this time. how are they getting along with the crops? Lide I want you to send me some stamps. I did not get eny and they cost 5 cents each. here I cant get my photegraf taken so I will have to wait until we go to other quarters.

I want you to write soon as you get this for we don't know how long we will stay here. you must excuse this for I have to write siting in my buk with my paper on my lap.

give my respecs to my neighbors. lide you must direct to barrix N.1. nothing more this time. tell Lana Cook and all the rest of the folks to write me.

good by lide and children.
From Will

LETTER 3

Wensday Spt. 21. .64

Dear wife and childran,

I received your kind letter about 20 minutes ago and hasten to answer it. I was very glad to hear from you. You did not say whiher you was ill or not. I am well and hope you are all the same.

Ned Posn is here and he says you talk of coming down here to see us. I would very much like to have you come if I could have the privelage of going out with you. there is a great many Ladys comes in here but all ther friends can do is walk around the camp with them; and that is not much satisfaction! if you come you had better come soon for I dont know how long we shall stay here. I think we will stay this week although we may stay two or three weeks.

we have just got our cloths today. dont be alarumed about my losing. I have plenty to eat and have got used to it so it goes pretty good. Sam Kor [?] and Sol Moyer bunks with me so with all our cloths and blankets we have a very good bed. So you se I can get along very well.

tell Mrs. Lowe she ned not trouble herself about me. I dont think I shall write to her rite away for I have to meny others to write just now.

tell the children to be good children and Ill write to them soon. they must write me. I wish you had sent me some dollars worth of stamps for I had borrowed half half of those you did send. I have to write so meny letters that I use a good meny. Lide I wish you would write every day or two for I tell you I want to hear from home often and you have not so meny to write to as I do. while I stay here you can put a letter in the offis in the morning and I will get it at night.

I mailed each of you a picture last sunday. let me know if they went through or not. you will find your one each.

I cant think of much to write today but will try and write something as often as you do. We have prayer meetings here every night. tell Mr. Kratts folks to write to me. nothing more this time. so good by to all

From Will

4. Private William Whitlock, New York State Volunteers, 188th Regiment, Company A, 1864. William married Mary Eliza Trowbridge on September 9, 1850, and enlisted for military service in Allegany, New York, on September 7, 1864. Courtesy of Mark Whitney, Allegany, New York.

The camp at Elmira, New York, was used as a collection and initial training point for newly formed regiments before they were moved south to battlefields. It consisted of four military barracks, two military hospitals, a military police headquarters, military warehouses, artillery ranges, and drill fields. Although Elmira had a population of only 13,130, it was a busy city during the war. By the time Will arrived there, thousands of Union soldiers had gone through organization and training at this camp to become fighting regiments.

All was excitement at Elmira, Barracks North 1 (Arnot Barracks), the night of September 13, 1864. Company A of the newly formed 188th Regiment of the New York Volunteers was the first company to arrive. This company was made up of the recruits of the 183rd Regiment (Company C) that had failed to organize, mostly men from the Allegany area (Anderson 2010; Phisterer 1890, 513–14). It is obvious from the letters given here that Will was a bit more subdued than some of the men, for he had trouble concentrating on his writing because of the noise. Men were excited by enthusiasm for the cause, by being with comrades, and perhaps by the "freedom" from domestic responsibilities because most were hard-working farmers. Among the eleven soldiers mentioned in Will's letters and including Will, the average age was almost twenty-nine, with five individuals from nineteen to twenty-three years of age and six from twenty-seven to forty-two. It might be expected that these two groups might have responded quite differently to these initial days in the military.

With the exception of George Strohuber and Robert Wright, the men who enlisted at Allegany were in the older group (ages thirty-five to forty-two) and may have had concerns for their families. In these initial letters from Will to Lide, Will sets the themes for most of his letters back home, especially to his wife: he misses his family; he is concerned for their well-being (physical, spiritual, and financial); and he provides reassurance to Lide that he is doing well and tells her not to worry. Will also begins the theme, connected to missing his family, of his need for Lide and others to write to him as frequently as possible. He quickly found bunkmates near his age from Allegany, Samuel Roe and Solomon Moyer, who were willing to share clothes

TABLE 3.1
MILITARY FRIENDS OF WILLIAM WHITLOCK
(MENTIONED IN LETTERS)

Soldier	Age	Date Enlisted	Location of Enlistment	Date Mustered
William Whitlock	35	Sept. 7, 1864	Allegany	Sept. 26, 1864
Ashbel Bozzard	23	Sept. 12, 1864	Sherman	Sept. 26, 1864
Charles Colvin	19	Sept. 3, 1864	Persia	Sept. 26, 1864
George Hughes	38	Sept. 5, 1864	Allegany	Sept. 5, 1864
Alanson Jones	37	Sept. 6, 1864	Allegany	Sept. 26, 1864
Solomon Moyer	42	Sept. 5, 1864	Allegany	Sept. 26, 1864
Harrison Newell	27	Sept. 19, 1864	New Albion	Sept. 26, 1864
Samuel Roe	37	Sept. 6, 1864	Allegany	Sept. 26, 1864
Charles Smith	19	Sept. 15, 1864	Olean	Sept. 26, 1864
George Strohuber	19	Sept. 5, 1864	Allegany	Sept. 26, 1864
Robert Wright	21	Sept. 6, 1864	Allegany	Sept. 26, 1864

and blankets. Will enjoyed the "fair" at Elmira and mentions that he has plenty of good bread and coffee for breakfast, bread and bean soup for dinner, and bread and coffee for supper. Fresh beef was also available twice a day. A year earlier Charles Biddlecom of the 147th had reported similar "tolerable" victuals but had suffered from the cold temperatures (Aldridge 2012, 47).

Will had already noticed that some soldiers had visitors from home. Knowing that guards were patrolling the camp perimeters, he adds a little humor to his letter by suggesting that it might be very difficult to be absent without leave in order to see the family. He also indicates that he has seen ladies in the camp and that it would be nice if Lide could come to Elmira. The opportunity to be alone with her would not be possible, he says, and all they would be able to do is walk together. Her coming to Elmira was not thought possible because Will was not sure how long they would be stationed there. It is noteworthy that desertion occurred among these recruits in the first few weeks of service. It is quite possible that at this stage of the war some of these recruits, especially those who were paid substitutes, were having second thoughts. Desertion became a major problem in 1864–65 (see chap. 10) as more soldiers were killed and wounded. Confederate soldiers especially were fighting without proper food and clothing and had great concern for the destruction of their family homes and loved ones.[1] Will mentions that even in training camp the penalty for desertion was quite high, including death by gunshot.

Not all was excitement and celebration when Will arrived in Elmira on September 13, 1864. As the war had progressed before Will's arrival, the US War Department had noticed that several of the barracks at Elmira were at less than capacity. The number of prisoners of war (POWs) on both sides in 1864 had increased in number to where most prisons were overcrowded. This situation had in part resulted from a failure to have a lasting policy on prisoner exchanges. Following several attempts, on August 10, 1864, the Confederate government made an offer for a "man for man" exchange accompanied by a description of the conditions at the infamous Andersonville Prison in Georgia.[2] Disagreement over prisoner exchange continued until January 1865, when the Confederacy agreed to exchange all POWs, including blacks (Thompson 1912, 97–122; Ward 1990, 337–38). General Ulysses S. Grant refused the proposal because he reasoned that if soldiers were exchanged, they would continually rejoin the fight, and every Confederate soldier would have to be killed, thereby prolonging the war.[3] As a consequence, the number of POWs continued to increase with no hope of release. The US War Department then ordered that Barracks Number 3 at Elmira be turned into a prison camp. This change was especially important because conditions in several federal prisons were overcrowded and not suitable. Camp Number 3 (Post Barracks) was

1. Ellen Johnson, "Memoirs of Ellen Cooper Johnson," 1920, unpublished paper, no. 73972, Horry County Memorial Library, Conway, SC.

2. For a detailed account of Andersonville from both Rebel and Yankee viewpoints, see Roth 1989.

3. Ulysses Grant to Benjamin Butler, Aug. 18, 1864, in Jesse Marshall 1917, 71.

to the west of Elmira near the Chemung River and at least two miles away from Camp Number 2 (Arnot Barracks), located north of the city. Lieutenant Colonel Seth Eastman was placed in charge of setting up Barracks Number 3 as a prison.[4] Following construction, Quartermaster General Montgomery C. Meigs reported that eight acres were now enclosed by a board fence twelve feet high with sentry boxes and an elevated platform for the guards.

There were twenty barracks in the camp (Barracks Number 3) when first constructed, each sixteen-by-one-hundred feet, each with double bunks to comfortably house 95 to 100 troops. Therefore, if crowded, the camp could hold 4,000, plus 1,000 more in tents within the compound. Quartermaster General Meigs, however, reported that the camp could hold 8,000 to 10,000 POWs.[5] By the time Will Whitlock arrived two miles away, 9,600 Confederate soldiers were imprisoned at Elmira.

The transfer of prisoners from the crowded Point Lookout Prison in Maryland did not go well. The prisoners were transported in old rail cars that were used for cattle. On July 15, 1864, an eighteen-car train loaded with 853 Confederate POWs crashed into a coal train near the hamlet of Shohola, Pennsylvania, killing 64 Confederate troops, Union guards, as well as the engineer and crew (Robertson 1962, 83; Boyd 2012). Moving from Point Lookout to Elmira was like jumping from the frying pan into the fire.

Once a significant number of prisoners had arrived in Elmira, it was clear that problems would quickly arise. Most of the Confederate soldiers, used to life in the warm South, were poorly clothed for the coming winter, and any available tents were filled by the time Will arrived in North Barracks Number 1. As in Andersonville Prison in Georgia, Elmira Prison—or "Hellmira," as many Confederate

---

4. Seth Eastman to Lorenzo Thomas, June 30, 1864, available through the Elmira Prison Camp Online Library at http://www.angelfire.com/ny5/elmiraprison /siteindex.html; Robertson 1962, 81.

5. Seth Eastman to William Hoffman, Aug. 7, 1864, Elmira Prison Camp Online Library.

prisoners named the prison—had open water in the middle of the prison yard.[6] Foster's Pond in Elmira, 12-by-580 yards in size, quickly became polluted because it collected garbage and an estimated 2,600 gallons of urine per day.[7] This amount of nitrogen and warm summer days resulted in the multiplication of algae covering the pond's surface, an increase in putrification, and the attraction of vermin. Rats were used as a bargaining tool in that one rat could be traded for five chaws of tobacco or one haircut (Horigan 2002, 140).

At about the time Will arrived in Elmira, sexton John Jones of the nearby Woodlawn National Cemetery, a cemetery created for the deceased Confederate prisoners, was busy burying an increasing number of Confederate soldiers (Coddington 2008, 187). Sexton Jones, a former slave who had escaped from Leesburg, Virginia, twenty years earlier, was responsible for burying the soldiers and maintaining records of camp prisoners.

One of the soldiers who died at Elmira, Private Philip Evan Thomas, Company E, Fifth South Carolina Cavalry, was buried about the time Will Whitlock arrived. Private Thomas was taken prisoner on May 16, 1864, at the Battle of Drewry's Bluff and serves as an example of the Union's prison system and the harshness of life at Elmira (Coddington, 2008, 187–88). After capture, he spent ten weeks at Fort Monroe in Virginia and then was transferred to Point Lookout Prison in Maryland. In July 1864, he was transferred to Elmira, where he died of typhoid fever in September, just two months later; he is buried in Grave Number 527 in the cemetery (Coddington 2008, 188). Sergeant G. W. D. Porter of the 44th Tennessee Regiment was also transferred in August 1864 from Point Lookout after spending forty-five days at that prison. His description of the horrible conditions at Elmira included an observation tower outside the wall that, for a small fee, people could climb up and then watch the prisoners. That winter,

6. Eastman to Thomas, June 30, 1864.

7. Eugene F. Sanger to Thomas R. Lounsberry, Aug. 13, 1864, Elmira Prison Camp Online Library.

with temperatures as low as minus thirty-five degrees, Sergeant Porter observed, "Prison authorities could tell a tale if they would. They surely can remember an order that was to deprive a prison full of half-starved wretches of all food until they produced a barrel of beans which had been stolen by their own underlings. They can recall the fact that only one stove was allowed to each hundred men, and only half enough fuel for use, while hundreds of wagon-loads were stacked on the premises. But the graves of dead Southern soldiers at Elmira tell a tale, before which every utterance of the lip or pen is dumb in comparison" (Porter [1878] 2009). From July 1864 to August 1865, the time the camp was open, 2,973 Confederate soldiers were buried at National Woodlawn Cemetery. The overall death rate was 24.4 percent, compared with an average rate of 11.7 percent in Union prisons and 15.3 percent in Confederate prisons (Reese 2010).

In at least one case, Union officials determined to make a prison housing Confederate soldiers even less comfortable. The prison on Johnson's Island, located in Sandusky Bay in Lake Erie just thirty-five miles west of my home in Lorain, Ohio, had drawn the attention of Confederate sympathizers working out of Canada. If the Confederacy could capture and control the prison, it could be used as a base against Union forces as well as inhibit the flow of escaped slaves on the Underground Railroad. The prison held 2,500 Confederate soldiers, most of whom were officers ("Johnson's Island" 2011). It was poorly built and had no running water in the barracks or drainage to the latrines. To match the conditions in Confederate prisons, the Union's War Department intentionally cut the rations in half; eliminated coffee, tea, and sugar; captured any food parcels; and refused any supplements to the prisoner's rations (Foreman 2010, 678, 679).

In approximately 160 prisons of different types used by both sides in the war, more than 56,000 men died in confinement because of poor sanitation, hunger, lack of clothing, poor medical care, extremes in temperature, and neglect from fellow humans (Hall 2010).

4

On the Move

Washington, D.C. Sept. 28 . . . 64

you may be somewhat supprised when you get this for I am now in
Washington. we arrived here about 30 minutes ago and I thought I
would write a few lines to you. we have bin on the cars since night
before last and am pretty well whipt so you must excuse me if I
dont write a very long letter this time.

I am well and hope you are the same. we stayed in Baltimore
last night. I sent my cloths to Olean from Elmira. directed to me
and you must call at the station and get them.

I got 33 dollars in Elmira and can let it on interest to our second leutenant. if you dont want it to use I will let him have it for I
dont like to risk it in a letter. he says he will get it for me. any time
you want it I will send it right off.

you had better not write until you hear from me agan for I
dont know whither we are a going to stay here or not. Our Captin
has gon to hed quarters and will likely know something when he
comes back.

Lide I have received only one letter since I left home and I dont
see what the reason is that some of you dont write me. I am shure
I write enough letters and think I out to receive some now when I
get settled so you can. I wish you would write twice a week.

I cant tell you much about Washington yet fore we have had no
chance to look around yet maybe when I write agan I can tell you

more. Now Lide if you want this money just let me know and you shall have it. excuse me this time.

give my love to all, nothing more this time so good by
Will

Lide I have just seen the captin and he says if you direct to Washington, D.C. 188 reg, Co A in the care of Capt. Curtis it will be all right. so now Lide write as often as you can answer this as soon as you get it.

> Washington D.C. 188 reg.
> Comp. A care of Capt. Curtis

LETTER 5

Sity Point Oct. 5 . . . 64

Dear Wife

I and more attenate to write a few lines to you to let you know that I am well but traveling pretty fast. We landed here about one o;clock yesterday. We are 8 miles from petersburg and could hear the booming of cannon all night. They say they have bin fighting there five days.

there is only one company of our regiment here. we had a pleasant voig here from Washington. we came down the Potomac and through the Chespeak bay past fortris Monrow and the rifrafs and from there to Newport news and then up the James river. the sene was rather novel to me; the gunboats lay all along the river and through the bay. I wish I could explane it all to you but I cant with the pen.

I am more contented than I expected I could be so near the front. we are encamped two miles from sity point and it is one solid encampment from thare to here and they say it is just the same clear through to petersburg. as I am writing I can hear the canon as plain as you can hear thear little pop guns from Olean. so you see we are about as good as in the front but never mind; I guess it will all come out right yet. we will hope so at any rate.

the more I travel around and the more I see of soldiering the more I am resined to put up with it. so make yourself as conted as you can and dont lay awake nights thinking about me for it will do not good. I will try and take care of myself.

The wether hare is about as warm now as it was up thare last summer in haying. so you se we dont suffer with the cold. I dont know what it can be here in the summer time. We proley shant have to make as long marches as our soldiers used to mak so I think we can stand it pretty well.

I sent you a letter last satterday before we left Washington with ten dollars in money in it and wish you would let me know whither you got it or not.

I have had no letters yet from eny one; onley that one I received from you before we left Elmira. so you must know I am in a hurry to hear from home so Lide write and let me know how you are getting along. Direct your letters now to:

Sity Point Verginy

Co.A 188 Reg. N.Y. V. in care of Capt. Curtis.

nothing more this time so good by once more.

Will

LETTER 6

Sity Point Oct. 12 . . . 64

Dear Family

as I was doing nothing this after noon I thought I would write a few lines to you to let you know that I am still in the land of the living and am well and hearty. can eat all the hardtack I can get and hope your helths are all as good as mine.

there is none of our company received any letters since we left Elmira. we think it is rather strange. we look for our names every night when the male comes in. as for war news you perhaps get more than we do. we hear the canon every day and knight too but dont hear the results as soon as you do. we are now throwing up breastworks within a quarter of a mile of our camp. the line is from 12 to 15 miles. it reaches from the James to the Appomatix. it is about 7 miles from Petersburg. we wont know what it is for but the officers seemes to be in a hurry to get it don.

I was on gard last night and dont have to work today. I went down to Sity Point this morning to get my picter taken but it would cost four dollars to get six and it would take two weeks to finish them so I thought I wouldnt have it taken now.

Lide write and keep writing until I do get a letter. I cant write much of the time but will write again in a few days.If you dont get eny letters it isnt because I don't write them for I write every chance I get and I hope you get them if I dont get yours.

give my love to all, I must close.

yours truly
Will

As the evening temperatures of Elmira, New York, began to chill in the fall of 1864, the time for troop deployment approached. Company A of the 188th Regiment of the New York Volunteers, because of its early arrival, waited for the rest of the regiment to assemble. Will Whitlock had been in Elmira since September 13 and did not get his army uniform, blankets, and so on until more than a week later (letters 1–3, chap. 3). The rest of the 188th was organized in Rochester and mustered in on various dates from October 4 to October 22, including Company K as late as November (Anderson 2010; Phisterer 1890, 513–14). Seven companies left New York State under Major Christopher Davison on October 13, 1864 (Anderson 2010; Phisterer 1890, 513–14). By then, Will, along with his Company A comrades, had been at the front near City Point, Virginia, for a week.

Based on the information in Will's letters, we can surmise that Company A boarded cars of the Northern Central Railroad on the night of September 26, 1864. The railroad went south out of Elmira, through Harrisburg, Pennsylvania, and on to Baltimore to join the Baltimore and Ohio (B & O) Railroad. In Baltimore at that time, railroads were not permitted to travel through the city, so troop trains had to stop, and the soldiers were transferred to coach cars that were pulled by horses across town to the Baltimore and Ohio. This transfer was accompanied by difficulties earlier in the war. Three years before Will arrived, the 6th Massachusetts Volunteer Militia was involved in such a transfer. While in their horse-drawn cars on Pratt Street headed for the Baltimore and Ohio depot, they were attacked by a mob waving the Confederate flag and throwing bricks and stones (L. Johnson 2006; Rhodes 1917, 17–19). The 6th responded with gunfire, and four soldiers and twelve civilians were killed (M. Williams 2011). Because of the danger in passing through Baltimore, troops coming from the north had to reach Washington via Annapolis for several weeks thereafter. In April 1864, just five months before Will Whitlock came through Baltimore, President Lincoln, in an address given at the Baltimore Sanitary Fair, a fund-raiser for the US Sanitary Commission, reminded the citizens of how the city's safety had improved since just three years earlier in 1861. This increase in safety, he stated, was owing to the war's progress.[1] Some of that "safety" may have been owing to the fact that a large number of the leaders of industry in Baltimore depended on the Union war effort and the fact that many pro-secessionists had been thrown in jail earlier.

As Will traveled into Baltimore, because of the timing of his arrival, he may not have seen much of Baltimore except as he was leaving for Washington on the morning of September 28, 1864. The railroad between Baltimore and Washington (B & O Washington Branch) was crucial to the Union's success. Not only was this railroad important

1. Abraham Lincoln, "Baltimore Address," 1864, manuscript, Rosenbach Museum and Library, Philadelphia, available to view at http://www.21stcenturyabe.org/2009 /01/13/manuscript-of-lincoln%E2%80%99s-baltimore-address-ca-april-1864c.

for the passage of troops and materials to the South, but several towns along the tracks served as Union camps and hospitals. As the soldiers of Company A rode between Baltimore and Washington in September 1864, they would have passed through Relay, a town that was formed where the horses of horse-drawn railroad cars (before the locomotive) were replaced with fresh horses. Between Relay and the next town on the railroad, Elkridge, the troops would pass over the Patapsco River on the Thomas Viaduct. The bridge was the largest in the United States at the time and the first railroad bridge to be constructed on a curve. Opened on July 4, 1835, it had a span over the river of 704 feet at a height of 59 feet above the water (Dilts 1993, 161; Stover 1999, 102–3). On one side of it, the passengers would have seen the Relay House, a popular hotel for B & O customers. Between May 6 and June 13, 1861, Cook's Battery of the Boston Light Artillery was guarding the railroad at Relay House. When Company A went by in September 1864, the hotel was occupied by Union troops under the command of General Benjamin Butler, whose responsibility was to guard the bridge and the railroad. Because of the presence of the railroad, a large number of military forts and camps existed in the immediate area, including Fort Dix, Camp Essex, and Camp Morgan.

Closer to Washington, Will's train passed through Annapolis Junction, where a branch of the railroad went to Annapolis, Maryland. The 109th Regiment of the New York Volunteers (known as the Binghamton Regiment, Railway Brigade) had been stationed at the junction and at Laurel, Maryland, for two years (1861–63), guarding the railroad (Phisterer 1890, 462). This relatively boring duty certainly changed for the 109th's troops when they were called to battles at the Wilderness and Spotsylvania Court House. They later were to join the 188th around Petersburg, where they were involved with that regiment in the Weldon Railroad Raid and the Battle of Hatcher's Run I (Phisterer 1890, 462).

Will mentions very little about Washington in his letters to Lide except a promise that he might do so in a later letter. He did have some time in Washington to buy a new watch, as indicated in letter 19

(November 23, 1864, see appendix C). Will also reports in the same letter that in less than an hour after their arrival in the capital, Sam Roe's money was stolen. The boys got together that night and took up a collection of $11.50 for him. It is uncertain how much Will contributed to the pot, but he had already lent Sam $2.50 while in Elmira that had not as yet been returned. In their brief stay in the capital, Company A's Captain James M. Curtis went to "headquarters" to get the company's orders. These orders apparently were to continue on to City Point, Virginia, without the remaining companies of the 188th Regiment. Travel to City Point was to be by ship via the Potomac River, Chesapeake Bay, through Hampton Roads, and up the James River. By the fall of 1864, the Union strategy had been forced into a siege on Petersburg. General Grant hoped to block all supply routes from the South and eventually capture Petersburg and then the CSA capital, Richmond.

Travel by train and then by ship was certainly a novelty to Will Whitlock. He was passing through areas of the country new to him on unfamiliar means of transportation, all in a military setting. As the ship began to sail south on the Potomac in late September 1864, Will sailed past several of the sixty-eight forts that surrounded Washington. Several of these forts were constructed in response to the possible dangers to Washington that the battle in 1862 between the Monitor and the Merrimac presented to the Union. To guard specifically against an attack up the Potomac, Fort Foote on Rozier's Bluff, about one hundred feet above the river, and Battery Rogers in Alexandria, Virginia, were constructed (US National Park Service 2010b). In 1864, Fort Foote had eight 200-pounder Parrott rifles and two 15-inch Columbiads (Rodman guns).

The effort to unload a Rodman gun from a flatboat and haul it up the hundred-foot cliff to Fort Foote required several hundred men. These guns were trained on the river and were capable of shooting more than a mile up and down the river.

Farther down the river, about sixteen miles from Washington, the ship carrying Company A of the 188th New York Volunteers would have passed between Fort Washington on the east bank of the river

5. Rodman gun at Battery Rogers, Alexandria, Virginia, 1864. The battery was located on the Potomac River to protect Washington, DC, from Confederate attacks along the river. The gun, with a fifteen-inch bore, was capable of sending a two-hundred-pound projectile a distance of 5,000 yards. Courtesy of Library of Congress, Washington, DC.

and Fort Foote on the west. Fort Washington, an older fort, had been the only fort in place to protect Washington when the war began. With the addition of Fort Foote, any vessels attempting to attack Washington coming north on the Potomac would have to survive superior firepower.

It is certain that Will saw the other major defense of the capital and the Northern war effort: the various ships belonging to the Potomac Flotilla. The flotilla was organized by Commander James H. Ward and departed the New York Navy Yard on May 16, 1861. It originally

TABLE 4.1
GUN PERFORMANCE AT FORT FOOTE, 1864

	Eight-Inch Parrott Rifle	Fifteen-Inch Rodman
Weight of gun (tons)	8	25
Weight of powder per projectile (lbs.)	16	40
Weight of projectile (lbs.)	200	440
Distance of shot (yds.)	2,000	5,000

US National Park Service 2010b.

consisted of three vessels, the *Thomas Freeborn* (flagship), the *Reliance*, and the *Resolute*.[2] In one of the flotilla's first engagements with the Confederacy at Mathias Point on June 27, 1861, Ward was killed.[3] The flotilla became much larger with the addition of myriad types of vessels, including ironclad monitors, screw sloops, sidewheel and screw gunboats and tugs, and sailing schooners.[4] Some of these vessels were originally Confederate vessels that had been captured and were recommissioned. In 1864, as Will's company sailed down the Potomac and into the Chesapeake Bay, the protective flotilla was commanded by Commander Foxhall A. Parker Jr., who served in that position from December 31, 1863, through July 1865 ("The Potomac Flotilla" 1864).

Although the flotilla had been successful in minimizing Confederate blockade runners and reducing the danger to Union vessels using the Potomac, the Chesapeake Bay, and the James River, Confederate forces were still sinking flotilla ships on occasion. For example, the Union had stationed a steamer to block the Piankatank River, the second major river south of the entrance of the Potomac that empties into

2. Samuel Breeze to Gideon Welles, May 12, 1861, in "Operations on the Potomac and Rappahannack Rivers," *Official Records of the Union and Confederate Navies in the War of the Rebellion (ORN)*, series I, chap. 4, p. 458.

3. Stephen Rowan to Gideon Welles, June 27, 1861, *ORN*, series I, chap. 4, p. 537.

4. "List of Vessels in the Potomac Flotilla," 1899, *ORN*, series I, chap. 5, pp. xv, xvi.

the bay. On October 4, 1864, about the time that Will landed at City Point, Confederate forces attacked the blockading steamer.[5] Master William Tell Street, commander of the USS *Fuchsia*, responded and unloaded troops onto smaller boats to chase the Confederate forces upstream. The Union forces destroyed four Confederate boats and captured five. Just four days later, however, on October 8, 1864, Confederates captured and destroyed US *Picket Boat #2* on the Potomac. The Union ships *Commodore Read* and *Mercury* chased the rebels into the Great Wicomico River. The Confederates destroyed the picket boat and captured twelve officers and crew as well as a twelve-pounder howitzer.[6] Even though the rivers and the bay certainly were safer than they were earlier in the war, the flotilla was necessary to protect and monitor the progress of troop ships delivering Union soldiers to City Point.

The flotilla's ships were sometimes called upon to rescue troop ships in trouble in situations other than Confederate attack. On October 8, 1864, the US transport steamer *Nellie Pentz*, carrying a detachment of the 36th Regiment of the New Jersey Volunteers to City Point, floundered because of rough water. It was rescued by the USS *Don*. Because the master of the *Nellie Pentz* appeared to be incompetent, personnel of the *Don* had to be transported aboard the *Nellie Pentz* to bring the steamer to safety.[7]

Having safely sailed down the Potomac and through the Bay, Will told Lide at home about sailing around Fort Monroe and by Rip Raps. A small, fifteen-acre artificial island at Hampton Roads, Rip Raps had been built in 1817 and named after the Rip Rap shoals and the type of rock used in its construction. Fort Calhoun, later renamed Fort Wool, had been built on the island, and from 1831 to 1834 Second Lieutenant Robert E. Lee had served there and at Fort Monroe as an assistant to Captain Andrew Talcott (Freeman 1934, 119–26).

---

5. William Street to Foxhall Parker, Sept. 26, 1864, *ORN*, series I, chap. 5, p. 484.

6. Foxhall Parker to Gideon Welles, July 31, 1864, *ORN*, series I, chap. 5, p. 486.

7. Ibid., pp. 485–86.

Fort Monroe, located just across the water at Old Point Comfort at the tip of the Virginia peninsula, remained in Union hands throughout the war. It was key to battles at Petersburg because of its strategic location. CSA president Jefferson Davis was held prisoner at the fort for two years following the war. Fort Monroe does look more like a prison than a military base because its six sides are surrounded by a moat. It remains the oldest continually garrisoned military post in the United States. In the early days of the war, Burrahe Rice of Bath, New York, enlisted at the first call for men under a three-month service duty. His family had moved to New England, and he joined the 1st Virginia Regiment and then was transferred to Fort Monroe (Rogers 1865). By the time Will Whitlock arrived in the trenches around Petersburg in 1864, Rice was captain of the 189th New York Volunteers and brigade inspector under Brigadier General Edgar M. Gregory of the 2nd Brigade. Rice was killed on a foraging raid on January 11, 1865, a raid that Will Whitlock was on and describes in a letter (letter 33, chap. 9).

For Will and his comrades in Company A, arrival at City Point (now Hopewell), Virginia, must have opened their eyes to see what they had volunteered for back in Allegany.

In October 1864, City Point, on the James River, was one of the busiest ports in the United States (Zinnen 1991). Ships carrying troops and war materials were unloaded as fast as the hundreds of dock workers could find temporary storage. Then the war materials were loaded on trains and wagons for shipment to the front lines. According to Will's letters, City Point was certainly close enough to Petersburg to hear the boom of cannon fire.

Inland from the busy docks, City Point was a typical military town with numerous entrepreneurial businesses that would attract a soldier. In addition to being a place for the relatively new technology of photography that blossomed in the Civil War, the town had several restaurants and saloons at the corner of Water and Pecan streets. The town was alive with sutler outlets (Jensen, Underwood, and Lewes 2003). Sutlers were businessmen with contracts with the Union military to sell food, clothing, writing materials, and other essentials. Their businesses were located in tent cities as well as in isolated tents

6. City Point, Virginia, 1864. Railroad yard and transports. City Point (now Hopewell, Virginia) became one of the busiest ports in the world during the Civil War. Courtesy of the Library of Congress, Washington, DC.

or huts in the trenches around Petersburg. At this time in the war, one of the greatest aims among the Confederate soldiers at Petersburg—certainly underfed and lacking sufficient clothing and currency to purchase necessities if available, which they usually were not—was to capture a sutler wagon or hut from the Union. In a letter that CSA general James Conner wrote to his mother on April 3, 1864, he told of his men complaining about General Grant's orders to remove the sutlers from the field before the impending Battle of the Wilderness. The men complained that the removal was the "meanest, cheapest trick" that ever was done because they had dreamed of capturing a sutler wagon or hut.[8] The high prices of goods from the sutler hut or wagon quite often dictated borrowing from one's comrades, capturing goods from the enemy, or foraging in the surrounding area (Delo 1998, 107).

8. James Conner to mother, Apr. 3, 1864, in Rhea 1994, 25.

7. Pontoon Bridge over the James River, 1864. On June 16, 1864, the 5th
Corps crossed the James River toward Petersburg, Virginia. The bridge was
constructed at Weyanoke Point and stretched for 2,000 feet across the river.
It was removed two days later after General Grant's forces had crossed.
Courtesy of Library of Congress, Washington, DC.

City Point was to remain the most important collection point for
men and materials for the Army of the Potomac for the duration of the
war. Because of its strategic position with respect to the plan for the
siege of Petersburg as well as a port on the James River, General Grant
made his headquarters on the bluff above the river.

The union's quartermaster Rufus Ingalls had his office in the
adjacent Eppes Manor House, part of a 2,300-acre plantation that had
existed since 1635. At the time of the Civil War, Dr. Richard Epps,
owner of 130 slaves, became a contract surgeon at a Confederate hospital in Petersburg and later moved his family to Philadelphia when
the Union gunboats arrived on the James River. After the war, in 1866,

8. Headquarters of General Ulysses Grant at City Point, Virginia, 1864. The Union Army used these headquarters during the Siege of Petersburg. Courtesy of the Library of Congress, Washington, DC.

Dr. Eppes and family returned to rebuild and start over (US National Park Service 2010a).

The long journey from New York to City Point was over by September 13, 1864, and Company A set up camp about two miles from City Point. Will believed that the Union encampments now stretched from City Point to Petersburg in one solid line. Will's letters indicate that when time allowed, he visited City Point to check on the possibilities of getting a photograph of himself done and of buying a few essentials.

5

Life in the Trenches

Oct 16 . . . 64

Dear wife and children

I am foarsed to write another letter without receiving one. I tel you Lide, you dont know how I would like to hear from home. it will be five weeks tomorrow morning since I left home and have received one letter. I am well and getting fat as a hog—it agrees here with me first rate. Lide I hope this will find you all well and hope you get my letters even if I dont get yours. we expect to get a lot of them when they come.

I cant think of much to write for I write so often but if I was home I could tell you a good deal but I guess we will have to wate a while. tel the boys and all the rest of the folks I wont write any more to them until there is some communication opened between hear and thair and then I will write lots. tell them all to write to me for I think we will get our letters after a while.

Lide let me know whither you got the ten dollars I sent from Washington or not and those picters I sent from Elmira. have you got the potatoes dug and how meny is there and how much Buck-sheet did you have? How is the pigs getting along and how is the corn? will you have enough corn to fat the pigs good? Write all the news. I have none to write. Every day is a like here. we have got used to the booming of the canon that we dont mind it at all. we can hear it night and day, Sunday also. I can hear them all the way up the James river while I am writing.

46

Lide I think I will send my vot to Rus Martin and if they think I am not another have Mr. Kratts tel them I am a resident of that town and so that it goes in.

we are still at work on those forts and breastworks; they will be a strong thing when finished. I think the Rebs cant break through them. I hope we can stay in them all winter.

excuse me this time and I will write again in a few days. tel Lana Cook that I thought her spark was going down in tenisee but I saw him at Elmira going for a soldier. tel her to write me a letter and I will be very much obliged to her.

Lide, I want you to answer all my letters as fast as you can get them by and by. I will send you the directions on a slip of paper in this. nothing more. good bye.

Will Whitlock

LETTER 8

City Point . . . Oct. 19 . . . 64

Well Lide,

I begin to feel pretty well for I have got so I get a letter every night. yesterday noon when we came in from work the order came for us too move. a part of our regiment had come and had encamped about three miles from us and we had to move to them. we are only about one mile farther from City Point than we was. there is sevan campings of us now.

I hope this will find you all in as good helth as it leaves me I never was eny helther in my life than I have bin since we left Elmira. I hope Hanks folks and all the rest had a good time a thear party. Tel them I would like to have bin there but never mid tel them to enjoy them selfs as best they can.

Well Lide I am just relieved from gard. it is one oclock. I will have to go on agane at five. we all like to be on gard for we are then excused two days from working on the ditch.

Lide tel Father and Mother and all the rest not to worry about me but tel them all to write. I have so much writing to do I cant write very often to them all. I think I must try and write to Morris and Hank this week. I have not written to them nor Austin yet, whenever I get a chance to write I feel as though I want to write to you.

tel Lin I have not lost my knife yet. Lide I wish you would write oftener now for when the male came in to day noon ther was no letter for me and you dont know how disapointed I felt. It seems I out to get a letter every male now the rout is open but I cant find much falt for I have got six letters the last three days. they come so fast they make me lonesome if I dont get one every day now. Lide write as often as you can and I will do the same. How is your Mothers health? I have got no answer to the letter I wrote her. Who stole uncle Sinns money? if you se eny one that I ever se just tel them to write to me for it makes me feel good to hear from eny one in that Cuntry.

A. Buzzard and H. Newell is here in our company and all the Allegany boys and I have got aquainted with the whole company. they are a good divel lot of boys.

Lide I heard some of our officers say this morning that they thought we would stay here this winter and I hope we will for I think if we dowe shant se any fighting. [but] they think there has got to be a big battle at Petersburg this fall. You probely have heard of the victry in the Shenendo valley by Sheridan. I hope the battle at Pietersburg and Richmond will be as grate a victry. I would like it if this thing co could be got along with this fall so we could come home next spring.

Lide I must close. tel the girls in the Winfal to write me another letter for I think I dill get the next one.

give my love to all and resurve a large shair for yourself and family. no more write soon.

good by all of you from

Will to Lide

When the 187th, 188th, and 189th regiments of the New York State Volunteers arrived at City Point, Virginia, in October 1864, they joined the 5th Corps of the Army of the Potomac under the command of General Gouverneur Warren. By then the 5th Corps, along with most of the Army of the Potomac under General Ulysses Grant and General George Meade, had been forced into a strategy of siege warfare around Petersburg by Confederate victories accompanied by tragic loss of life. For example, in a seven-week period beginning on May 5, 1864, at the Battle of the Wilderness, the 5th Corps, which Will joined in October, had a high number of casualties (table 5.1). At Spotsylvania, General Warren experienced 4,480 total casualties in just that one battle.

The Union army's battle strategy of attacking entrenched forces received extensive criticism in the North. In one month, beginning at the Wilderness and ending at the Battle at Cold Harbor, the Union had 50,000 casualties, whereas the Confederacy suffered 32,000. One of the Union casualties at Cold Harbor was the former Baptist minister at Westfield, New York, Colonel Jeremiah Drake of the 112th New

TABLE 5.1

5TH CORPS CASUALTIES IN SEVEN WEEKS, UNION ARMY OF THE POTOMAC, 1864

Battle	Killed	Wounded	Missing	Total
Wilderness (May 5–6)	487	2,817	1,828	5,132
Spotsylvania (May 8–13)	657	3,448	375	4,480
Cold Harbor (May 29–30, Bethesda Church)	?	?	?	750
Petersburg Attack (June 18)	389	1,899	38	2,326
Total	1,533	8,164	2,038	12,788

Sources: Fox 1889, chaps. 12, 14; W. Powell [1896] 2010, 352–61.

York Volunteers from Chautauqua County (W. Hyde 1866, 83, 135). June 1, 1864, was a terrible day for the 112th in that they lost Colonel Drake; his assistant adjutant general, Lieutenant Gurdon Pierce; and 150 other members of the regiment (W. Hyde 1866, 83). One of the soldiers killed that day was Corporal J. Munroe Potter from Hanover, New York. A memorandum book was found in his pocket, where he had recently written the following verse:

> Whether on gallows high,
> Or in the battle van,
> The noblest place for man to die
> Is where he dies for man. (quoted in W. Hyde 1866, 84)

Private Henry Charles of Company C, 21st Pennsylvania Regiment Cavalry, who was then on foot, described the Battle at Cold Harbor in his diary two days after the battle was initiated. "Some of the dead were bloated so bad that the buttons tore off their coats. All of us that had blankets took them to cover the dead next day and shoveled a little dirt over them and that is all the burial they got. It was horrible for a human to behold and what we tell, human ears cannot understand" (Charles 1969, 200). Unfortunately for the Confederacy, although fewer men in its army were killed or wounded, they could not be replaced as easily or not at all.

Once the siege strategy had been adopted, Warren's 5th Corps fooled the Confederate forces by moving toward Richmond, then quickly moving south and crossing the James River. At 6:30 AM on June 16, the corps crossed the James River on a 2,100-foot pontoon bridge, a triumph of Civil War engineering (Field 2009, 20–22; Hess 2009, 14–17; Jordan 2001, 166). The James was 90 feet deep in the middle where the bridge was constructed and had steep banks and a tidal current of 4 feet (Jordan 2001, 166). It was not until the night of June 17 that General Lee learned of the pontoon bridge and the mass movement of Union troops. At the time, Petersburg was hardly being defended at all by the Confederacy. General Pierre Beauregard, in command of the defense of the city, had only elements of the dismounted North Carolina 4th Cavalry supported by Graham's Virginia Battery (Field 2009, 24; Jordan 2001, 166).

At this point in the war, Union troops had seen too much of the results of attacking fortified Confederate troops and so were not eager to attack the fortifications around Petersburg (Glatthaar 2008, 378–79). Union general William Smith, in command of the 18th Corps, arrived on the scene in the late morning of June 15. If he had immediately pressed an attack, the Confederate trenches and fortifications around Petersburg (the Dimmock Line) would have been destroyed. Unfortunately for the Union, General Smith was overly cautious after experiencing so much bloodshed at Cold Harbor (Field 2009, 25). When General Winfield Hancock arrived on the scene with the 2nd Corps, he assumed that General Smith knew more about the situation and deferred to Smith's assessment of battle conditions. Although earlier attacks that day had captured Batteries 3–13, no major attack was made until June 17, and opportunities were missed (Field 2009, 24–27; Glatthaar 2008, 378–79; Jordan 2001, 166). General Smith was relieved of duty on June 19 and placed on "special service" for the remainder of the war (Field 2009, 25). General Lee then moved his troops south of Petersburg and joined up with Beauregard's defenders.

Before arrival of the 188th Regiment of the New York Volunteers in October, several important battles around Petersburg had already occurred. Knowledge of these battles certainly assists in understanding the atmosphere that Will was to face on arrival. Will told Lide about General Philip Sheridan's victory over Lieutenant General Jubal Early's Confederate troops in the Shenandoah Valley and hoped that the battles for Petersburg and Richmond were just as decisive (letter 8, this chapter). The victory in the Shenandoah allowed General Sheridan, one of General Grant's favorites, to move south to join Grant at Petersburg.

The first major battle of the Siege of Petersburg began on July 18, 1864, on the City Point Road (see table 5.1). The siege lasted for nine and a half months. The Confederacy had placed the Dimmock Line, a ten-mile breastwork around the south side of Petersburg, to protect the city from attack and to assist in keeping open all of the roads and railroads that brought men and materials from the south. The line was named after Captain Charles Dimmock, who had overseen the building of defenses around Richmond. This fortification of Petersburg consisted of fifty-five batteries, each open to the rear. Between the batteries, infantry parapets were constructed along with deep ditches measuring fifteen feet wide and up to six feet deep (Hess 2009, 10–14).

In spite of overwhelming odds (the Confederacy had approximately 44,000 men compared to the Union's approximately 100,000 men), the Union forces were repelled in front of the trenches, in part owing to lack of Union coordination. General George Meade, in command of the Union efforts, continued to push the men forward with great loss of life and had serious disagreements with General Warren on the performance of the 5th Corps (Jordan 2001, 168–69). The Northern army recorded 10,000 casualties during the battle, and the entrenched Confederacy lost approximately 4,000 (Field 2009, 27).

There is nothing better to enhance a person's career than to have a superior present when great success is achieved. General Lee sent out numerous reconnaissance forces to locate Union construction of breastworks opposite or flanking the Dimmock Line. Upon location of Union troops near the Petersburg and Weldon Railroad, General Lee decided to go on the offensive on June 21, 1864, the Battle of Jerusalem Plank Road (or First Weldon Railroad, June 21–24, 1864). General Billy Mahone, a South Carolina hero with no military training, had been a surveyor and railroad engineer before the war. He knew the area around Petersburg and suggested a flanking operation, which General Lee agreed to and was present at the battle (Field 2009, 27; Glatthaar 2008, 423). The attack was a great victory for the Confederacy, resulting in 3,000 Federal casualties as well as the capture of four guns and the added glory of eight regimental flags.

Again at the Battle of Globe Tavern (or Reams Station), just south of the city on August 18–21, General Mahone's Southern troops were victorious (Calkins 2010; Field 2009, 60–62; Hess 2009, 129–35). Mahone's reputation quickly spread so much so that Union officers were greatly concerned as to his location. Fortunately for the Confederacy, his troops remained in Petersburg when General Lee sent others to protect Richmond from a diversionary move by General Grant. This faint to the north, reasoned Grant hopefully, would decrease the support of the Confederate forces in the trenches around Petersburg.

The stage was set for one of the most famous battles of the war, again characterized by much confusion on the part of the Union army: the Battle of the Crater on July 30, 1864 (Field 2009, 37–59; Hess 2009, 90–106; Glatthaar 2008, 424–25; Jordan 2001, 176–80). A group of noncommissioned officers and men from mining country in Schuylkill County, Pennsylvania, persuaded their commanding officer, Lieutenant Colonel Henry Pleasants, an excellent mining engineer, to build a tunnel under the Confederate line and explode a mine to break open the breastworks (Field 2009, 37). The mine exploded, killing or wounding about 350 of the Confederate force, but the Union armies were not organized to take advantage of the situation (Field 2009, 37). Northern generals, including Warren, had been using newly arrived black troops to dig trenches and build breastworks in place of white soldiers, so these hard-laboring troops arrived on the scene with only about two weeks of training for combat (Jordan 2001, 177). In addition, two Union officers of the forces fighting in and near the crater were drinking rum in nearby "bomb proofs" (Field 2009, 51; Hess 2009, 89; Jordan 2001, 177). Several significant aspects of this well-reported battle were important to the future of the war. The Confederate army encountered black soldiers for the first time in a major battle in the eastern theater; they did not allow the black soldiers to surrender and killed them based on General Mahone's order to give "no quarter" (Glatthaar 2008, 424–25; Hess 2009, 99–102). Some of the black soldiers were even killed by Union soldiers who feared being captured by the Confederacy while being associated with black soldiers (Field 2009, 56). The Union soldiers' concern was well founded. Phoebe Yates Pember, a matron at Hospital Number 2 of the Chimborazo complex in Richmond, reported that after the Battle of the Crater, wounded Confederate soldiers had a change in their attitude toward Union soldiers. Before the Crater, wounded Confederate soldiers spoke respectfully about the enemy. Now they pictured the Crater as a "mean trick," and they were angry about the use of black troops (Pember [1879] 2002, 48).

With the battle resulting in 5,000 Union casualties to only 1,500 on the Confederate side, an inquiry was ordered in which General Warren of the 5th Corps testified against General Ambrose Burnside, who was in command (Jordan 2001, 179–80). The defeat at the Crater led to the resignation of General Burnside, who already was in disfavor after his failure at Fredericksburg. Mahone, in contrast, was promoted to major general because of his leadership.

Will Whitlock arrived at Petersburg as a raw recruit with very little training for battle, especially the techniques of fighting in trenches. He quickly found out that one of the major functions in trench warfare, especially at the level of private, was digging. It is clear from his letters that he was involved in digging more than any other aspect of training, especially during the time that trenches were being extended to the west. After Company A's arrival in City Point at 1:00 PM on October 4, 1864, the company settled in about two miles from the city in "one solid encampment" from City Point to Petersburg. That particular summer had been hot and dry, and everything was covered with a layer of dust. The two to ten inches of dry powder on the ground resulted in clouds of dust when anything moved. As expected, rain quickly resulted in a sea of mud (Glatthaar 2008, 381–82; Hess 2009, 65). Private Benjamin Mason of Company F, 60th Alabama, wrote to his wife that when it rained, everything and everyone were in four to eight inches of mud.[1] On October 12, Will's company was heavily involved in digging breastworks about a quarter of a mile from their camp, which was part of a line that extended twelve to fifteen miles from City Point on the James River, south around Petersburg, and eventually to the Appomattox River, just west of Petersburg. From a private's point of view, Will did not know what the breastworks were all about, but he knew that the officers were in a hurry to finish the construction. Four days later, in letter 7, Will informs Lide that Company A is still working on the

1. Benjamin Mason to wife, Aug. 16, 1884, Mason Family Papers, Auburn Univ., quoted in Glatthaar 2008, 381–82.

9. Bomb proofs at Fort Sedgwick, Petersburg, Virginia, 1864. Bomb proofs were underground rooms reinforced with logs and covered with soil and sandbags. They served as protection from artillery shells. Courtesy of the Library of Congress, Washington, DC.

breastworks but this time mentions that these works connect with numerous forts that were being constructed as well. Will thinks that the works and forts are strong enough that the "Rebs can't break through them."

The normal routines in the day-to-day life of the Civil War soldier were altered depending on a number of factors, such as stage and style of warfare, weather, and specific orders from officers. Will was initiated into a relatively static siege situation in which he believed he would not do much marching (letter 5, chap. 4). Will thought that any movement of troops was related to movement within the trenches caused by enemy attacks and the ever-increasing length of the breastwork westward.

With construction of breastworks and more permanent fortifications, several changes in a soldier's typical day were brought on by the necessity of digging and the cutting and hauling of lumber. Some of the events of a typical day scheduled for troops in large camps out in the open were also maintained in trench warfare except when the soldiers were on the march. Camps were set back from the trenches at least some distance from sharpshooters and the enemy's picket lines.

Members of the bugle and drum corps signaled each event daily (Casey 1862, 227–72). For almost every activity during the day—for instance, fix and unfix bayonet, tempo of march (stand, march, double time, quick time, and run)—there were specific drum beats and bugle calls, and there was even a call for the musicians to assemble. To be a bugler, a man or boy, as the case may be, had to be able to play at least the following melodies: reveille, fatigue call, assembly, sick call, and taps. Reveille was sounded at about 5:00 AM or an hour later in winter and was quickly followed by a company roll call by the first sergeant. About thirty minutes later, there was a breakfast call, followed by a sick call and a fatigue call. Sick soldiers were either returned to their campsite for rest or sent to a hospital if necessary or were deemed fit for normal duties. When Will came down with a severe cold, he reported to the doctor on the morning of October 26 and was excused from duty that day (letter 9, chap. 6). If diagnosed as extremely fatigued, the soldier was often ordered to police up the area around the camp. By 8:00 AM, the guards were selected and posted. If assigned to guard duty, the Union soldier served two hours out of every six (Wiley 1951, 45–49). In the trenches, Will reported (letter 6, chap. 4) that after serving guard duty at night, he was excused the next day from digging. In letter 8 given in this chapter, he wrote that they all enjoyed guard duty because, at least in the first weeks of October, they would get two days off from working on the "ditch."

If the army was in camp, training and drilling followed until the call for the noon meal. After the meal, there was usually a short free time before the call for more drilling. Late in the afternoon, the camp became active in preparation for the "retreat exercise," which involved dress parades and ceremony. After a call to supper, as dark approached and eating was finished, taps was the final call of the day. As mentioned earlier, in active warfare a number of these calls might be omitted, and drilling time considerably reduced or eliminated. Sunday activities were different from the routines of the rest of the week, as dictated by officers' preferences as well as by the stage of battle. In most cases, Sunday meant cleaning up the camp and their equipment (Wiley 1951, 45–49). When knapsack inspection occurred on Sunday, Will found that being in Company A was a great advantage. The regiment lined up with Company A on the right, Company B on the left, and the other companies in between (based on the rank of each company captain). Inspection started with Company A and went down the line, with Company B last. After a company was inspected, it was dismissed, and its soldiers picked up their stacked rifles and marched back to their tents. With about one hour required to inspect ten companies, soldiers of Company B had to be very patient (Casey 1862, 10). After the noontime meal, Sunday afternoons were free time, although some officers required church attendance. Every other month soldiers expected pay ($16 per month for Will Whitlock) on Sundays, which required muster exercises and inspection (Wiley 1951, 45–49). As described in his letters, Will tried to send most of his money home rather than spend it on personal items that were not absolutely required. Pay was frequently late, as much as six months at various times during the war.

Trench warfare in 1864 certainly differed from armies on the move or in large camps in more open areas. If the camps were far enough behind the trenches, tents might be used, especially if the company moved frequently. Regulations indicated certain arrangements for quarters that were altered because of the fighting or terrain or both. By the time Will arrived at the trenches in October 1864, the typical use of tents in the summer had evolved not only as to the form of the tent, but also into other structures depending on ambient temperatures and climate. At the beginning of the war, Union armies used the Sibley tent, which was a cone of canvas eighteen feet in diameter that when supported in the middle by a pole, was about twelve feet high. The top could be left open for ventilation or covered to trap any heat in the winter made by an interior conical stove. Each tent was designed to house twelve men, but more were often assigned (Billings 1888, 46; "Life in a Civil War Army Camp" 2010; Wiley 1951, 55).

As the war wore on, however, with the exception of very large camps, tents decreased in size, so that the typical tent was the dog tent for both Confederate and Union troops. Union troops were issued a shelter-half, a four-by-six-foot piece of canvas that when buttoned together with a mess mate's or buddy's formed the canvas for the dog tent (Billings 1888, 53; McGinley 1897; Wiley 1951, 56). At a distance back from the trenches at the front, quarters for the soldiers and officers were arranged according to army regulations. Just behind the trenches, the privates' tents or huts were placed by company on either side of a road running away from the front. Behind the privates' quarters were quarters for noncommissioned officers, then company officers, and finally, at the rear, regimental officers. The baggage trains were placed behind the officer quarters (Wiley 1951, 55).

The soldiers of the Confederacy, as the supply of canvas got very low, often slept in open-air beds made of straw or leaves between two logs. Tents were rarely seen unless captured from the enemy. Two men usually slept together with an oil cloth between them and the ground. They placed over them their two blankets with a second oil cloth over the blankets to keep them dry (McCarthy 1882, 25).

The small community in which a soldier lived often had to be guarded, with tent entrances restricted even among members of the same company. The invader most likely to succeed, though, was *Pediculus vestimenti*, the body louse (Billings 1888, 80–85). These "graybacks" were a difficult problem to solve. When idle, an infested soldier would often go "skirmishing"—removing each pest by hand, one at a time—in an attempt to escape the bothersome invaders. Soldiers found that the best method was washing their clothes and bed materials in hot water, often in the same pots used for cooking (Billings 1888, 80–85). Another reason for restricting visitors to tents or huts was *Pulex irritans*, the human flea. Ben Robertson wrote to his sister on February 2, 1862, that when he inquired about noise he had heard in the regiment, he was told that two fleas had "taken holt" of a man and carried him halfway to the river to drown him because he had sworn vengeance against them.[2]

In a war in which insects were involved in more deaths than cannons, rifles, and bayonets, it is noteworthy that one of the persons so enthusiastic about going to war was Edmund Ruffin (see chap. 2). He was an entomologist who studied grain moths (Lockwood 2009, 65). Two-thirds of the deaths in the Civil War (thus, approximately 327,000 out of a total of 488,000) were owing to insect-borne pathogens, so advancement of the sciences of entomology, parasitology, and medicine in general would have saved thousands (Lockwood 2009, 65). Flies that carried enteric pathogens played a major role in deaths from diarrhea. Both Union and Confederate armies suffered more than a million cases each of diarrheal disease, resulting in 44,558 Union deaths and an estimated 30,000 Confederate deaths (Lockwood 2009, 66). Near the end of the war, a Rebel soldier suffering from diarrheal disease remarked to a Union cavalryman who seemed to be quite healthy and well dressed, "Oh my, oh my! you look like you wuz sich a happy man. You got on sich a nice new uniform, you got sich nice boots on, you ridin' sich a nice hoss, an' you look like yer bowels wuz so reglar" (quoted in Wiley 1943, 252).

Confederate ingenuity actually resulted in the use of insects as weapons. As Union forces approached Richmond, General Joseph Johnston was criticized repeatedly for not deploying his small force against the Union troops. He chose instead to keep the Yankees pinned down in the swamps along the Chickahominy River so that, owing to the deaths caused by the great population of insects in the swamps plus deaths in combat, the Union lost a regiment a day among General George B. McClellan's sickly troops (Lockwood 2009, 71–72). Although scientific knowledge was lacking, the Confederacy was in fact planning to use disease as a weapon. Dr. Luke Blackburn,

---

2. Ben Robertson to sister, Feb. 2, 1862, manuscript photostat, Univ. of Texas, quoted in Wiley 1943, 250.

known as Dr. Black Vomit, tried to spread yellow fever by smuggling clothes from yellow fever victims to the Union troops. The good doctor also sent clothes from yellow fever victims to President Lincoln in an assassination attempt. He was later elected governor of Kentucky (Lockwood 2009, 75–76).

Siege warfare around Petersburg resulted in the disappearance of much of the area's vegetation. In addition to the use of wood for heat in the winter time, especially the winter of 1864, both armies' trenches and forts required logs and lumber for fortification. The landscape around Petersburg was desolate and void of vegetation.

10. Fortification and dugouts at Petersburg, Virginia, 1864, showing the lack of vegetation characteristic of trench environments owing to the use of wood in construction and damage done by artillery. Courtesy of the Library of Congress, Washington, DC.

Depending on the season, entire trees were used in the camps. In the hot autumn of 1864, Will found Petersburg as hot as haying time back home in Allegany. Shades were constructed in the camps in the open for meetings and cooking or even used to shield tents from the sun. The branches of trees were used on the top of logs to form a roof under which soldiers were shielded (Billings 1888, 54).

During the wintertime around Petersburg, shelters for the officers and men, especially in a siege situation, evolved into huts. Both Union and Confederate huts were typically designed for four men, made of notched logs or planks, and had one door cut into one of the sides. The hut was warmed by a small fireplace that was connected to an external chimney. The floor of the hut was either planks or soil. Hundreds

11. Summer shade construction, Petersburg, Virginia, 1864. Summer construction back of the trenches used the entire tree. Courtesy of the Library of Congress, Washington, DC.

of these huts were constructed during the siege (Wiley 1943, 59–61). Will was happy to be back in his hut when he returned from the first Battle of Hatcher's Run (letter 17, chap. 9).

Some of the digging in the building of breastworks around Petersburg was part of the construction of more elaborate, permanent fortification by both armies. Using lumber, soil, sandbags, and metal, simple trenches became significant protection for the troops. Some construction included abatis, which were trees or planks inserted into the ground with pointed ends toward the enemy; ramparts of piled soil that contained a honeycomb of trenches; and barbettes, which elevated the guns for firing over the parapets.

More skill was required to construct other structures to supplement the trenches, including gabions, fascines, and *chevaux-de-frise*. Gabions were cylindrical weaved bundles of vines and small branches (two to three feet tall and two feet in diameter) that were packed and integrated into walls of soil along the trenches. Fascines were bundles of brushwood or sticks approximately one to two inches in diameter bound tightly with wire and as long as required by the wall being strengthened (ten to twenty feet long and one foot in diameter) (Ethier and Pawlowski 2008, 1–9; Hess 2009, 54–61; McGinley 1897, chaps. 1–2). They were often used in between rows of gabions, such as those constructed at Fort Sedgwick. One of the more exotic but deadly constructs in the Petersburg trenches for both armies was the *cheval-de-frise*. The structure was made of a central log (sixteen feet long), with drilled holes into which seven-foot-long stakes sharpened at the points were inserted (Hess 2009, 54–61; McGinley 1897, chap. 1; Miller and Lanier 1911, 103–218). They were frequently used at night, several of them wired together along the front. The 50th New York Engineers put together 10,000 gabions and 1,200 fascines in just five weeks.

In addition to these major constructs, the ground around and in the trenches was filled with small rifle pits just large enough for an individual soldier and often filled with mud. These small holes could be covered with a canvas for some protection from the elements. If a pit was to be used for any extended time, side "rooms" could be dug for sleeping or even fires so that only the smoke was visible (McGinley

12. Gabions below a fascine, 1864. Gabions were cylindrical, weaved bundles of vines and small branches and filled with soil. Fascines were bundles of sticks one to two inches in diameter and up to twenty feet long that were packed with the gabions into the walls of the forts. Courtesy of the Library of Congress, Washington, DC.

1897, chaps. 1, 4; Wiley 1943, 61–62). Larger structures, especially on the Union side, included bomb proofs constructed with large supporting logs and often having wood-lined floors and walls. These structures formed the main residences of the officers and men within the fort.

In Will's letter of October 16, he tells Lide that army food is making him "fat as a hog." This was not a response to any questions from home about food because he had received only one letter during the five weeks he had been in the army. The mail problem was solved in the next few days, and the letters began pouring in from home. Later on in Will's war, the increase in weight was also solved, but in

13. *Chevaux-de-frise*, 1864. As a barrier to attackers, the *cheval-de-frise* was constructed of a sixteen-foot log drilled with holes into which seven-foot sharpened stakes were inserted. They were often found linked together to cover more frontage along the trenches. Courtesy of Library of Congress, Washington, DC.

a negative fashion. Not all Yankee soldiers agreed with Will. One Union soldier wrote the following poem that was published in a Nashville newspaper:

The soldiers' fare is very rough,
The bread is hard, the beef is tough;

14. Officer's winter hut, 1864. The hut was often built around the summer tent. Fireplaces made of mud/sticks or brick/clay had chimneys of mud-packed wood, such as pork barrels. Most huts held two to four officers. Courtesy of the Library of Congress, Washington, DC.

If they can stand it, it will be,
Through love of God, a mystery. (*Nashville Daily Union*, Apr. 16,
    1863, quoted in Wiley 1951, 224)

While Will was reporting his gain in weight, just across the trenches Confederate soldiers were lucky to have anything to eat. The strategy of cutting off all supply lines to Petersburg from the south was already at work in the fall of 1864. Confederate troops had little to eat, and their clothing was minimal.

At the beginning of the war and under the best circumstances, the official allocation of food was quite similar for both armies.

Per soldier/day
12 ounces of pork or bacon, or 1 lb and 4 ounces of salted or
fresh beef
1 lb and 6 ounces of soft bread or flour or 1 lb hard bread or 1 lb
and 4 ounces of corn meal

To every 10 rations:
15 lbs of beans or peas and 10 lbs of rice or hominy
10 lbs of green coffee or 8 lbs of roasted coffee or 1 lb and 8
ounces of tea
15 lbs of sugar
4 quarts of vinegar
3 lbs and 12 ounces of salt
4 ounces of pepper
30 lbs of potatoes when practicable
1 qt of molasses[3]

No private in the infantry of either army received the listed allocations. Even Union soldiers did not see these allocations when called
out of the trenches for long marches before a battle. Confederate soldiers in the trenches around Petersburg saw little of the allocated food
for as much as three or four days at a time, and only some of the
items arrived, thus prohibiting the preparation of a healthy meal. Soldiers ate almost anything, including corn meant for the horses and
whatever they could capture from the enemy and forage from farms
near the trenches. Based on a soldier's cooking skills, members of the
mess (usually three or four soldiers who lived and worked together)
would turn cooking responsibilities over to the "cook." Will served as
cook during the winter of 1864. Confederate cooks across the trenches
from Will had to come up with recipes that used very little and could
be stretched to meet their comrades' needs. Such Southern delicacies

3. *Army Regulations* (1863), art. 43, para. 1190, available at http://www.archives
.org/stream/regulation.

as "slosh" or "coosh" and "slapjacks" were too common (McCarthy 1882, 57–59; Wiley 1943, 104–5).

> slosh: available bacon is fried until pan is one half filled with grease. A mixture of flour and water that flows like milk is poured into the grease and rapidly stirred. When the whole mixture is a dirty brown color, it is ready to be served.
> slapjacks: reduce the amount of water with the flour to form a paste, reduce the amount of grease and pour into the bottom of a pan. Brown on the underside and flip. (Wiley 1951, 237–38)

The most common form of bread was the flour and water cracker or pilot biscuit that both armies called "hardtack." Ten or twelve of these hard, flour-and-water crackers were considered a full bread ration. Hardtack, also called "teeth dullers" and "sheet-iron crackers," was justifiably named (Wiley 1951, 237–38). Jokes recorded about hardtack were numerous: they would make good breastworks because they could stop a musket ball; one soldier made a bridge of one for his violin; they required beating with musket butts to make them soft enough to eat. One reported dialogue focuses on hardtack:

> SERGEANT: Boys I was eating a piece of hard tack this morning, and
> I bit on something soft; what do you think it was?
> PRIVATE: A worm?
> SERGEANT: No, by God, it was a ten penny nail. (Wiley 1951, 237–38)

Hardtack was packed in boxes and became stale and moldy or sometimes infested with worms or weevils when the boxes were stored too long or under humid conditions (letter 19).

There were no major food shortages among the Union soldiers around Petersburg. As evidenced in Will's letters, the boys in blue frequently received care packages from home, could buy food from sutlers, and could forage if need be. In letter 19, Will tells Lide that they bought tea, cheese, butter, and apples if they got their pay. He purchased tobacco with his change. On Thanksgiving Day 1864, Will tells Lide sarcastically that it was a big thing that he had an apple and a half and a little turkey bone (letter 21, app. C). On that day, there were only about two pounds of cheese for Company A's seventy-five soldiers. In Will's tent, they had one little turkey for six men. Will tells Lide that the general donation of food for the army did not feed the private in the trenches. It all went through the hands of officers and "nigger" waiters. One negro in Company A told Will that he had a whole duck, almost a dozen apples, and as much as he could eat in two meals. Word spread across the trenches about the Union's Thanksgiving "feast," so a committee of Richmond citizens planned a big Christmas dinner for the Confederate Army of Northern Virginia (Power 1998, 229–30). The date was changed to New Year's Day when the committee realized the enormous task at hand. Newspapers in Richmond announced the "Soldiers' Dinner" to be held on January 2, 1865 (Power 1998, 229–30; "Proposed Dinner" 1864).

Delivered very late on January 2 or one or two days later, the actual "dinner" disappointed most soldiers. Although some units received some of the dinner as promised, others received just bread or nothing at all. Private John Armfield of the 30th North Carolina wrote to his wife, Lydia, on January 10, 1865: "and when it was sent out to us it consisted of 3 or 4 bites of bread and 3 bites of meat and it was quite a snack for a feast. Somebody stole my part, but I did not grieve very much" (quoted in Power 1998, 232).

Will concluded that the best way to get food was to have it boxed by friends at home and sent to the specific soldier. Confederate soldiers, in contrast, had trouble getting packages from home either because the folks back home did not have much to send or because the packages frequently were broken into or stolen at depots (Wiley 1943, 99–100). Even with volunteer organizations back home, such as the Soldiers Relief Association in South Carolina, food and clothing were difficult to come by for the hungry and cold Rebels. The typical ration for the Confederate private in the trenches was one-third of a pound of cornbread and three ounces of bacon or less (McCarthy 1882, 56–57). As a consequence, foraging was a military assignment, and any opportunity to share a friendly family's dinner was a life-saving experience.

When thousands of men were gathered into a relatively small area, sanitation and contamination of water supplies immediately became of pressing importance. Soldiers who used open streams, rivers, and lakes for drinking water were warned to boil the water first, but many ignored the warning and so went straight to the hospital. Latrines or "sinks" were often open shallow trenches that were frequently left uncovered too long and for convenience were too close to the camp (Glatthaar 2008, 70–75). Unwelcome guests in the trenches included rats reported to be the size of squirrels (Hess 2009, 217). At night, the rats came out of the trenches to look for food and ran over soldiers who were trying to sleep.

Trench warfare was characterized by the hum, whistle, and buzz of bullets and the scream of artillery shells called "camp kettles," "iron foundries," and "tubs" (Wiley 1951, 78). Will said that he eventually was not bothered by the booming of canon and the artillery shells as they whistled overhead. Owing to disease, poor nutrition, and the danger of picket and sharpshooter rifle fire day and night, life in the trenches was an ever-swinging pendulum between sheer boredom and sheer terror (Glatthaar 2008, 78–79; Hess 2009, 72–76).

6

Life Back Home

Camp near the Dansvil Railroad, Oct 26 . . . 64

Dear wife and children

I hope you will excuse me for not writing sooner for we have bin moving and have bin very bissy for three or four days. I am well excepting a hard cold. I have gin pretty near sick with a cold ever since we commenced moving. I went to see the doctor this morning and he excused me from duty today so I thoughed I would write a few lines to you. we have orders to march again tomorrow morning at day brake. I dont know whare we shal go this time but I will let you know as soon as I can. my head aches pretty hard today and my hand trembles so I dont know if you can read this or not.

Lide there has got to be some fighting done within a few days near here but we dont know whither we shall be engaged or not. now Lide don't worry about me for I will take care of myself and if I dont feel eny better tomorrow, I shal try and get excused from marching with my napsack.

Lide it is strange that I dont get more letters from home. I thought when they began to come I would [get] letters every day but I have not received one in over a week and it makes me feel lonesome (but they must be delayed somewhere).

Lide we have pleasnt wether ever since we come hear. there has ben no storm to speak of yet: rather cool nights but warm days. the day we marched hear was the dustyes time I ever saw. You couldnt tel what culler our clothers was when we stoped. how is the wether up there? I suppose there isnt much dust flying! have you eny snow yet? how is Mr. Kratts folks and all the rest of the neighbors? tel them I would very much like to have them to write to me. has Mr. Kratts found out wither his farm is sold yet or not and who is the man that talked of buying him out? has Hanks folks ben down to se you yet and dos Marshs folks come to see you often? Lide write about every body for I guess I will get your letter by and by and I want to hear all the news.

Lide I cant think of much to write today and my hed aches so you will have to excuse me if I dont write much of a letter today but I guess I will feel better in a day or two. dont worry about me because they dont ask a man to do much if he dont feel well hear.

Lide I will close for the male is going out and I want to get this in it. Lide direct as befour onley addd First Division, Second Brigade, Fifth Corpse. Write as often as you can. and I will the same.

good by all
From Will

LETTER 11

Rebels Farm Oct. 30 . . . 64

Dear Lide

I received another letter from you this morning and was glad. I tel you. to think that your letters begins to come through pretty regular and hope they will continue to do so. I mailed a letter to you yesterday in which I attempted to cinder halfway describe a littel brush we had on the 27th with the Johneys but I did not feel very well and my hand trembled so I couldnt write. So you will have to write til I can carry a stideyer hand. My cold is a good deal better. I feel now as though I should be all right in a few days but my hand trembles today. I write you a short ong this time. I was very glad to hear that you got your cloth and it suited you. I hope you will try and enjoy yourself as well as you can this winter.

all the objection I have to joining the Church is this: if I live to come home I dont think I shal stay in that country. if you think best I am willing. you can do as you like and you will suit me.

Lide you must ansur Fernands letter. tel him that I was glad to hear from him once more. tel him I will write to him if I can get time but I have so much writing to do I dont think I can.

Lide you did not say whither you had got the crops gathered or not nor how they are. I wish you would [tell] all about those things. where is old Jack and every thing else? I gave Jim five hundred dollars in one roe and then I lent him five to get home and think that was all. he did have fifteen and that morning we left Dunkirk I bought a watch for that sum. I think he had just five hundred. if they dont want to come and se you let them stay at home. you can get along I guess. how is prices there now, have they come down eny yet? when you write agane let me know all about those things. if I was worth a shit to compose I could get off Quite a letter but you know I cant and so you will have to wate til I come home.

well Lide I stoped to eat my dinner and then went to meeting and now will finish my letter. we had a first rate meeting and will have preaching agane at four oclock and I have not changed my shirt yet so I must hurry. I hope nerves will get stil befour I have to wrie eny more for it is hard work and I dont believe you can read it. it is the bust I can do so excuse this. I like your dress and ribbon first rate.

now Lide write all the news and often to for I would like to get a letter every day. My love to all; good by.

from Will

P.S. Lide don't worry on my account.

Will Whitlock wrote these two letters to Lide one day before and one day after his involvement in the first major battle of his military career. He had been in Virginia with Company A only since the first week in October. Most of the 188th New York Regiment arrived during the two weeks before these letters. Although it is obvious that he did not know that on October 27 and 28 he would be fighting in the Battle of Hatcher's Run I (also known as the Battle of Burgess' Mill or the Battle of Boydton Plank Road; see chapter 7), he knew that he was under marching orders and that the digging and drilling were to come to a halt. These two letters reflect a continual concern, as in most of his letters, for Lide and the children back on the farm and his need for communication not just to ease his loneliness, but also to keep up with the operation of the farm. It is possible to determine Will's concern for conditions at home not only directly from his questions, but also through his replies to comments and questions that Lide must have expressed in her letters to the battlefield.

The frequency of certain requests and questions in Will's letters indicate that his major concerns regarding his family back home in western New York were communication, health, and finances. For example, he expresses his need to hear from home in all of the recovered letters but one, his concern for the family's health in all but three letters, and his wish to know about the family's finances in about half of the letters. The financial concerns, as might be expected, focused on the farm animals and crop production in the fall of 1864 and early spring of 1865.

From the beginning of his enlistment and his short time at Elmira, Will expressed to Lide that he missed her and the family and the need for letter writing. Being a family man, he apparently did not have his younger comrades' wild enthusiasm for the "freedom" of being away from home and in the military service. He found the noise distracting, making it difficult to concentrate on his writing.

Correspondence during war time is made difficult by numerous factors. In letter 2 (chap. 3), Will was able to give Lide his address at Barracks Number N1 at Elmira so that she could begin to write. He was very conscious of the effect of moving camps and location on the timely reception of mail and reminded Lide repeatedly of his current address. Even at the start of the war (1861), the US Sanitary

Commission reported that many regiments sent out six hundred letters per day on average. With more than eight million letters being sent per month, postal reforms were necessary (Wiley 1951, 183). Following secession and the removal of mail to the Confederacy, free delivery of mail in the larger cities in the North was in place. When Will arrived at City Point in October 1864, the mail was even being sorted on the train to speed up delivery. Even with some delays owing to battles and troop movement, most soldiers in the Union received their mail within two weeks after its being sent (Wiley 1951, 183). For example, Matthias Mosman of the 188th New York (Will's regiment) received a letter on November 23, 1864, from Charles Ganung that was postmarked in Olean just five days earlier. With all the letter writing going on, Union soldiers were often short on paper and stamps. In a letter to his brother, Mosman reports that Charles Reynolds was now in Company A and had brought some paper to sell and that he had purchased some.[1] Will mentions the shortage of writing paper several times in letters to Lide (letters 33 and 35, chap. 9). The paper used was typically lined to make it easier to write legibly because of the frequent problem of not having a solid platform to support the letter. Will was concerned about this problem because he had to write several times using just his knee as backing. Paper and envelopes could be purchased or obtained from home, sutlers, the US Sanitary Commission, and the US Christian Commission. Will obtained several envelopes from the two commissions.[2] In 1864, the US Mail Service announced that Union soldiers could send letters home free if they wrote "Soldier's Letter" on the envelope or used one from the Christian Commission that had "Soldier's Letter" already printed on the envelope.

So what are we to make of Will's reminders to Lide to write as much as she could and complaints about not getting a letter almost

---

1. Matthias Mosman to Charles Ganung, Nov. 23, 1864, available at http:// home.swbell.net/jcanders/index.html.

2. Two envelopes were among Will's letters, and they are included in Mark Whitney's collection, Allegany, New York.

every day? Was Lide too busy to write, or was the postal delivery not improving at all? With the exception of a few delays in delivery probably caused by troop movement, Will admits to Lide on January 22, 1865 (letter 35), that he has received more letters than any soldier in Company A. It would appear that if Will did not receive letters as often as he wished, it may not have been Lide's fault. Will's biggest disappointment related to communications from home at the beginning of 1865 was not receiving an expected box of food and other items. Soldiers on both sides of the conflict looked forward to "care packages" from home containing food, clothing or other personal material that they could not get on the front lines. On December 13, 1864, upon returning from the raid on the Weldon Railroad during very cold weather, Will first asks Lide for a "small box if you are a mind to," with some butter and cheese "if you please" (letter 26, chap. 8). In his next letter to Lide on December 16, he adds other items to the list. In addition to the butter and cheese, he hopes that Lide will have his brother-in-law Marshall Trowbridge add a pound or two of dried berries, a chunk of maple syrup candy, and other "little things that would be quite a comfort to me." In addition, he asks Lide to see Mr. Gray for a little piece of honey to add to the box. Most important, he requests that she include some wool gloves because of the weather. They must be gloves, he indicates, and not mittens because he cannot handle his rifle with just mittens. Will also wants Lide to make the box as strong as possible and sent to the same address as her letters. In the next letter home (letter 27, app. C), Will suggests that if the box costs her too much, she should just send the gloves because he needs them and they cost too much at the front lines. The day after Christmas he again mentions the need for getting something from home, at least the gloves. In this same letter, he complains about Marshall's not going to see Lide very often and wonders if her family even want to see her: "if they dont want to come let them stay away. I have never have had a letter from him since I left home." All of this concern for the box and its possible contents finally paid off for Will. In a letter Lide wrote the same day (as can be gathered from Will's response), she told Will that she had started getting the box ready. She did not tell him what was in the box, but he wishes it had arrived that very night (December 31). By January 10, 1865, the box had not arrived, and Will reminds Lide that she posted it December 28, 1864. He suggests that the box was detained somewhere because he has seen the arrival of boxes to other soldiers posted after December 28. As evidenced by a letter to Lide on January 10, 1865 (letter 32, app. C), Will knew that Lide had made a sacrifice by selling some of her potatoes to get enough money to prepare the box.

When one is expecting a gift from home, and it is delayed, the situation is made more frustrating when other individuals, especially close friends, have received boxes on time. On January 15, 1865, Will tells Lide that four big boxes from western New York arrived at headquarters, and his was not one of them. Boxes arrived for Alanson "Lont" Jones, Ashbel Bozzard, and Harrison Newell. His friends shared some of the contents with Will, so he had some "home vittles," which may have eased the pain. Ashbel Bozzard told Will that his box weighed more than a hundred pounds and cost only $3.00 to send. Lide paid $5.50, so Will thought Lide had sent him a really big box. "but never mind the cost if it onley comes" (letter 33, chap. 9). Even though more boxes arrived, as many as 150 for the brigade, not one was addressed to Will. In a letter written January 29, 1865 (letter 37, app. C), it is clear that Will has given up on the box: "Lide I think I might as well give up looking for that box for it has ben over a month since you started it. I think it has got destroyed or it would have ben hear befour this time. George Hughs got one last Thursday that was started the 13th. since his come I have give mine up as lost. I feel wors about it on your account than I do on mine for I know you worked hard and the expence it was to you and I know you need the money for your own comfort but it cant be helped. We are not to blame."

Subjects covered in Will's letters were typical of Yankee letters to the folks back home. They focused on battles (Will wrote about three battles and a foraging incident), health, weather, the land and people of new regions, Negroes, comrades from the same hometown, rumors of future battle plans and possible peace, food, and officers (Wiley 1951,

185). Because of the differences in the weather between western New York and Petersburg, Virginia, Will was very conscious of the family's health as the days became shorter and colder. He expresses a concern that Lide dress herself and the children comfortably and warmly. He does not want Lide to do much work outside in the cold weather and asks if the older children, Euzetta and Stanley, can do more of the outside work on the farm.

These letters occasionally reflect on reports from home, some quite personal. Will responds quite strongly to information from Lide about an affair discovered in a well-known family on the Five Mile in Allegany. He says that if he were in the husband's shoes, he would have shot the man and kicked the woman in the face (letter 29, app. C). Two days after Thanksgiving, Will tells Lide how he fared for Thanksgiving. He is not happy with the amount of food for all the men. He doesn't think that two pounds of cheese was nearly enough for the seventy-five men of Company A. He doesn't think that the mechanism for sending large amounts of food is getting food past the officers and their "nigger" waiters (see Chap 5). Four days later on November 29, he complains about having to drill so much and that he only has time to write just a few lines; "but we have to put up with it and there is no uce complaining for we are not concidered as good as the negro" (letter 22, app. C). Perhaps Will was still troubled by all the food that the black waiters had received at Thanksgiving. On Christmas night, when Will returned from the picket lines, the boys told him that he had some mail. He ran with great excitement to get the letter but tells Lide that he was disappointed that the letter was from Mrs. Lowe, not her. He mentions to Lide that after reading just a little of the letter, he told the boys he had read enough and was ready for supper (letter 29, app. C). Lide was apparently troubled by the gossip back home. She had heard that Mrs. Lowe intended to write to Will and tell him that Lide was jealous of a supposed relationship that Will had with Mrs. Lowe (a person first referred to back in September in letter 3, chap. 3). Will responds that if the rumor were true, he would like to hear what Mrs. Lowe had to say about it. People were saying that the reason he joined the army was that Lide had "driven him off." Will's response is, "What do we cair for what folks say. We know whether you drove me off or not and this is enough so let er rip" (letter 34, app. C). It is possible that in closing this letter by saying "let us hope we shal come out all right yet," he is not just referring to the war. Both Will and Lide were lonesome. Even as early as when Will was still at Elmira, he got word that Lide would like to come to the camp and see him. Will answers (letter 3, chap. 3) that such a visit would be nice, but all they would be able to do, as he observed other women doing, is walk around the camp, which would not be "much satisfaction." Just after Thanksgiving, Lide asked Will who was doing his washing. "Now you ask if I get wimon to do it?" The only women that he had seen since leaving Washington were about six women being escorted around the camp by officers (letter 22, app. C). As 1864 gave way to a new year, the couple missed each other even more. On January 1, 1865, Will writes to Lide about the end of the war and his return home. "I think we will know how to enjoy each others company if that time ever comes dont you Lide?" (letter 30, app. C). Lide expressed the need to see Will, and he responds that if he made it safely through the war, they would enjoy themselves "first rate" (letter 35, chap. 9). Just three days later Will has a dream about being home on furlough and kissing her (letter 36, app. C). In letter 37, January 29, 1865, he writes, "I tel you Lide I think it would be the hapeist part of my life to be shiped for home once more."

Writing home and getting letters from home were just as important for soldiers of the Confederacy—possibly even more important because their families were in the path of devastation created by Sheridan's march to the sea. Members of the middle and lower levels of the Southern socioeconomic ladder became more articulate for the first time (Wiley 1943, 192). Southerners with the same writing skills as Will begged their relatives to send news from home. Thomas Warrick of Alabama wrote home to his wife on February 12, 1863, "Martha I waunt you to write often and send me all the nuse for I am one of the Glades[t] fellows that you Ever seen when I git a letter from you you dont no how much good it dus me to here from you." Four months later he wrote, "I haint got nary letter from you for sometime when you fail to Rite . . . it ceeps mee uneasy all the time."[3]

In the early stages of the war following secession, only federal stamps were available to the Southern letter writer. The Confederate Post Office was established on June 1, 1861, and federal stamps were no longer allowed for postage. For a short time, Southern businesses that owed money to Northern corporations paid off their debts with federal stamps accepted as cash (Norris 2009, 80). To send a letter in the South, a person had to pay in cash a flat rate of ten cents at the local post office. By 1862, stamps were being produced in Richmond, Virginia and Columbia, South Carolina, but were printed in uncut sheets so that individual stamps had to be cut or torn from the sheets (Norris 2009, 81).

For the South, the supply of letters and envelopes rapidly disappeared as the war continued into 1863 and beyond. Letters and envelopes could be obtained from a sutler, but for an inflated price. William Stillwell of Georgia reported that he was spending as much as $11 a month just for writing materials.[4] Because of the cost, soldiers resorted to using the inside of envelopes, wrapping paper, and wallpaper, to writing joint letters to the community, and to having the letters posted in the community. Ink became scarce and was made from the red juice of pokeberries *(Phytolacca americana)* and the gallotannic acid from oak balls, a gall produced by the plant in response to an invading insect (Karnes 1999; Wiley 1943, 196). One of the best ways to obtain writing materials was to capture them from defeated Yankees. Perhaps the best illustration of the boon of Yankee captured materials is given in the letter from Confederate lieutenant Leonidas Polk to his wife after Confederate troops took Plymouth, North Carolina: "I am seated in an old field surrounded by men . . . dividing

3. Thomas Warrick to wife, Feb. 12, June 23, 1863, manuscript, Alabama Archives, quoted in Wiley 1943, 193.
4. William Stillwell to wife, Apr. 11, 1863, manuscript, Georgia Archives, quoted in Wiley 1943, 388.

out their captured spoils. I write to you on Yankee paper, with a gold pen, and Yankee envelope, with Yankee ink smoking Yankee cigar, full of Yankee sugar coffee and c [*sic*] with a Yankee sword, navy repeater and other 'fixins' buckled about me" (quoted in Noblin 1949, chap. 3). After the war, Polk was credited with founding the North Carolina Department of Agriculture.

By autumn of 1864, the Confederate army was suffering acutely from lack of supplies owing in part to a reduction in productivity. Farm products were reduced because of the lack of manpower. The Confederacy had placed 18 percent of its white male population in uniform, and at least 50 percent of these recruits were farmers. Like Lide Whitlock, farming wives in the South had to take over the management of the farm in addition to looking after children. The farmers' wives who had slaves found that the slaves worked less, deserted to the Union lines, or were required to work on the Confederate railroads or for the military (Glatthaar 2008, 467).

Samuel Wiley, a large plantation owner from Mt. Zion, Georgia, just west of Atlanta, wrote to his mother, Eliza DeWitt Wiley, on November 26, 1864, concerning the future of the plantation because of the war. Interestingly, he places most of the blame for decreasing productivity on his slaves. "It is the presence and expense of an idle, lazy, sickly, deceitful, discontented family of negroes. I believe they have been a sponge to soak up all the substance and increase and profits of a few who have always rendered reluctant, compulsory service . . . so many sick, the demand of the Government for a tenth of what is produced when the negroes do not produce enough to support themselves, and when every article of necessity which is not produced at home commands such a fabulous price; how can I drive the thoughts away and find any comfort in the future?"[5] Wiley's job in the Confederate quartermaster's office apparently was as frustrating as owning a plantation. With General Sherman's Union troops plundering and

---

5. Samuel Wiley to Eliza DeWitt Wiley, Nov. 26, 1864, Samuel H. Wiley Papers, Southern Historical Collection, North Carolina Univ. Library, Chapel Hill.

burning their way through Georgia toward Savannah, people without food and hope for victory stripped the countryside as they moved in front of the advancing Union troops. Similar situations were observed in most border states, where Union soldiers who took livestock and crops were followed by Confederate troops needing the same supplies.[6] Plantation families were exposed and defenseless against trouble coming from Yankees, undisciplined Confederate soldiers, and former slaves (Golay 1999, 54–55). Joseph LeConte was a successful physician in Macon, Georgia, who had graduated from the College of Physicians and Surgeons in New York City in 1845. An income from his Syfax Plantation in Liberty County, Georgia—worked by around fifty slaves—allowed him to study natural history at Harvard with Louis Agassiz. He then accepted a teaching and research position in chemistry and geology at South Carolina College. With the arrival of war, he found it difficult to "stay up" with his science because of travel difficulties and a decreasing availability of books, journals, and supplies (Golay 1999, 54–55). With General William T. Sherman headed toward Georgia, Dr. LeConte left Columbia, South Carolina, to rescue his relatives and move them to safety in central Georgia. He wrote that Sherman was approaching Savannah and would certainly ravage the whole coast. LeConte's widowed sister's plantation, where she lived with her two daughters and where his own daughter was staying, was in great danger (LeConte 1903, 185). The rescue of his relatives included dodging Yankee troops through swamps and mud to what was left of the railroads. When Dr. LeConte returned to his childhood plantation and his home in Charleston, he found wilderness and destruction (LeConte 1903).

Mary Boykin Chesnut, famous for her descriptions of the Civil War as seen through the eyes of a wealthy plantation owner, also remarked on the devastation the war had even on the wealthy and

---

6. For an excellent account of farm life in a border state, see the diaries written by George Browder, a Methodist minister-farmer from Logan County, Kentucky, who owned slaves (Browder 1987).

politically connected. At the start of the war, the Mulberry Plantation, near the Wateree River just south of Camden, South Carolina, was a cotton-producing plantation with more than five hundred slaves. Mary Chesnut, very fond of the plantation and the lifestyle it afforded, also eventually became a refugee because of the war. She had to leave the parties she attended in Richmond while visiting President Davis and his wife and return to Mulberry. As the war moved to South Carolina, she left the plantation behind for Columbia and eventually, as the Yankees arrived, to Lincolnton, North Carolina. By then, she had little money, and her friends brought her food. Her husband met up with her after ending his governmental connections in Richmond, and they tried to return to Mulberry but had difficulty in coming up with the ten-cent ferry fee to get across the Wateree. At Mulberry, they found windows broken, furniture destroyed, doors smashed, cotton mills and gin destroyed, and all the cotton burned. Because of increasing taxes and having to pay the freed slaves whom they employed, they eventually used the bricks from some of the destroyed outbuildings at Mulberry to build a home in Camden (DeCredico 1996, 17–19, 119–22, 130–32, 153–54).

Will and Lide Whitlock were very fortunate that they and their children did not become seriously ill. At a time when the medical treatment and scientific understanding of infection were undeveloped, concern for each other's health was high. Will refers to his family's health in almost all of his letters home, and it is apparent that Lide did the same in return letters: "be careful of your helth for that is the main thing and I want you to tend to your helth if nothing else" (letter 17, chap. 9). Although he is in a more dangerous environment, he expresses gentle wishes for Lide to dress warmly and comfortably (letter 3, chap. 3), to have Stanley help Euzetta (Zety) with the milking so Lide will not have to spend too much time outside in the cold (letter 36, app. C), to avoid work outside (letter 17), to make sure the children are clothed properly (letter 13, app. C), and to "doctor yourself right off." He tells her, "dont wate til you are clear down" (letter 17) and to be quick to the doctor and stop working outdoors (letter 21, app. C). This concern for health extended to his mother-in-law, Olive Sackett

Trowbridge, who did become ill. In a short letter to his children on November 29, Will asks Euzetta to be kind to Lide, to keep her still, and not to let her go out in the cold or work anymore than necessary (letter 22, app. C). Will's concern comes to the surface when he hears that Lide does have a few health problems. She wrote that she was troubled with a toothache, and Will warns her about taking cold (letter 16, chap. 7). The day after Thanksgiving in 1864, Lide told Will that she had been suffering from neuralgia, a disease that had been recently described by Silas Mitchell, a pioneer in the treatment of nervous disorders (Kreth 2010). It is interesting to note that Will's advice to stay in out of the cold may have been on target because cold sensitivity leading to pain can be experienced by individuals suffering from some types of neuralgia. In addition, tooth decay may also trigger neuralgia attacks (Hershey Medical Center 2010). Lide also reported that their youngest son, Henry, was ill, and Will wants to know what is wrong and if he is better yet (letter 38, app. C). This news is important to Will because each of the family has chores to accomplish to help Lide in his absence.

One of the greatest differences between the North and the South during the war years was the financial situation back home away from the battlefields. By the fall of 1864, both countries were in the throes of inflation in which farmers and laborers were finding most goods and everyday items far too expensive. Farmers were forced to consider little profit for crops and an increasing self-sufficiency as the war continued. Will wrote home about finances and related topics in most of his letters. He received $33 in pay while he was in camp at Elmira, and out of fear that it would get lost in the mail, he "let the money on interest" to his second lieutenant (letter 4, chap. 4). By the time he reached Washington, he decided to chance the mail and sent $10 home in the mail (letter 5, chap. 4). If Lide has more of certain crops than the family needed, Will is very concerned about the prices she is getting with the rising inflation. In some cases, especially hay, he wonders if she has enough for the winter and if she is planning on purchasing any. At one point, he tells her that she should get some money from the "boys on the hill," perhaps relatives living on "Howe Hill" in Humphrey, New

York (letter 23, app. C). Later on, in January 1865, he mentions that he has $4 if she needs it (letter 33, chap. 9) and soon thereafter tells her that he might not get paid for the month of January. If she receives some money from her brother Marshall and he sends home the $10 he lent Harrison Newell, she and the family might make it through January (letter 34, app. C). With some assistance from relatives and friends and continued good health, the Whitlocks might survive the winter.

The farm family in the Confederacy was usually not doing as well and was often near starvation. Mrs. W. W. Mize, the eldest daughter in a Georgia family of six children, recalled in an interview in 1939 when she was eighty-seven years old that her father was shot in the arm in battle and returned home, but then died of typhoid fever. His death left no male family member to run the farm. The women of the family had to do all types of field work and make their own clothes. Because of the lack of salt in the South, they obtained their salt by taking the soil out of the smokehouse and boiling off the added water. Owing to the lack of sugar, anything that was to be sweetened had to have cane, corn, or sorghum syrup. Flour was not available or too expensive, so wheat or rye was parched and used to make biscuits, but only twice a week. Mrs. Mize had seen people in tears because of the lack of food (Mize 2010). For Ida Baker in Union, South Carolina, one of the things missed most at any meal was good coffee. "Everybody had to use parched wheat, parched okra seed or parched raw sweet potato chips for coffee. If sugar was missed, it was never mentioned" (Baker 2010).

By the middle of 1863, the average family living in the cities of the South was experiencing inflated prices and the scarcity of necessities. Colonel Robert R. Stewart of the 2nd Indiana, a prisoner in Richmond, looked out his window on April 2, 1863, and saw, as he later describes, a riot of about 3,000 women armed with clubs and guns ("Reported Bread Riot" 1863). In what are now known as the "Bread Riots," the women protesting the high cost of bread proceeded to break into shops and carry away various necessities.

The wealthy of both nations were affected by the war's inflation, a fact most noticeable in the Confederacy, especially with the loss of

slave labor. For example, the increases in cost, the decrease in supplies, and the increase in population in the capital during the war
resulted in a crisis for the housewife in Richmond. In 1864, the cost
of the "finer things in life" for the women who had been raised to
take pride in their appearance was very high: boots $200, shoes $125,
a coat $350, and calico $10 per yard (Roberts 2003, 80). Even as late as
the fall of 1864, however, parties and banquets were still taking place
among the wealthy and politically connected plantation owners such
as Mary Boykin Chesnut, as she reports in her diary. She remembered
the menu for a lunch served in Richmond by President Davis's wife,
Varina: gumbo, ducks and olives, *supreme de volaille*, chickens in jelly,
oysters, lettuce *salade*, chocolate jelly cakes, claret soup, and cham-
pagne (DeCredico 1996, 102). Even if a family had an income of $600
a month, they were still poor because flour was $300 a barrel, meal was
$50 a bushel, and fresh fish was $5 a pound (DeCredico 1996, 103).

Inflation was worse in the South because the war was being
financed with bonds and Treasury notes. Devaluation of the Confederate Treasury notes was extreme. For example, in Richmond one
dollar in gold cost $1.10 in 1861, but in 1864 the same dollar of gold
cost $20 ("$100 for a Barrel of Flour" 2010). The new Confederacy
attempted to fund the war by various types of taxes but was forced to
depend on the various states to collect the revenue. Most states did
poorly in collection and either borrowed or printed money. Adding to
the problem was the issue of 8 percent bonds that Southerners could
not afford, plus a minimum of 12 percent inflation. Problems escalated
because the bonds were purchased using Confederate Treasury notes.
Therefore, the financing of the war included $1.5 billion in new dollars
that fell in value immediately (Tax History Project 2010). The currency eventually declined so much in purchasing power that $60–70
equaled only one gold dollar ("Cost of the American Civil War" 2002).

In the late months of 1864, most if not all the citizens of both the
United States of America and the Confederate States of America were
subject to the costs of war: inflation, depression owing to the war's
longevity, as well as dead and wounded loved ones and friends.

7

"The Bulits Whistled Right Smart"

Battle of Hatcher's Run I (Boydton Plank Road)

L E T T E R 10

Oct. 29 . . . 64

Well Lide,

I have seen the elephant. I wrote you a letter dated the 26 in which I stated that we was ordered to march the next morning. we was called at four oclock and ordered to get our breckfast and pack our napsacks. about an hour befour daylight we started and marched about six miles and was drawn in line of battel. we drove in the Reb picketts and stoud and fought about two hours and then fel back about 60 rods and stoped. we sent out two old regts. of old soldiers skirmishing and we threw up rifelpitts and set there all night and until about noon the next day. then [we] was ordered in line and marched back to our old camp. I came through all right with the exception of two days hard marching and no sleep and I tell you Lide I am about faged out but I guess we will have a chance to rest some now. I tel you the bulits whistled right smart. there was about 18 kild/wonded in our compiny but only three or four kild; none that you know. George Strowhover was wounded in both feet. I believe he was the only one wounded you knew.

Lide I dont know as you can read this. my hand is so stiff that I cant get it around whare I want to. Lide I was perfectly cool all through the fight. I dont feel a bit as I expected I should. I was not a bit scaird.

our mail was sent up that morning befour we left and I got a letter from you. you dont know how glad I was. I dont know as I shal be abel to ansur all of your questions in this letter but I will write agane in a few days. I hope I shal feel more like writing than I do today and will try to ansur all of them.

oh I forgot to tel you that our Captin was wonded soon after the engagement commenced. he [was] shot through the body near the left lung and it will very likely kill him. he was alive yesterday morning and was sent to City Point. we have not heard from him since. we feel to morn for he was a fine man and a good officer. he stood at the hed of his company when he fell.

Lide I am glad to learn you get all of my letters for I know how to pity you if you didnt get more than I do but I guess they will come now. keep sending them eyn how. you wrote in the last letter I got that you would not write much for feer I would not get it now. Lide I dont want you should do that way for when I get a letter I like to get a good big one. write all the news; fill it up with some thing.

you will have to excuse me this time for I have got to clean my gun. if I can I will write agane tomorrow. I am as well as usual excepting a hard cold but I guess I will get over that in a few days now.

Lide write often. I hope this will find you all well. give my respecs to all. I thank you very much for those verses. no more.

from Will

LETTER 16

Camp Near the yelow house Nov. 13th . . . 64

My Dear wife

. . . we was within forty or fifty rods of the rebs the day we had the fight. our pickets drove thairs in the brestworks and we followed them until we got to the edge of the woods. from whare I was the brush was so thick I could se nothing, but the brestwork. I could se the smoke and hear the bulits whistel right smart. I lay behind a little nole and fired 20 ronds and then croled back behind a tree to fill my catrige box and by the time I was redy to go back the order came to fall back. so that was all the shooting I done. we retreted about 30 rods and throde up brestworks but the bulits flew like hale while we was at work and just at dark it commenced raining and there we set on the grond and in rain all night expecting at daylight the rebs would make a charge on us. when daylight came they fired a few ronds at our pickets and then fel back and we went at work on our brestworks until about ten oclock and then was ordered to march. we went back to our old camp pretty well faged out I tel you. I was pretty near sick enyway but Lide I was as cool as a pickel all the time. it did not scare me a bit to se a man fall. I felt a littel ancous while waiting for daylight to come but it dident last long. when we marched back the rebs followed us and when they got out of the woods they fond some of our Artilary and our rear gards and they opened on them and we took about 60 prisners and marched them to City Point but I did not se them for we was in the advance.

During the Overland Campaign and the subsequent Siege of Petersburg in 1864, General Grant had learned the hard way that Union troops could not defeat the Army of the Confederacy by directly attacking entrenched troops. Perhaps the most innovative attempt to penetrate the Confederate lines resulted in the Battle of the Crater on July 30 that year. Pennsylvania coal miners dug a secret tunnel underneath the Rebel lines and exploded a mine beneath Confederate troops. The tremendous force of the blast opened a hole 30 feet deep, 60 feet wide, and 170 feet long. The brunt of the explosion was borne by Brigadier General William H. Wallace's ragged and hungry troops from South Carolina (see table 7.1) ("The War for Southern Independence" 2010).

TABLE 7.1

SOUTH CAROLINA CAUSALITIES AT BATTLE OF THE CRATER, 1864

Unit	Killed	Wounded	Total
17th South Carolina	25	8	33
18th South Carolina	43	43	86
22nd South Carolina	?	?	170
23rd South Carolina	14	41	55
26th South Carolina	?	?	72
Total	82	92	416

Sources: Field 2009, 48; "The War for Southern Independence in South Carolina" 2010.

Although the explosion provided an opportunity for the Union to break the Confederate line, last-minute changes and incompetent Union leadership resulted in disaster for the Federal attackers (Field 2009, 51). In August and September 1864, the Union continued the siege around Petersburg, sidling to the left and trying to cut off supplies from the south for Petersburg and Richmond. As discussed in the next chapter, these battles included Globe Tavern on August 18–21, Reams' Station on August 25, and Peebles' Farm on September 30–October 2, 1864. The Union attacks were usually rebuffed but allowed Union control of the Weldon Railroad for twenty miles south of Petersburg to the Stony Creek Station. The Yankees were able to extend entrenchment westward from the railroad. Movement out of the trenches by the Union forces was designed to outflank the Confederate breastworks on the Rebels' right and take control of the Southside Railroad that ran parallel with the Appomattox River.

Will and his comrades spent most of October digging breastworks and forts west of the Weldon Railroad. These Union lines extended from the railroad across Vaughan, Squirrel Level, and Church Roads going west and then directed south and back east to the railroad. While the Yankees were constructing these extended breastworks and forts, the Confederate forces, under General Henry Heth, were also extending their trenches and battle lines along the Boydton Plank Road, a road running east and west, north of the Union lines (Hess 2009, 167–69). These Confederate lines were angled to keep control of the road and protect the Southside Railroad, which ran between the road and the Appomattox River.

With the November presidential elections coming up in a few weeks, General Grant and other Union leaders were concerned with handing President Lincoln a battlefield victory to help his election chances. Lincoln's opponent was General George McClellan, who had been sacked by President Lincoln in 1862 and was now a "peace" candidate ("The Removal of General McClellan" 1862). Many on both sides of the conflict thought that if McClellan were elected, the war would be over.

On October 24, 1864, General Grant ordered General George Meade to march early on October 27 to take the Southside Railroad and hold and fortify it back to the Union troops' present position. Success in carrying out this plan would shut off another railroad to Petersburg and give the Union a notable victory (W. Powell [1896] 2010, 736–38). General Meade sent three columns to accomplish this goal: General John G. Parke's 9th Corps (General Ambrose E. Burnside's replacement), General Winfield S. Hancock's 2nd Corps, and General Warren's 5th Corps.

The Confederate forces were entrenched in the breastworks along the Globe Tavern line south of the Southside Railroad and were commanded by General Ambrose Powell, General A. P. Hill, and General Edward Johnson. The infantry in the trenches was supported by cavalry commanded by General Wade Hampton, General William Butler, and General Fitzhugh Lee. In preparation of the advance to the Southside Railroad, Union troops were quietly withdrawn from the trenches starting on the morning of October 25. General Nelson Miles was left with his division to hold the trench positions of the 2nd Corps.

At this same time, other secret preparations were under way. In Montreal, Canada, the actor John Wilkes Booth was meeting with a group of Confederate spies and planning to kidnap President Lincoln.

Booth received at least $1,500 for his part in the plot that changed from kidnapping to murder in the next year (Titone 2010, 335–36). In a letter to Lide written on October 26, Will tells her that they have orders to march the next day. Because of a bad cold, he is hoping to be able to march without his knapsack (letter 9, chap. 6). In a letter on October 29, he says that he had to fill his knapsack and march, so he did not get his wish. Although the 188th New York Regiment had been drilling numerous times a day, they had no experience in battle. Most of the regiment had been at the front only two weeks. An analysis of battle readiness of the 5th Corps under General Warren reveals a very inexperienced group of soldiers (table 7.2).

The original order from General Warren to march was for 5:30 AM but was altered to 4:00 AM by General Meade. Will was called at 4:00 AM to get breakfast and to pack his knapsack. He was part of a fighting force that consisted of General Gregory of the 1st Division, General Ayres of the 2nd, and General Crawford of the 3rd.

Brevet Brigadier General Edgar Gregory of the 1st Division, 2nd Brigade, certainly had his hands full of newly organized troops. He commanded New York Volunteer Regiments 187, 188, and 189. The original battle plans fortunately called for the 5th Corps to back up General John Parke's 9th Corps and, if Parke was successful, to follow up by moving to the left of the 9th Corps. If Parke was not successful, the 5th Corps would have a much more difficult assignment

TABLE 7.2
LACK OF BATTLE PREPARATION IN THE 5TH CORPS, 1864

Division	Commander	Total	Number Ignorant of Manual	Number Never Firing a Musket before Battle
1st	Charles Griffin	4,707	1,247	2,803
2nd	Romeyn Ayres	4,704	104	812
3rd (two brigades)	Samuel Crawford	596	298	298

Source: W. Powell [1896] 2010, 737.

that involved outflanking the enemy to its right (W. Powell [1896] 2010, 737). The total fighting force of bluecoats for this action was 43,000, approximately 75 percent of the Union forces in the Petersburg trenches at the time ("First Hatcher's Run" 2010).

At 3:00 AM on October 27, 1864, the 9th Corps under General Parke initiated the Battle of Hatcher's Run I (Boydton Plank Road) by moving out westward toward the road. Because his troops were the closest to the enemy, it was expected that they would be in battle very soon. However, movement was slow, and at 9:00, after marching for four miles, they discovered a well-entrenched force in front of them. This unexpected situation caused Parke to stop and entrench, fearing an attack by the southern forces on his front.[1] The 5th Corps, under command of General Warren, started off at approximately 4:00 AM and, according to Will, marched about six miles before joining up in a line of battle. Captain Daniel Loeb, of the New York 187th, reported an even earlier time of 2:00 AM at which the troops were awakened quietly to "strike their tent" and pack up for the march (Martin 2001, 124; W. Powell [1896] 2010, 739). Although Will did not mention it, this march was very difficult because the troops were marching west, but all the roads ran north and south. Some of the regiments in the 5th Corps had to cut down trees and brush that blocked their intended path. Many men got lost in the thick brush, and communication was confused and minimal throughout the corps.[2] The march was made even more difficult because visibility was inhibited by clouds and rain that started around 4:45 AM.

Private Henry Didcock (from Killbuck, New York) of the 187th New York, Company I, who had enlisted at Salamanca, New York, on September 20, recorded that he was up at 3:00 AM getting ready for the

1. Daniel Loeb to editor, *Dunkirk Union*, Oct. 29, 1864, available at http://dmna.state.ny.us/historic/reghist/civil/infantry/187thInf/187thInfCWN.htm.

2. Henry Didcock to father, mother, and brother, Nov. 21, 1864, quoted in Anderson 2010.

march with full knapsack, haversack, a canteen of water, and sixty-five rounds of cartridges.[3] Through the gray morning, Didcock saw other regiments moving with infantry and artillery. During the march, the 187th passed an open farm area where no army had camped, as evidenced by unharvested corn and Chinese sugar cane or sorghum (J. Hyde 1857, 16–18), undug sweet potatoes, and untouched rail fences. The regiment's inexperience is evident in Didcock's description of a stop in a wood as they got closer to the Confederate lines: "Order is to Stop Marching and load our Musketts in case of an emergency. Our Musketts are Loaded for the first time. Then March on."[4] It is possible that the phrase "for the first time" meant that the muskets were loaded for the first time for this particular battle, but it might mean that it was the first time some of the soldiers had ever loaded their rifles because of their lack of training.

Finally, at about 9:00 AM the 5th Corps came under fire by Confederate skirmishers. Brigadier General Charles Griffin immediately ordered Brevet Brigadier-General Edgar Gregory's 2nd Brigade (made up of the three new New York regiments, the 187th, 188th, and 189th) to line up and advance through the woods.[5] A report from General Warren to General Meade at 9:30 AM indicated that his forces had found a road leading directly west and found the enemy. He also reported that he did not think, because of the enemy forces, that it would be practicable to cross Hatcher's Run above Armstrong's Mill.

General Gregory established a battle line with clear knowledge of the inexperience of the three regiments from New York. He placed them behind experienced skirmishers from the 91st Pennsylvania and the 155th New York and surrounded them with experienced soldiers from both of these regiments. On the far right of the line, General

3. Ibid.
4. Ibid.
5. Charles Griffin to Fred Locke, Oct. 29, 1864, in *General Griffin's Report* 2010 (quoted in Anderson 2010).

15. General Gouverneur K. Warren, 1861–65. General Warren commanded the 5th Corps of the Army of the Potomac and was the army's chief engineer. He was a hero of the Battle for Little Round Top when his forces helped save the day on July 2, 1863, at Gettysburg. He was in command of the 5th Corps while William Whitlock served but was relieved of duty when he was falsely accused of poor performance by General Philip Sheridan at the Battle of Five Forks on April 1, 1865. Courtesy of the Library of Congress, Washington, DC.

Gregory placed General John F. Hartranft's brigade of experienced Yankees, most from Pennsylvania. General John F. Bartlett's brigade of experienced soldiers, predominately from Massachusetts, was in reserve at the rear. While Gregory's brigade was in the woods lining up, he came to the front of the lines and told them that they had a short job before them that would take about twenty minutes of work. Henry Didcock wrote home that it was more like twenty-four hours of work and that these new soldiers were told not to fire until ordered for fear of hitting the men of the 91st Pennsylvania.[6] When Gregory's Brigade began to march forward out of the woods, Will watched as the pickets in front of the line drove the Rebel pickets into the breastworks across the field. When he arrived at the edge of the woods, he had difficulty

6. Didcock to father, mother, and brother, Nov. 21, 1864.

16. General Charles Griffin, 1861–65. General Griffin commanded the 1st Division of the 5th Corps under General Warren. William Whitlock served in the 2nd Brigade under General Griffin. The general replaced General Warren during the Battle of Five Forks. Courtesy of Library of Congress, Washington, DC.

seeing because of the brush. He could see the breastwork and smoke and heard the bullets whistle by "right smart." As the firing began, the captain of Company A, 188th Regiment, James Curtis, was hit in the chest near a lung and went down. He was still alive the next morning and was taken to City Point. Will tells Lide later about how much they missed the "fine man and a good officer": "He stood at the hed of his compiny when he fell." In a letter written on November 1, 1864, Will reports that Captain Curtis is still alive and gaining slightly. On December 16, he informs Lide that Captain Curtis is doing well and is talking about going home soon. Captain Curtis came to visit the troops one more time before going home on January 30, 1865. He looked better than Will expected but was quite thin. Will wished the captain could stay but realized he will not be able to take the field ever again (letter 37, app. C).

Will found a small hill near the edge of the woods and fired off twenty rounds. He then crawled back behind a tree to fill his cartridge box. At about 150 yards from the enemy breastworks, strong firing from the Confederates forced General Gregory's men (the new New York regiments) back about 50 yards, where they reformed and again advanced. This advancement sent the Confederates into their rifle pits. During this advancement, Henry Didcock of the 187th moved forward about twenty-five feet behind the 91st Pennsylvania. At 1:00 PM, General Warren ordered General Griffin to have his skirmishers (155th Pennsylvania) on the left to press up against the enemy and commence firing. The woods south of Hatcher's Run was so dense that Griffin's men needed to hear the sound of battle to guide them. Under heavy fire, Didcock moved forward about 150 yards to join the 91st Pennsylvania even though his own regiment, the 187th New York, fell back. The first person he saw was George Fowler, who had enlisted from Freedom, New York, and was up front from the 188th. Didcock describes the encounter:

We then was in front of the enemys brest works. There was a few trees in front of us and then a field clear of every thing. We could not see any Rebs but there Balls was passing over us. I asked George what we was agoing to Shoot at. We concluded to direct our fire in the direction that the Reb fire came. We could see the blaze of there guns, George and I being in the front so the Balls passed over us. My opinion is that there is more men hit by Skulking than by being in there proper place. We were there perhaps 2 or 3 hours, cool and calm, Loading and firing. I did not see but one dead man as I know of and some wounded. The most that was killed and wounded was in the rear.[7]

Some amazing aspects of war occurred to these inexperienced New York soldiers that October afternoon. Private John Anderson of Allegany (188th) was hit in the chest by a musket ball. The ball fortunately did not kill him because it hit the Bible and a pocket watch he had in his jacket pocket (Anderson 2010). Andrew Helser of Machias (188th) was hit twice during the battle; one bullet went through his pants, and another stopped in his blanket. Neither bullet broke the skin (Anderson 2010). Perhaps the most amazing incident was what happened to John Lovewell of Ellicottville (188th). Private Lovewell was shot in the face about one and a half inches above his eyes. At the hospital, when he regained consciousness, he was told that the bullet had been removed. After he complained of painful headaches, later surgeries removed some pieces of bone, but the pain continued. The pain was so great that on September 9, 1901, Mr. Lovewell took a pair of nippers and finally removed the ball that had been there for almost thirty-seven years (Anderson 2010).

Back in the trenches vacated by the 2nd Corps near Petersburg, General Nelson Miles, who was left behind to protect the Union breastworks, asked for one hundred volunteers from the 148th Pennsylvania to check on the strength of the Confederates across the trenches from them (the 46th Virginia). Armed with Spencer 7 shooters, the one hundred volunteers took the fort and captured four commissioned officers. They held the fort for only thirty minutes, though, because the 46th Virginia received reinforcements. Perhaps

7. Ibid.

with greater force, this action might have been one of the breaks in the Confederate line that Grant desired ("The Virginia Campaign" 1864, 741).

The major object of the attack on October 27, 1864, was the Southside Railroad and control of Boydton Plank Road. General Hancock's men crossed the flooded Hatcher's Run about 8:30 AM, but General Thomas Smyth's brigade lost fifty men to Confederate cavalry that had been protected by a deep ditch (Hess 2009, 192–98; Walker 1887, 616–18). Hancock found the Confederate forces much more organized and entrenched than expected. His men pushed forward and reached the Boydton Plank Road about 10:30 AM and even controlled White Oak Road, which led to the railroad. This action separated his troops from the rest of the Union forces, and he received a message at 1:00 PM to wait for instructions (Hess 2009, 192–98). However, as described earlier, General Warren's troops were not able to support Hancock. Warren had sent troops under General Samuel Crawford (3rd Division), but because of the thick woods and underbrush this connection was never made, leaving the 2nd Corps' right flank exposed (Hess 2009, 192–98). At 1:30 PM, General Hancock was visited in the field by Generals Grant and Meade and told to hold his position until noon the next day ("Burgess Mill" 2010). That night General Crawford's men were able to capture more than two hundred Rebels, who were then taken to the rear (Hess 2009, 135–40).

It was obvious, though, that the overall Union plan was not going to work because of the slow going through dense brush, the rain, and the Confederate forces' unexpected strength. General A. P. Hill's experienced Confederate forces, commanded by Generals Henry Heth and William Mahone, were entrenched north of Hatcher's Run in front of Hancock's Union forces and supported by experienced cavalry under the command of Generals Wade Hampton and Matthew Butler. General W. H. Fitzhugh Lee's cavalry was behind Hancock's Union forces blocking the crossing of Gravelly Run. Hancock could move his men only to his right along Dabney's Mill Road ("Burgess Mill" 2010). The Union's 2nd Corps was almost surrounded, and so General Hill called for a Confederate attack at about 4:00 PM.

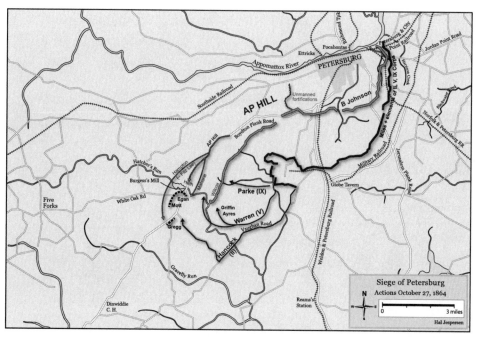

Map 1. Siege of Petersburg and the Battle of Hatcher's Run I (October 27, 1864). Map by Hal Jespersen, www.cwmaps.com.

At 4:00 PM, Heth and Mahone moved across Hatcher's Run. General Hampton attacked on Hancock's left flank, and General Fitzhugh Lee attacked across Gravelly Run at Hancock's rear. This was certainly a better-coordinated attack than what the Union forces were able to muster. The Confederate attack placed great pressure on Hancock's 2nd Corps, which had not performed very well at all at the Battle of Reams' Station (or Globe Tavern) (Hess 2009, 135–40). To add to the pressure, the skies opened up with a strong rainstorm. With Confederate forces on three sides, Hancock arranged his forces in an oval, with the long axis on the Plank Road.[8] The northern end of the

8. Winfield Hancock to Seth Williams, Nov. 10, 1864, *Official Records of the Union and Confederate Armies in the War of the Rebellion*, series I, chap. 42, pp. 230–38; see also Trinque 2010.

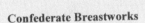

Confederate Breastworks

Open Field   100-200 yds to breastworks

Advanced Union line- -

Gregory's Brigade
91st PA (skirmishers)
↕ 25 ft

155th PA   188th NY   91st PA (first line)   Hartranft's Brigade
(skirmishers)   187th NY   155th PA (second line)

Bartlett's Brigade

Map 2. General Gregory's Brigade at the Battle of Hatcher's Run I. Map by the author.

oval was near the Burgess Tavern on Hatcher's Run, commanded by General Thomas Egan with Colonel Robert McAllister's brigade in support. The western side of the oval was in the command of Brigadier General Regis de Trobriand and Colonel Michael Kerwin's dismounted cavalry. The southern portion of the oval was occupied by General David Gregg's cavalry facing General Lee's cavalry to the south. The eastern side of the oval was manned by Brigadier General Byron Pierce facing toward the west (Trinque 2010).

Just when the battle was going well for the Confederacy, tragedy struck. As General Butler's men advanced on Hancock's left, Butler noticed a group of Confederate officers riding too close to the front and drawing dangerous fire from the Yankees. He recognized two of them as his brother Oliver and Preston Hampton, General Hampton's son (Brooks 1994, 568–69; Field 2009, 69; Martin 2001, 127). General Butler signaled for them to drawback and get out of range of the Yankee muskets. Before they could, however, Preston was hit and fell off his horse. Wade Jr., Hampton's eldest son, quickly rode to the scene but was also hit as he tried to help his brother. General Hampton rode up and gathered Preston in his arms and found that he had been shot in the groin, usually a mortal wound. Soldiers and officers assisted Hampton in placing Preston on a wagon and Wade Jr. on his horse. The general accompanied the wagon for a short distance to the rear, and then, realizing that his boy was dying and it was too late, he returned to battle. The next day the general, after leading a pursuit of the retreating Yankees, buried Preston and was thankful that Wade Jr. was not seriously injured (Brooks 1994, 569; Martin 2001, 128).

Confederate forces now faced a tactical turnabout as General Matthew Butler's forces were greatly slowed by Union fire. Lee's attack along the Boydton Plank Road was also inhibited by General Gregg's dismounted cavalry. Commanding General Heth's charge across Hatcher's Run was stopped by General Smyth's forces (Field 2009, 68–69; Hess 2009, 193–94).

General Meade, after hearing of the Rebel attack, ordered General Hancock to withdraw, which Hancock initiated at 10:00 PM.

Hancock's forces had left the area of battle by 1:00 AM the next morning (Hess 2009, 193–94).

Back to the east in the late afternoon, Will loaded up cartridges to return to the small hill from which he had been firing. While he was reloading, the order came to fall back, so he did no more shooting. The troops under General Gregory pulled back about 160 yards and began to throw up breastworks under heavy fire from the enemy. Because of the lowering clouds, darkness arrived early, and the rain returned. Henry Didcock reported hearing skirmishers shooting throughout the wet night. Will, after lying on the ground all night in the pouring rain, expected that the Rebels would attack in the morning on October 28.

When daylight came, the 188th went back to work on their breastworks, receiving some Confederate fire at their pickets. At 10:00 AM, Gregory's forces were ordered to retreat to their old camp. In the letter dated November 13 (letter 16), Will tells Lide that he was a little anxious during the night waiting for the morning Confederate attack, but that through the whole skirmish he remained "cool as a pickel." In the morning, when Gregory's troops started to march back to camp, the Confederate forces followed them out of the woods into the open. When they saw Union artillery and rear guards, the Rebel soldiers opened fire, but with little consequence. Will reported to Lide that Gregory's forces took about sixty prisoners, but that he did not see them because the 188th New York was in the advance on the retreat back to camp. In thinking back on the battle, Will tells Lide on November 29 that he would not want to be taken prisoner but that he came very close to it in that the "Rebs" were flanking the 188th New York as the regiment left the woods (letter 22, app. C).

In the letter written on the day before the battle, Will complained that he had a bad cold with headaches and that his right hand trembled so much he was concerned that Lide might not be able to read the letter. Two days after the battle on October 29, Will is still complaining about his right hand: "my hand is so stiff that I cant get it around whare I want to. Lide I was perfectly cool all through the fight. I dont feel a bit as I expected I should. I was not a bit scaird." In a letter written just three days after the battle, however, Will admits to Lide that he wishes his nerves would settle down so he could write more legibly (letter 11, chap. 9). In a letter on November 17, 1864 (letter 17, chap. 9), he again complains about his trembling right hand. The news that Lide received from the front was apparently told to all the Whitlock and Trowbridge family members. Will's brother-in-law, Marshall Trowbridge, may have told Lide that the reason Will's hand was shaking was that he was frightened. Will writes Lide in response, "Lide tel Marsh that when in theat battel I felt just as I wrote I did and if he thinks I was scaired becose my hand trembled tel him that I have to drink a good deal and have to cary my gun in my right hand so much that my hand trembels all the time. for two weeks I felt so bad that it was worce and I dont have as good a place to write as when I was at home but I have to wrtie and I do the best I can."

William Whitlock had "seen the elephant" (letter 10).

8

Wrecking the Weldon

Dec. 13th . . . 64

My Dear wife

I have just recied two letters from you about ten minuts ago and was right glad to hear that you was all well. I am well but some lame from the long march we have just returned from. I received a ltter from you the night befour we marched and wrote a short ansur stating we was ordered to march. we started the next morning and got back last night. we are within four miles of our old camp but dont expect to stay. we may have to go on another rade. some think they are looking up winter quarters for us. I hope they are. Lide if I had time I would like to give you a detale of the rade we made for I think it would be interesting to you if I could explane it just as it was but I cant. I will do the best I can in giving a few detales. we started about fifty thousand strong, marched south fifty or sixty miles within a few miles of North Carliny. [we] burnt buildings and fences tore up about 25 miles of railroads burnt up tyes and spoiled the iron. we was gone just a week but saw no fiting. the cavlery had a few little shots. we drove quite a drove of cattel and some negroes. I tel you Lide it was a splendid part of the contry. rich bildings but they had to come down. we went down one road and back another and it would be hard matter to estimate the damage. Perhaps you will get the amout befour we will. I stood the march first rate did not loose eny thing but befour we

104

had marched two days half of the boys threw away thear knapsacks and almost all thear clouths. we were gone just a week. we started tuesday and got back mondy night.

I cant ansur your questions today for I have not time but I thank God that I am spaired to hear from you once more and to write a few lines back to you. Now Lide you must excuse this time for I am in a hurry. write as often as you can. I will do likewise. if we get whare we put up for the winter in a few days I will Write and you may send me a small box if you are a mind to. [include] some butter and a few things, just what you are a mind to—a little cheas if you pleas.

Lide write soon. I dont know as you can read this ; I was in a hurry and I didnt stop to get ink. Now good by to all.

yours in true affection,
Will

LETTER 26

Dec. 17th. . . . 64

Dear Lide

as I am on picket and stood on post last night we are held as reserve to day and nothing to do. so I thought I would write you a few lines. I am well and do hope you are all the same. Lide I dont know as you can read this for I have to sit on the ground with my paper on my lap and I have nothing to stidy my hand on but you must figure it out some how or other.

Lide I am going to try and tel you something about our march but you must not expect a ful detale for I am not capable of giving it. The first day nothing occurd of note. we marched until about 'fore oclock in the afternoon and halted for a pontune bridge to be put across the Notoway river and at two the next morning started on our march agane and cept it up until four oclock that day then we halted and rested until dark then started agane and five miles and struck the railroad. we stacked our guns and slung our knapsacks and went to work taking up the track. it was hard work and we was tired but we made it fly I tel you! we worked about two hours and then moved on past two or three brigads and went at it agane and worked until two oclock in the morning. then we had orders to rest so we layed down on our blankets until daylight. that was at Larits station. we burnt the station and everything around it. in the morning we kild three or four cattel and had some fresh beef. then we moved on til about two oclock and halted and made some coffe and kild some sheep and had some fresh mutton. then [we] stacked our knapsacks and marched up the road three miles. [we] tore up track until ten oclock then went back whare we left our baggage and pitched our tents and tried to get a little rest but it rained and haled and blew so we could not sleep nor keep dry. the next morning at daylight we started back and marched hard all day through the rain and mud about half knee deep til after dark. [we] did not halt during the day to get enything to eat. we ate a few hard tack on the march. I tel you we was a tierd lot of men. that night. it rained all night and we had to lay on the wet ground but I enjoyed some sound sleep. the next day we did not march only ten or twelve miles [and] got across the Notoway. the rebs made an attack on our rear but was drove back. the next day we got whare we are now. none of our brigade fired a gun on the whole march. I stood it first rate. I was some lame and tired but not half as bad as some of them. I did not throw away eny of my things but there was not half of the knapsacks brot back thatt was taken out. But Lide thank God we are ordered to put winter quarters and I think if we move agane this winter they will be short marches and will return to our old camp agane. I will have to write on another sheet.

During the summer of 1864, several direct attacks on the Confederate trenches south of Petersburg (one being the Battle of the Crater on July 30) had resulted in disastrous defeats for the Union army. Although forced to set up a siege around Petersburg, as opposed to more direct attacks on entrenched Confederate soldiers, General Grant recognized that to maximize the effects of a siege, supply lines, both roads and railroads, must be completely shut down. One of the major links that the Confederate army had to supplies and war equipment from the south, primarily from the port of Wilmington, North Carolina, was the Weldon and Petersburg Railroad. This railroad used to run south along the present Route I-95 in southern Virginia. Closer to Petersburg, the Weldon ran south out of Petersburg along the Halifax Road, present-day Route 604. At that time, the Union lines were located just north of Flank Road (approximately 2.9 miles south of Petersburg) before the line curved southwest toward Hatcher's Run. Flank Road intersected the Weldon Railroad's north–south lines and the important north–south roads: Vaughan (Route 675) and Squirrel Level (Route 613).

Several attempts to destroy the railroad's northern connection to Petersburg occurred in the summer of 1864 and had allowed the Union fortifications to proceed westward toward Hatcher's Run. To maximize the effectiveness of Union attacks south of Petersburg, Grant put pressure on Confederate fortifications between Petersburg and Richmond to force General Lee to withdraw some troops from the trenches around Petersburg to protect the Confederate capital.[1]

The first battle specifically aimed at the Weldon Railroad was the Battle of Jerusalem Plank Road on June 21–24 (Field 2009, 27–28; Hess 2009, 38–39). The Union army attempted to extend its line farther west and at the same time destroy the railroad south of Petersburg. The battle was initiated by cavalry forces under the command of Generals James H. Wilson and Augustus Kautz (5,500 cavalry and twelve guns), who began to tear up tracks. The cavalry forces were followed by the 2nd Corps, which was supported by the 6th Corps. In addition to wrecking the tracks, the Union soldiers established breastworks adjacent to the railroad on the night of June 21.

1. Ulysses Grant to Benjamin Butler, Aug. 18, 1864, in Jesse Marshall 1917, 5:71; George Meade to Theodore Bowers, Nov. 1, 1864, *Official Records of the Union and Confederate Armies in the War of the Rebellion (OR)*, series I, chap. 36, pp. 188–95; Walsh 2002, 387.

Late that evening the Confederates returned to their breastworks, leaving a small force of sharpshooters to engage any pursuing Yankees. In retreating, the Rebel sharpshooters saw a small road that would assist their rapid return to their forces. Unfortunately for the Rebels, the Yankee pursuers also saw the road, and the race was on. One Rebel sharpshooter arrived at camp panting and laughing. "Lord God! You ought to see them fat Yankees run. They run arter me, a-hollin' 'Stop you damned rebel! Cut off the damned rebels!' I heerd em blow. Says I to myself, 'You too fat, Yankee! You get too much to eat over your side. You don't catch me!' And you ought to a seed me as I slid past em" (quoted in Caldwell 1866, 165).

The next day the Union forces were met with Confederate infantry and cavalry under the command of Brigadier General William Mahone. General Mahone had an advantage because he had been a railroad engineer and knew the region's topography very well. Fierce fighting went back and forth most of the day, with the Union forces pushed back to their breastworks and farther back approaching the Plank Road. On June 23, Union forces again reached the railroad and began taking up the track. Once again, the Confederates under the command of General Mahone counterattacked with some success. At the end of the battle, although the Union forces had been forced to retreat twice, they had advanced westward, destroyed some of the railroad, and taken 1,700 prisoners (Field 2009, 28).

The second major battle aimed at the Weldon Railroad was the Battle of Globe Tavern on August 18–21, 1864. In the early hours of August 18, the 5th Corps, under the command of Major General Warren, attacked the Weldon Railroad at Globe Tavern, and troops of the 1st Division led by Brigadier General Griffin began to tear up tracks and destroy any structures the enemy might use.[2]

Brigadier General Romeyn Ayres led the 2nd Division southward along the railroad destroying the tracks and soon made contact with

2. Field 2009, 60; Ulysses Grant to Henry Halleck, Aug. 18, 1864, *OR*, series I, chap. 42, p. 18; Meade to Bowers, Nov. 1, 1864.

Confederate troops. On a very hot summer day, Confederate major general Henry Heth quickly moved Davis's brigade and Walker's brigade from Petersburg. They deployed on both sides of the railroad facing south and waited for the Union troops (Hess 2009, 129–135). With a loud Rebel yell, Davis's brigade charged and overlapped both flanks of the Federal line. Fighting continued back and forth until at about 2:30 PM when the Confederates were stopped by a deadly volley of artillery. On the next day, August 19, both sides poured more troops into the area. In the afternoon, two of General A. P. Hill's brigades slipped through the woods behind the Union lines and captured 2,700 Federal soldiers, with many casualties.[3] Once again, Major General Mahone was hurried into position on the opposite (eastern) side of the Union line from Hill's brigades. With heavy fighting, Mahone's five infantry brigades gained ground but were repulsed later in the day by Warren's 5th Corps (Field 2009, 61). After a day of entrenchment and relative inactivity on August 20, General Hill's troops attacked an entrenched Union army near the tavern on August 21. During the back-and-forth advances, Brigadier General Johnson Hagood led his brigade of South Carolinians into the Federal works, only to find that one of his officers, without consultation, had already surrendered his regiment (Field 2009, 61). He ordered his men back to battle or to fall back, every man for himself. General Hagood escaped but had two horses shot from under him during his retreat. Unfortunately for the Confederates, one of the soldiers killed that day was Brigadier General John Caldwell Calhoun Sanders. Sanders had left the University of Alabama and enlisted in the Confederate Guards (Company E), 11th Alabama. As captain, Sanders had led his troops at the Battle of Seven Pines, and at Frayser's Farm where he was wounded on June 30, 1862 (Goellnitz 2010b). With promotions because of leadership and bravery, Sanders led his Confederate troops at Second Bull Run, Antietam, Fredericksburg, Chancellorsville, and Gettysburg, where he was

---

3. Hess 2009, 131; Ulysses Grant to Henry Halleck, Aug. 21, 1864, *OR*, series I, chap. 42, p. 18.

wounded again. He returned to command his regiment at the Wilderness and Spotsylvania. He was promoted to brigadier general and led his men in the counterattack at the Battle of the Crater. In the Battle of Globe Tavern on August 21, 1864, he was mortally wounded when a minie ball severed both of his femoral arteries. His exact burial place in Hollywood Cemetery (Richmond, Virginia) is not known (Goellnitz 2010a). In the Battle of Globe Tavern (August 18–21), the Union forces were successful in stretching the siege lines farther west and cutting off the northern part of the Weldon Railroad from Petersburg. The price was high, however, in that more than 2,000 prisoners were taken, and there were 4,300 casualties. It was estimated that the Confederates suffered 2,300 casualties (Hess 2009, 134).

On August 24, Major General David Gregg's cavalry moved south along the Weldon ahead of General Hancock's 2nd Army Corp in an attack on the railroad about eight miles south of Petersburg, initiating the Battle of Reams' Station (Hess 2009, 135–41). While destroying the railroad, the troops moved into fieldworks that had been constructed by the 6th Corps earlier in June. These works were poorly constructed, with openings for the railroad and Depot Road, and had been further deteriorated by the weather (Dauchy 1890, 2). In the early afternoon of August 25, Confederacy forces (3rd Army Corps) under General A. P. Hill (13,000 infantry) and General Hampton's cavalry attacked these poorly constructed fieldworks. General Hill, a frail individual in part owing to a lifelong battle with venereal disease acquired while he was a cadet at West Point (Goellnitz 2010b; Walker 1884), was in so much pain that he commanded his forces while lying on the ground in front of the Union's fieldworks. In charge of General William "Rooney" Lee's division because of Lee's own illness, General Rufus Barringer led his troops from North Carolina. General Barringer had been shot in the right cheek while he was leading his men at the Battle of Brandy Station in June 1863, and the bullet had come out his mouth. After the war and after being held captive at Fort Delaware, he returned to Republican politics and was a supporter of Reconstruction and black suffrage. D. H. Hill, an elder of the First Presbyterian Church of Charlotte, refused to serve Barringer communion because

"Republicans were not fit to sit at the Lord's Table." Barringer transferred his membership to the Second Presbyterian Church, where he
was welcomed and later became an elder (Barringer 2010).

As the Confederates advanced, the members of the 116th Pennsylvania were about to fire when General Hancock ordered the men
at double quick through a cornfield to the poorly constructed breastworks. Because the breastworks were so low, the Rebel skirmishers
were having a "hot time," so the 116th Pennsylvania was ordered to
charge out of the breastworks. The fighting was so severe that the regiment lost both Captain Garrett Nowlen of Company B and Captain
Samuel Taggart of Company I in quick succession. Even though the
Southern troops were being raked with grape and canister as well as
the "Buck and Ball" of the 116th's older muskets, they advanced within
twenty paces of the Yankee line (Chisholm 1989, 35–36).

At 5:00 PM, the Confederate troops mounted an assault, resulting in major confusion in the Union troops. Private Patrick Ginley,
Company C, 1st New York Light Artillery, found himself between
the lines in grave danger. He crawled back into the fieldworks and
single-handedly loaded a cannon with charges of canister and fired
point-blank into Confederate troops. He received the Medal of Honor
for his actions (Field 2009, 63). During the confusion, Confederate
troops accidentally fired captured Yankee cannons loaded with canister—formerly belonging to the 2nd Division, Battery B—into their
own men (Rhodes 1894, 326–33). By the end of the day, both Hancock
and Gregg were forced to withdraw. The number of prisoners captured by the Confederate forces was so large (2,150) that the officers
of the Confederacy originally thought that this large group marching into Petersburg was their own retreating soldiers (Field 2009, 64).
Owing to previous losses and the large number of troops mustered
out of service, numerous Union outfits were much reduced in quantity
and quality. The presence of some men who were drafted—bounty
men and jumpers, foreigners, and untrained soldiers—served to spell
the doom of the once proud 2nd Corps. The Southern troops had
stopped the Union from further destruction of the Weldon but had
not retaken the railroad from Reams' Station north to Petersburg. As

a consequence, General Lee had to depend on supplies coming up the Weldon as far as Stony Creek Station, sixteen miles south of Petersburg, and then being hauled across country thirty miles out of the way via Dinwiddie Court House and up the Boydton Plank Road to Petersburg. During the rest of August and September, up until the arrival of Will Whitlock at City Point in the first week of October, numerous battles occurred in this same area, including the Beefsteak Raid (September 14–17) led by CSA general Wade Hampton, in which 2,468 head of Union cattle were rustled (Field 2009, 64; Mewborn 1864, 6–17, 44–50), and a major struggle at Peebles' Farm on September 30–October 2, 1864. Most of these skirmishes were Union attempts to outflank the Confederate entrenchments toward the west.

Following the Battle of Hatcher's Run I, Will wrote several letters in which he indicates to Lide that his company was in camp near the Rebel's Farm and the Yellow House (tavern) during the first week of November (letters 12–17). Will was very tired of moving around and wanted to find a place to settle down for the winter. It was during this time of boredom and drilling that he found time to write about politics (the national election, Copperheads) and that he was very happy to know that Lide was getting out into the community, attending church and political rallies. He was also able to catch up in his correspondence about his experience in the Battle of Hatcher's Run I (October 27–28, 1864).

The approach of winter brought all major operations to a halt as both armies settled into the trenches, with the usual dangerous artillery shells overhead and the buzz of musket shells from pickets and sharpshooters. Based on the condition of the Confederate troops, the siege was working for the Federals in that the food, ammunition, and clothing supplies were getting lower. The first really cold weather occurred on November 23, 1864, when snow and cold resulted in frostbite for Confederate troops with no shoes, blankets, or coats (Hess 2009, 215). Desertion became a major problem for the Confederacy because of lack of food and lack of pay. Jesse Hill of the 21st North Carolina said of his comrades, "Tha say it hant of any use to stay here and be kiled for no thing tha all say we are whiped and tha all no it" (quoted in Hess 2009, 224). Captain Gabriel Floyd of the 11th Florida had heard through the grapevine that a six-man picket post was thinking about desertion to the Union lines. To combat the possible desertion, he placed two reliable men at either end of the pit to watch the other six. On returning to his command post, however, Captain Floyd heard that all eight men had gone over to the Union lines.[4] Many of the starving Rebel troops stuck to their guns despite the hardships even when letters from home told of looting and burning by General Sherman's troops. Although W. E. Leak of the 22nd South Carolina knew Sherman was burning his way through South Carolina, he stayed through the rain, sleet, and snow with daily rations of a tin cup of cornmeal and some beef. He was captured and later died at Point Lookout Prison.[5] Although not so much of a problem as experienced by the Confederacy, desertion did occur in the Federal lines as well. Major E. M. Woodward, in recording the history of the 198th Pennsylvania Regiment, described the execution of Private Charles Miller of the Maryland 2nd, who had deserted and was captured by the pickets of the 198th Pennsylvania. To make an example of Mr. Miller, his entire division was present at the execution. Following a death procession that included the prisoner, his coffin, a priest, and the guard, the prisoner was shot while seated blindfolded on his own coffin. Despite this warning, the next night, the 198th Pennsylvania pickets captured another Yankee deserter who had witnessed the execution the previous day (Woodward 1884, chap. 4).

During the month of November, Will was involved in winter activities such as picket duty, drilling, and patrolling. This routine was disrupted in the first week of December. In a letter written to Lide on December 5 (letter 23), while he was on relief from guard duty, he informs her that he is under marching orders once again and that he

4. David Lang to Joseph Finegan, Jan. 21, 1865, *OR*, series I, chap. 46, part 2, pp. 1146–47.

5. W. Leak to wife and children, Jan. 30, 1865, Leak Letters, Petersburg National Battlefield Archives, Petersburg, VA; Hess 2009, 225.

must leave the relative warmth of winter quarters and be exposed to the dangers of war outside the trenches.

On December 5, General Grant issued orders to General Meade, commander of the Army of the Potomac, to prepare to move down the Weldon and destroy it all the way to Hicksford, Virginia (present-day Emporia) or farther. General Meade was to take a force of "not less than 20,000 infantry, 16–20 guns and all your disposable cavalry; six days rations and 20 rounds of extra ammunition will be enough to carry along."[6] As a consequence, General Meade ordered General Warren of the 5th Corps to command the raid with his three divisions. In addition, the 3rd Division of the 2nd Corps led by Brigadier General Gershom Mott and the 2nd Cavalry led by Brigadier General David Gregg were also involved, making up a total of approximately 27,000 troops. Each infantry division had an artillery battery, and this large fighting force also was followed by engineers with a 250-foot pontoon bridge (Woodward 1884, chap. 4).

Will and the rest of Company A of the 188th New York Volunteers heard the news of the campaign the afternoon of December 5. Very few of the rank and file knew where they were headed, but they packed their knapsacks with four days' worth of rations and their pockets with twenty rounds of extra cartridges. Rumors were flying throughout the trenches and camps that they were headed either west again or possibly down to Wilmington, North Carolina, where they supposedly would be involved, in conjunction with the Union navy, in attacking this important Confederate port (*Under the Maltese Cross* 1910). Charles Biddlecom of the 147th New York tells his wife in a letter written on December 6, 1864, that rumors included going south to either Georgia or the Carolinas to assist Sherman's troops (Aldridge 2012, 252). These rumors were somewhat supported by other rumors of extra rations and ammunition in regimental wagons. By early dawn on December 7, troops were looking for their companies and lining up in the camps. Getting ready to move out from entrenchment was

---

6. Ulysses Grant to Henry Halleck, Dec. 7, 1864, *OR*, series I, chap. 42, p. 24.

difficult in the early morning darkness, and Major Evan Woodward of the 198th Pennsylvania reported that the 198th did not leave camp until 9:00 AM (Woodward 1884, chap. 4).[7] The warm but wet and windy morning did not assist in assembling so large a fighting force on the Jerusalem Plank Road (current Route 301, South Crater Road). By this time, the infantry had surmised they were indeed headed south and not west to outflank the entrenched enemy. Given the size of the column moving south, Will (from a private's perspective) believed that the number of troops appeared to be about 50,000. Henry Charles, who had enlisted for the third time on February 23, 1864, in Company C, 21st Pennsylvania Cavalry, wrote in his diary that the cavalry started with just three days' rations no matter how long the expedition and were expected to "live on what we could capture, or rather steal." [8]Because the cavalry was ahead of the main body of the infantry, Charles's diaries contain a different perspective than Will's at certain times in the raid.

Will thought that nothing occurred on the first day except lots of marching. Because of the rain in the area, most of the streams and rivers were running quite high and slowed the long chain of soldiers. The first water obstacle of importance, not mentioned by Will, was the Warwick Swamp, approximately seven miles south of Petersburg. Army engineers built a 40-foot wooden bridge over the swamp, and so the raid continued (Calkins 2005b, 19). Just after crossing the swamp, the force moved slightly southeast farther away from the railroad following the Jerusalem Plank Road (currently Route 35, Courtland Road). This area of the Virginian countryside had seen a bit of the war during the successful Beefsteak Raid led by General Hampton earlier that summer (September 14–17). At Hawkinsville (currently nonexistent), the Union forces turned west, back toward the railroad, but were

---

7. See also George Meade to J. A. Rawlins, Dec. 4, 1864, *OR*, series I, chap. 42, part 3, p. 795; Jordan 2001, 201.

8. Charles 1969, 20; S. W. Crawford to Fred Locke, Nov. 2, 1864, *OR*, series I, chap. 42, pp. 495–97.

confronted by the swollen Nottoway River. The engineers were well prepared and put together a 140-foot pontoon bridge. Will arrived at the river about 4:00 PM after a full day's march. His company and most of the Union force crossed over the bridge during the night and rested as much as possible. The Union cavalry, which reached the river ahead of the main force, forded the stream about a mile above Freeman's Ford, downstream from where the pontoon bridge was constructed (Charles 1969, 20). At this point, the river was about 3 feet deep and caused a few problems. Henry Charles of the 21st Pennsylvania Cavalry reported that his comrade Adam Shelley's horse stumbled, and Adam found himself in the river, to the enjoyment of the rest of the men (Charles 1969, 20). In addition, Union units from Colonel Charles Smith's brigade destroyed a trestle bridge across the Nottoway River north of Jarrett's Station.[9] Those units in front of the long column of men, animals, and materials spent the night of December 7 in the yard at the Sussex County Courthouse. As discussed later in this chapter, the courthouse became the historical focal point for many because of the horrendous deeds committed by a few of the Union soldiers and local residents, especially on the return of the Union army to Petersburg. During the rest stop, gallows were observed behind the courthouse, but, more important, the Union soldiers found cabbages behind the village tavern ("Warren's Great Raid" 1864).

At 2:00 AM the next day, December 8, Will was up and marching south along the present Courthouse Road (Route 626). Based on Will's description of the march, the Union plans were to arrive at the railroad at night, fully rested and ready to go to work. Turning west and marching through the small village of Coman's Well, however, the advanced cavalry units ran into enemy cavalry. As expected, movement of such a large force attracted the attention of Confederate scouts, who had reported the force to General Lee. Lee had sent a warning message to guards along the railroad and to General Hampton's two

9. Gouverneur Warren to Seth Williams, Dec. 14, 1864, *OR*, series I, chap. 42, pp. 443–46.

divisions under Major General Rooney Lee and Major General Matthew Butler and had ordered General A. P. Hill to move out of Petersburg to attack and trap the Union raiders (Martin 2001, 129). After a fight near Halifax Road between the 4th Pennsylvania Cavalry and the 9th Virginia Cavalry, the Confederates retreated. General Butler then moved his cavalry south about ten miles to Belfield on the Meherrin River.[10] The Confederates had several forts on the south side of the river to guard the tracks. Butler planned to use his men to replace and support some young boys who had been pressed into service to guard the rails. Apparently hearing that the Yankees were coming, one of the boys became frightened and began to cry. When told by an officer that he was crying like a baby, he said, "Yes, I wish I were a baby, and a gal baby at that" (Martin 2001, 129). To defend the railroad, the Confederates had forts located on the north side of the Meherrin River (where Battery Avenue, Barham Lane, and Tiller Street in Emporia are now). These forts consisted of three 20-pounder Parrots, two 12-pounder guns, one 6-pounder gun, and three 12-pounder howitzers.[11] In addition, the Confederates had rifle pits covered by trees. The trees' trunks were buried, and their branches, sharpened so that they resembled the pikes in the trenches at Petersburg, were pointed north to the invading Yankees (Hess 2009, 213).

Leaders in the long column of Union troops reached the railroad at Jarrett's Station at about 2:00 PM. General Warren's orders were to wait until the entire Union force was in the vicinity. Will reported that at about 4:00 PM, still some distance from the railroad, the part of the caravan in which he was marching rested until dark. As darkness approached, they marched about five more miles and arrived at Jarrett's Station. At 6:00 PM, General Warren sent parties north on the Weldon to destroy the tracks (Martin 2001, 129).

The organization for the destruction of the tracks was well planned and in fact, as Will described, somewhat competitive. Although quite

10. Martin 2001, 129; Warren to Williams, Dec. 14, 1864.
11. Warren to Williams, Dec. 14, 1864; Deutsch 2010.

tired from the march, the Union soldiers went to work in squads that were spaced along the tracks. When a squad reached a section of the tracks destroyed by another squad, they would leapfrog two or three brigades and start to work again. The squad in which Will was working tore up track for two hours and then leapfrogged. Will worked until 2:00 AM, when his squad was ordered to return to Jarrett's Station and rest.

Upon returning to Jarrett's Station, Will was involved in the burning of the station, destruction of the water towers, and the burning of several buildings in the village. This was the second time that the station had been burned that year. Union cavalry under Brigadier General August Kautz had attacked the station earlier, on May 8 (Writer's Project 2010). Gary Williams, current clerk of the Circuit Court at Sussex Court House, remembered talking to a very old woman whose last name was Jarrett. The woman told him that when she was a young girl, she stood on a very cold wintery night watching one of the Jarrett buildings burn.[12] William Nicholas Jarrett's home still stands at the site of the original station. Will, greatly impressed by the farms and acres of crops, told Lide that this area of the country was quite splendid and that it was a shame that the buildings of the enemy had to come down.

The next morning other regiments arrived to join the 5th Corps in the destruction of tracks south of Jarrett's Station. In a letter written on December 13, 1864, Captain Benjamin Oakes of the 1st Maine Heavy Artillery describes in some detail the techniques used to destroy the tracks.[13] As Will mentioned to Lide, the first thing the troops had to do was stack their rifles and hang knapsacks and jackets on them. First, a detail of men was sent out to remove the spikes from about four hundred yards of track (Chisholm 1989, 34). A line of men then marched to one side of the tracks, reached down together,

12. Gary Williams, interviewed by the author, Sussex County Court House, VA, July 17, 2009.

13. Benjamin Oakes to J. G. Richardson, Dec. 13, 1864, Virginia Military Institute Archives, manuscript no. 0392, available at http://www.vmi.edu/archives .aspx?id=12199.

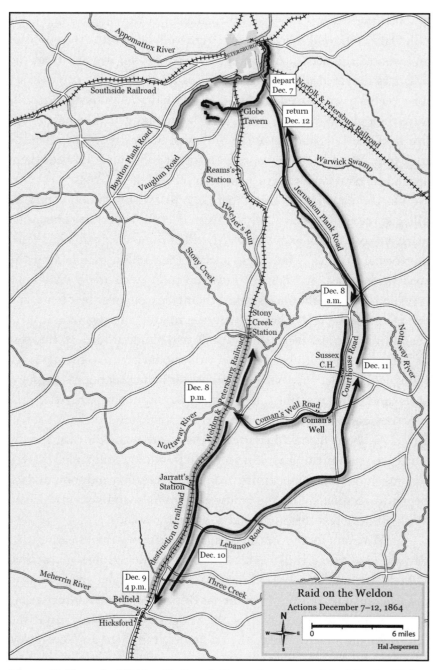

Map 3. Raid on the Weldon Railroad, December 7–12, 1864. Map by Hal Jespersen, www.cwmaps.com.

grabbed the sleepers (ties), and turned the track over. Although Captain Oakes reported that the tracks were well made with "the best iron and wood," the necessary leverage to separate the sleepers from the rails was obtained using telegraph poles from alongside the tracks.[14] The sleepers were placed in a pile along with dry fence posts. The rails were then placed over the wood, and the pile ignited. The heat of the fire bent the rails and made them useless. Several 5th Corps squads took four of the heated rails, one on top of the other, and bent them around trees to form the corps' symbol, the Maltese Cross.

On the morning of December 9, Will and his Union comrades killed three or four cows and had fresh beef for breakfast. They then marched south until about 2:00 PM, killed some sheep, and had fresh mutton and coffee. They then stacked their rifles, marched up the road three miles, and began to tear up track until 10:00 PM. They returned to where they had stacked their rifles, pitched their tents, and tried to get some rest. The same day, the 198th Pennsylvania arrived at the railroad, posted pickets in a woods two hundred yards to the west of the track, and with laughter and wild shouts began to tear up track (Woodward 1884, chap. 5). They arrived at Belfield at noon—feathers, sheep and calf skins, hides, and horns marking their path. After dinner, they continued destroying the track south toward the Meherrin River. At about 8:00 PM, however, the weather took a turn for the worse, the rain turning to sleet and then to snow accompanied by very strong winds. The temperature dropped to freezing, and snow and ice began to accumulate on the landscape, animals, and stationary men. Will got little rest that night and was wet and cold.

As Warren's forces continued south tearing up tracks earlier that day, ahead of where Will was also busy, the leading groups approached Belfield at about 3:00 PM. Warren's forces were under the command of General Henry Davies Jr. of the 1st Brigade of General Gregg's cavalry. His objective was to destroy the bridges over the Meherrin River. The regiments involved were the 1st Pennsylvania, the 1st New Jersey,

14. Ibid.

and the 1st Massachusetts, who were attacking the 5th North Carolina Cavalry and troops under Colonel John Garnett, commander of the Weldon Railroad Guard Brigade (Calkins 2005b, 21). The Weldon Guard comprised Junior Reserves from North Carolina as well as Zouaves from Louisiana (six of whom were killed in the fight). In a history of the 1st New Jersey written by its chaplain, Henry R. Pyne, the Confederate preparation on the north side of the river was "works covered with thick wood extending a mile along the road" (Pyne 1871, 300). Colonel Hugh Janeway initially sent Captain Joseph Brooks to clear the way. Under heavy rifle fire from the Confederates, Lieutenant Walter Robbins received a bullet through the hat that bruised his head, and Captains Samuel Craig and Gilbert Johnson had their horses shot from under them. Then Colonel Janeway and the rest of the 1st New Jersey dismounted and charged. They drove the Confederates out of their works and across the river (Pyne 1871, 301–2).

The Union troops were now located within easy range of the Confederate guns across the river but were not prepared to attack across the one remaining bridge. Lieutenant Colonel Lucius M. Sergeant of the 1st Massachusetts was then ordered to lead a retreat but was mortally wounded before he could even get his horse up to a gallop (Pyne 1871, 302). By 4:00 PM, Union forces had control of Belfield. At this point, the major problem facing the Confederate forces in Hicksford across the river was the remaining bridge that still would allow the Yankees to cross. The town of Emporia still celebrates the five courageous boys of the Home Guard, all under the age of eighteen, who under Yankee fire successfully set fire to the bridge (Wray-Welsh 2012).[15]

Major General Warren and Brigadier General Charles Wainwright (Artillery Brigade) arrived and assessed the situation. As reported by Wainwright, after a small attempt to get to the bridge, it was not feasible to attack the bridge because it was "likely to cost more loss of life than it was worth. It would cost us one day's delay, and probably 200 to

15. The five boys celebrated for burning the bridge were John L. Mitchell, Newett H. Ferguson, Marion Rideout, A. Turner Sanders, and Joe Sweeney.

300 men; half of our rations were gone, and the most dangerous part of our work, the getting back, still to do" (Wainwright 1962, 489).[16]

After staying all night in the worsening weather, the northern cavalry broke camp at 4:00 AM and retired. They overtook some infantry, collected stragglers, and returned to the vicinity of Coman's Well (Pyne 1871, 302). A little earlier CSA general Butler had heard that the Yankees were headed back north. He ordered his troopers to get on their horses in the snow and cold and said, "If we survive this weather . . . we need not fear the Yankees." As they began to follow the Yankees north, out of the dark and cold came a Confederate rider going the wrong direction. He was covered with ice and snow and asleep in the saddle. General Butler yelled, "Wake up, Thompson." The rider woke up and reversed his direction. When Butler was asked how he recognized the rider, considering that there were at least twenty-six Thompsons under his command, he said he recognized this Thompson's horse (Martin 2001, 131).

War often provides humans unique opportunities to exhibit their finest and worst behaviors. A number of Union officers and men exhibited their worst, so that the Weldon Railroad Raid is also called the "Applejack Raid." During the Virginia harvest time for apples and peaches, farmers fermented the juices and made applejack brandy by boiling off the water. When the Yankee forces moved south to destroy the railroad, several problems arose. Stragglers did not keep up with the moving column. Will told Lide that a number of his comrades in Company A of the New York 188th were getting tired and had lightened their load by throwing away their knapsacks and some clothes. This act is somewhat understandable because each soldier was carrying about fifty pounds of clothes and equipment (Chisholm 1989, xvii, xviii). The discarding of clothes and some equipment had occurred early in the raid when the weather was relatively warm. These soldiers may not have had to become stragglers, but they probably had to steal clothes to keep warm on the return to Petersburg. The stragglers, however,

16. See also Warren to Williams, Dec. 14, 1864.

unfortunately discovered kegs and other containers of applejack in barns, sheds, and under hay on the farms as they passed through on the way south. The supply of applejack was usually discovered first by the cavalry units ahead of the main column of infantry. Private Henry Charles of the 21st Pennsylvania Cavalry recorded that the applejack had to be taken quickly because the Provost Guard (military police) was usually right behind them, and the guard had been given orders to destroy any and all liquor found. He thought that more than half of his detail was drunk and wondered what would have happened if they had been attacked. Under the leadership of Captain William Boyd, Private Charles wrote that toward evening they found a great deal of applejack. Captain Boyd told Charles to take a keg of it back to the boys in their camp. He was stopped by a member of the Provost Guard, however, who destroyed the keg. The infantry complained that the cavalry got all the liquor, and "every time they saw us they would yell 'Apple Jack' and some would crow like roosters" (Charles 1969, 21). Captain Amos Judson records in *History of the Eighty-Third Regiment Pennsylvania* that almost every soldier filled his canteen and coffee pot with applejack, and by midnight the entire brigade was drunk ([1865] 1986, 110).

　　The Union forces quickly consumed the supply of applejack, resulting in drunken units loose in the Virginia farmlands. Brigadier General Charles Wainwright saw a man so drunk he could not stand by himself. His comrades tried to get him up and to march with them, but they gave up and left him there. Wainwright recorded in his diary that this man was lying there when the "Rebs" came through and that they, too, tried to get him on his feet. When they failed, they took his pistol, shot him in the head, and left with his boots. Wainwright reported that this incident took place in sight of where Brigadier General Gregg of the cavalry was waiting to talk with General Warren (Wainwright 1962, 488–89).[17]

17. Brevet Brigadier General Charles S. Wainwright reported that only one member of his artillery unit was intoxicated. That soldier was immediately arrested and punished.

During the raid's progress, according to the men of the 155th Pennsylvania, General Warren had issued orders prohibiting foraging and harming any "inoffending non-combatants" along the way (*Under the Maltese Cross* 1910, 328). The historian for the 120th New York indicated that no special order against pillaging and the wrecking of private property had been made, but from the beginning of the raid stragglers had been doing just that (Deutsch 2010). The foraging soldiers became a mob as more men discovered applejack. On the second and third day, every house along the road and beyond was visited and ransacked while women and children wept. It was also reported that in Coman's Well a drunken Colonel Edwin Byles of the 99th Pennsylvania and his adjutant Captain Washington Worrall were involved in raping two women, threatening to remove them from their home if they did not consent (Calkins 2005b, 20).

Farther south, on the night of December 9, Will was not able to get much sleep or to keep dry even in tents that were put up because of the weather. There is no doubt that Will was involved in tearing up track on the railroad and even was proud of his squad's success. He was also involved in burning buildings around Jarrett Station. At daybreak on December 10, Will and the 5th Corps began the trip back north to Petersburg. About five miles north of Belfield, the main force left the railroad and returned to Coman's Well through the countryside, using different roads than employed on the way south (letter 24). Will told Lide that on the return trip on December 10 they marched all day with nothing to eat but hardtack. By now the roads were a sea of mud up to Will's knees. The infantry frequently had to deal with swamps and thick underbrush in addition to the mud because the wagons and artillery had first use of the roads. The column was certainly slowed because the absence of rations and ammunition in the wagons allowed space for a large number of escaped slaves who had flocked to join the Union troops headed north. Will was so tired that night that even though the rain continued, he had a good sleep lying on the ground. The men of the 155th Pennsylvania, during a rest period on the way north, observed a soldier from another regiment of the 3rd Brigade who marched by in mud up to his ankles. He was hatless, and his canteen was full of applejack. He had a brace of chickens under his belt, his rifle over his shoulder, and a willow basket filled with honey on his head. Apparently unaware of the honey running down his face and shoulders, he walked by, singing patriotic songs to the cheers of the 155th (*Under the Maltese Cross* 1910, 329).

The Union forces were moving north through areas in which the citizens of Virginia had gathered small guerilla bands to capture, kill, and mutilate Union stragglers in retaliation for what the Union troops had done while on their raid. Privates James Flynn and Louis Schilling were apparently too drunk to keep up with the 83rd Pennsylvania. Flynn was captured and sent to Pemberton Prison in Richmond, and Schilling disappeared (Deutsch 2010). Union soldiers reported seeing bodies that had been stripped and mutilated. Some of them had their throats cut from ear to ear, and others were hanged by the side of the road. At the Sussex Court House, six Union soldiers were found lying dead on the grounds, and another was staked to the ground through his mouth (Woodward 1884). According to the men of the 155th Pennsylvania, General Warren withdrew the orders against foraging after hearing about troop mutilation (*Under the Maltese Cross* 1910, 329). Upon seeing these bodies, some of the Union soldiers retaliated in their turn and began to burn every building in sight. In addition, anything that wasn't fastened down was stolen for use or as a souvenir. Benjamin Oakes of the 1st Maine Heavy Artillery wrote in a letter dated December 13 that after arriving back at Petersburg, he had enclosed in the letter an ancient specimen of bookkeeping that he stole from a store near the Sussex County Court House.[18] Union soldiers also may have left graffiti on the walls of the original clerk's office across from the courthouse (Calkins 2005a, 62–63).

Numerous Union soldiers and officers were taken aback by and ashamed of their fellow troops' behavior. Although Will tells Lide about being involved in the burning of houses, barns, and structures related to the railroad and in the foraging for food, he makes no

18. Oakes to Richardson, Dec. 13, 1864.

mention of applejack, drunken soldiers, or mutilated bodies. Perhaps he wanted to spare her the horrors of war and the behavior of his comrades. Brigadier General Joshua Chamberlain, a Union hero of the Battle of Gettysburg and commander of the 1st Division under General Warren, later stated: "This was a hard night. . . . I saw sad work in protecting helpless women and children from outrage. . . . I invariably gave them protection which every man of honor will give any woman as long as she is a woman. But I have no doubt they were all 'burnt out' before the whole army got by. It was a sad business. I am willing to fight men in arms, but not babes in arms" (quoted in Trulock 1992, 223). Brigadier General Wainwright of the 3rd Division Artillery recorded:

> But now comes the worse. The story spread almost instantly through the column, and the sight of the burning house seem to raise devil in the men at once. Scores of men left the ranks, and seizing brands from the burning house, fired every building in sight. None escaped, large and small, pig sties and privies, all were burnt, with barely time allowed for the people themselves to get out, saving nothing. The Negroes fared no better than the whites. . . . For this barbarism there was no real excuse, unless exasperation and the innate depravity of mankind is one. . . . So pitiable a sight as the women and children turned adrift at nightfall, a most severe night, too. I never saw before and never want to see again. If this is a raid, deliver me from going on another. (quoted in Deutsch 2010)

On December 11, Will marched only ten or twelve miles through freezing rain and mud and crossed the Nottoway River. He was aware that the Confederate forces were following the Union column northward and had made an attack on their rear. In the early hours of December 10, the Confederate cavalry of Major General Rooney Lee's Barringer's Brigade had in fact come in contact with the rear of the Union column at the intersection of the Halifax and Sussex Court House roads (Calkins 2005b, 22). Although Warren's forces designed an ambush, the Confederate Cavalry discovered it and were not surprised. After shots were fired, the Union column continued north. In the ambush, two Southern soldiers were killed, two wounded, and six taken prisoner (Calkins 2005b, 23). General Grant had been concerned about Confederate forces under the command of General A. P. Hill leaving the trenches in Petersburg to attack the returning Union army, so Grant ordered General Meade to send Brigadier General Robert Potter's division of the 9th Corps to meet Warren's force on the Jerusalem Plank Road with ammunition and food supplies. The Confederate army under General Hill never caught up with the Union column, however, and the Confederate cavalry under General Butler was ordered back to Belfield, where he set up his headquarters (Martin 2001, 132).

On December 12, Will and Company A of the 188th New York returned to the camp they had left on December 7. Will was very glad to be back, although tired and a bit lame. He was proud that he did not feel as bad as many others did after the long cold march. He had stood it "first rate." He was also proud that he returned with his knapsack and all that he had taken on the raid. Most important, he thanked God that they had received orders to put up winter quarters and that any marches would be short. In his extended letter on December 17, he reveals to Lide his feelings about the war. Although he saw Confederate soldiers starving in the trenches at Petersburg, he also observed beautiful cornfields of thirty to two hundred acres. He longs for the Confederate soldiers to give up so he can go home.

Even in "small skirmishes" in the war, people were killed or wounded. Some twenty to thirty Union cavalry lost their lives in the Weldon Railroad Raid, as did the Louisiana soldiers and two cavalry from the South, making this raid no small matter to relatives and comrades.[19] In addition, women were raped, and numerous innocent civilians were put out in the cold, not just for one night, and faced

19. George Meade to U. S. Grant, Dec. 14, 1864, *OR*, series I, chap. 42, part 1, pp. 37, 38; Warren to Williams, Dec. 14, 1864.

rebuilding destroyed farms. General Butler was assigned to rebuild the railroad from his headquarters in Belfield. With 940 men, he reported the repair of six miles of track during a two-week period. An experienced superintendent of the railroad was then put in charge with three hundred slaves. By the year's end, the repair was completed but too late to save the starving and underclothed Confederate troops in the trenches at Petersburg (Martin 2001, 132). Overall, including the battles before the December raid on the Weldon, this railroad had cost the Union army 9,500 men (200 per mile of destroyed track), and Confederate losses were estimated at 2,339 (Taylor 1939, 4, 5).

9

Faith and Fighting

Rebel Farm Oct. 30 . . . 64

Dear Lide
 . . . All the objection I have to joining the Church is this: if I live
to come home I dont think I shal stay in that country. If you think
best I am willing. You can do as you like and you will suit me. . . .

Camp Near the yelow house Nov. 17 . . . 64

Dear wife
 . . . Lide, as far as joining the Church is concerned joyn it if they
will take us in. tel them to remember me in thear prayrs for I think
I need them. I dont think that I could write enything that would
be fit to read before the Church so I guess I wont try. . . .

Our old Camp Nov. 25 . . . 64

Well Lide
 . . . Yesterday was Thanksgiving. in the morning at nine oclock
we had a battalion dril then the whole Brigade marched to head
quarters and we had a good surmon and a number of officers and

privets spoke and then we were dismissed. I wish you could have heard our general speak. I find that most of our officers are good Christians and I am very thankful for it. . . .

FROM LETTER 33

Jan. 15th . . . 65

My Ever Dear Wife
. . . Lide acording to the acounts in the papers they are trying close up this war and God grant that they may for I tel you it is an owffal thing. . . .

FROM LETTER 35

Jan. 22nd . . . 65

My Dear Wife
. . . I tel you our General has ben at work bilding a church. today it was dedicated. I did not have time to go for I had to make been soup for dinner and boil poark this after noon. theay are having meetings this evening but I woint to write to you so you se I cant go to night but I can hear them for the church is not ten rods from the cook house. it is thirty feet wide and sixty feet long. it is coveard with tent cloth the same as our tents are but it is a big peace of cloth. the christian commision furnished the cloth for it. . . .

William Whitlock was born into a family that had a Christian heritage. One of thirteen children, he was raised in an atmosphere that focused on the church starting when his grandparents joined the First Presbyterian Church of what is now Ithaca, New York, in 1816.[1] As

1. Jean D. Worden, "Records from the First Presbyterian Church of Ithaca," 1983, p. 128, Tompkins County New York Church Records, Manuscript no. 4045, Box 27, Cornell Univ. Archives, Ithaca, NY.

he noted in his letters home to Lide, he continued to attend services regularly after he signed on to the 188th, starting in training camp at Elmira and extending through his military career in and around the trenches in Petersburg, Virginia. He was very pleased that numerous comrades as well as officers were fellow Christians. He recognized that he and his family were in the hands of "providence" with respect to both the ending of the war and his and his family's health and welfare. Soldiers on both sides of the war often referred to God as "providence" when describing God's action in the world (Woodworth 2001, 29). James Theaker, Company F, 154th Ohio, said in July 1864, when only one member of his company had been wounded and none killed so far in the war, "I sometimes think that I can plainly see a Providential hand connected with our company so far. I do not put my trust in any arm of flesh nor in heavy battalions of men, but in Him who rules the armies and holds the destiny of the nation in His hands" (Theaker 1974, 118–19). In a letter to his mother, Richard Crowe of the 32nd Wisconsin uses phrases from Christ's Sermon on the Mount to remind his mother that the "Supreme protecting power over us knows the number of our hairs and if a sparrow falls. Providence would only will what is best and good for us."[2]

In his letters home, Will mentions very little about his comrades' daily behavior. In fact, he has more comments on the behavior of folks back home in western New York. When he first arrived at training camp in Elmira, he was disturbed by all the shouting and energy displayed by his comrades, at least when trying to compose a letter home to Lide. Early on in the war, other Union soldiers also wrote home complaining about three major vices: swearing, gambling, and drinking (Wiley 1943, 174–91; 1951, 247–74). Private Henry Hagadorn from Minnesota, under the command of General Henry Sibley, wrote in his diary that he had not seen the depths of human wickedness and

---

2. Richard Crowe to "Dear Mammy," May 19, 1864, Richard Robert Crowe Papers, State Historical Society of Wisconsin, Madison; see also Woodworth 2001, 33–34.

depravity until he joined the army (Hagadorn 1930, 125). Private Delos Lake of the 19th Michigan wrote home to his brother, who was thinking about joining the army, and tells him that the army was the "worst place in the world" because of the opportunity to learn bad habits of all types. Several men in the 19th Michigan, he says, were "nice respectable men" when they enlisted and now were "ruined men."[3]

Swearing was widespread in the Union army, a habit from before the war or acquired from conversations around the camp. In fact, profanity was forbidden by the articles of war and involved a fine for officers of one dollar per incident and a fine of one-sixth of a dollar per incident for a soldier. If repeated, the soldier would pay an additional one-sixth of a dollar and serve a possible twenty-four-hour confinement. The collected money was to be made available to sick soldiers (*Revised Statutes* 1875, 234). No great sums of money were ever collected. Indeed, peer pressure and the pressure of the war often resulted in profanity by the officers themselves. Captain John DeForest, 12th Connecticut, recorded that he observed officers who were church members and who never even played cards "rip out" oaths when a drill was not correct or when discipline was not practiced (DeForest [1946] 1996, 43).

Although not mentioned in any of Will's letters home, gambling was just as prevalent as swearing, especially when and if the soldiers received their pay on time. In 1864, one soldier estimated that nine out of every ten card players played for money (Lane 1905, 217). When some card-playing soldiers went off to battle, they were apparently concerned that if they were injured or killed, the cards might be sent back home with their other belongings. Sergeant Michael Schroyer of the 147th Pennsylvania observed that to avoid the possible embarrassment, Yanks threw the cards away along the march and picked up what they found on the way back to replace a full deck (Lumbard 1868, 31). Playing cards was the main form of gambling, with poker (Bluff) and Chuck-a-luck (Sweat) predominating (Wiley 1943, 250).

3. Delos Lake to Calvin Lake, Feb. 12, 1864, Papers of Delos W. Lake, 1862–65, Huntington Library, San Marino, CA.

The use of alcoholic beverages, often whiskey, increased the problems of swearing and gambling and frequently was the direct cause of lack of discipline. It was more of a problem for Union troops than for Confederate troops because of the greater availability of alcoholic beverages in the North and the fact that the Union soldiers had the funds necessary to purchase them. General McClellan thought that drunkenness caused most of the disorder and court-martials (Wiley 1943, 252). The New York 48th was known as "Perry's Saints" because their colonel was James Perry, a minister. While they were stationed near Tybee Island off the coast of Savannah, Georgia, the cargo of a shipwreck, which included a large amount of wine, whiskey, and beer, floated ashore. The "Saints" quickly made generous use of their gift from the sea and became intoxicated. Colonel Perry ordered all of the alcoholic beverages collected and the drunken soldiers confined. This added stress may have contributed to the death of Colonel Perry, who suddenly died the next day while sitting in his office (J. Nichols 1886, 113).

Perhaps the spiritual condition of the Union army may be illustrated by a vote for chaplain that General Daniel Sickles allowed for the 73rd New York. Father Joseph O'Hagan, the winner, reported the vote to be "400 votes for a Catholic Priest; 154 votes for any Protestant minister; eleven votes for a Mormon elder; and 335 said they could find their way to hell without the assistance of clergy."[4]

As the Union army was being formed, gathering men from all over the North, numbers of women joined the movement to the larger cities, where they became or continued being prostitutes. By 1862, Washington, DC, a center for troop dispersal, had 450 bordellos and at least 7,500 full-time prostitutes (Clinton 1999, 14). Venereal diseases were widespread because although treatment with herbs and minerals—such as pokeweed, elderberries, mercury, and zinc sulfate—may have eased the symptoms, they did not cure the disease (King 2010). The

---

4. "Father Joseph O'Hagan," Nov. 11, 1861, Woodstock Letters, recorded in Maryniak 2003, 14.

US Surgeon-General's Office noted in 1870 that more than 180,000 cases of venereal disease had been reported for the period of May 1, 1861, to June 30, 1866 (US Surgeon-General 1870, 1:636–37, 710–11; 3:891–96).

The situation among the Confederate troops with respect to disruptive activities was somewhat different because Southerners of the 1860s were church oriented in most aspects of their lives. Rebel soldiers were sent to war with a word and prayer from the local minister and a Bible or Testament delivered by a pretty girl (Wiley 1943, 174). The minister sometimes even followed the local group of soldiers to the front (McCarthy 1882, 10–15). Once in their regiments, especially in the first two years of the war, numbers of Rebel soldiers became "religious rebels" from the church, and the army gained a bad reputation with the folks back home. Some of the preachers, who followed their hometown heroes to war, returned when confronted with the lack of moral behavior in the camps. Dr. John William Jones, the "Fighting Parson," reported a conversation with a mother at Louisa Court House, Virginia, whose sixteen-year-old son was leaving for the army. The mother said that she was in bitter anguish because her innocent son might return as a cursed man (Jones 1887, 17).

Richmond, Virginia, just like Washington, DC, became overpopulated with soldiers, which in turn contributed to an increase in the population of prostitutes and gamblers. A crime wave began in 1861 and continued to the end of the war in this center of prostitution in the Confederacy. There is no doubt that such activities had a negative influence on the visiting soldier away from home for the first time.

When letters from the front reached home describing the moral and spiritual conditions in the US and CSA armies and navies, various individuals and religious organizations began to take action. In the South, a law passed on May 31, 1861, gave President Jefferson Davis the authority to appoint chaplains. The salary initially was $85 per month, with no allowances for food and clothing. Just two weeks later the salary unfortunately was changed to $50 but included the rations available to a private in the army. This change resulted in the departure of some of the chaplains because they could not support their families. On April 19, 1862, the monthly salary was again raised to $80, with the rations included. Finally, in January 1864 the chaplains received funds for forage for their horses if forage was available (Wiley 1943, 187; Woodworth 2001, 145). In 1862, only 58 percent of the Union regiments had chaplains, and in 1863 only 50 percent of the Confederate regiments had them (Woodworth 2001, 148).

The denominational response to the need for chaplains varied with the denomination's size, denominational leaders' influence and commitment, and in general the importance of chaplains to governmental officials. At first, President Davis was lukewarm to the enlistment of chaplains because the Confederacy needed fighting men immediately. The overall response by the various Christian denominations is given in table 9.1.

The life of a conscientious chaplain was extremely busy, with duties including services, individual conversations concerning religion, care of the sick and wounded, letters to the families of the sick and wounded, sympathy letters for the families of dead soldiers, and even

TABLE 9.1
DENOMINATIONAL CHAPLAINCIES DURING THE CIVIL WAR

Confederacy		Union	
Denomination	Percentage of Total Registered (938)	Denomination	Percentage of Total Registered (2,154)
Methodist	47	Methodist	38
Presbyterian	18	Presbyterian	17
Baptist	16	Baptist	12
Episcopalian	10	Episcopalian	10
Roman Catholic	3	Congregational	9
		Unitarian/ Universalist	4
		Roman Catholic	3
		Lutheran	2

Sources: For the Union, Brinsfield 2003, 61; for the Confederacy, Maryniak 2003, 45.

the sorting and delivery of the mail. Most chaplains played important roles in the young soldier's life and in general were greatly appreciated.

A few of the chaplains, however, were not appreciated at all. One Union officer said that his chaplain was good for nothing and a waste of government money. "He never visits a sick man, but is always on hand when pay day comes" (Stuckenberg 1995, 103; Woodworth 2001, 151). Private Edward Edes of Company B, 33rd Massachusetts, wrote home to his father that he had lost all confidence in his chaplain (Reverend Daniel Foster) and reported that the chaplain just hung around his tent and sorted the mail and did not mix with the men. "I think he is nothing but a confounded humbug and nuisance."[5] Private Edes's assessment of Reverend Foster was based on the chaplain's performance as chaplain rather than on any knowledge of his background. It is quite possible that Reverend Foster was not pleased with his position in life. He was an ordained minister in both the Congregational and Methodist denominations and developed into an extreme abolitionist. After being asked to leave several churches because of his antislavery emphasis and following a sermon entitled "The Bible, Not an Inspired Book," he was recognized as a Unitarian for the rest of his life. William Garrison published the sermon in his newspaper *The Liberator*, which gained Reverend Foster recognition and friendship with Henry David Thoreau and Ralph Waldo Emerson. In 1857, he was appointed to the chaplaincy of the Massachusetts House of Representatives. Two months later, after hearing a speech by John Brown, he left Massachusetts for Kansas to join Brown and the Free Soilers. In 1862, he moved his family back to Massachusetts and joined the 33rd as a chaplain. Perhaps Reverend Foster did not want to be bothered by the mundane duties of a regimental chaplain. As soon as the 37th United States Colored Regiment was formed in 1863, he accepted the rank of captain and left the 33rd. Reverend Foster was mortally wounded at Chapin's Bluff outside of Richmond on September 30, 1864 (Garvey 2005).

5. Edward Edes to father, Dec. 19, 1862, microfilm, P-376, Massachusetts Historical Society, Boston.

A few chaplains had problems with their commanding officers when there was a disagreement about the chaplain's authority and interaction with civilians. One Confederate chaplain overstepped his authority and commandeered a horse from a farmer in Virginia who supported the South. When his commander told him to return the horse, the chaplain used the scriptures to defend himself, saying that the situation was similar to the incident preceding Palm Sunday when Jesus's disciples commandeered an ass from its owner to ride into Jerusalem. The commander responded by ordering the return of the horse because the chaplain was not Jesus, the horse wasn't an ass, and the chaplain was not headed to Jerusalem (DeFontaine 1864, 57).

It might be expected that most chaplains preached sermons that supported the soldiers' belief that they were fighting for a just cause and that God was on their side in the struggle. One Presbyterian leader in Virginia, Reverend Robert Dabney, opined that the sides in the coming war consisted of Christian people of order and regulated freedom against people who are "tongue-valiant brawlers who have inflamed the fued [sic] by their prating lies about the barbarism of slavery."[6]

A few chaplains, however, believed that perhaps God did not take sides in the war, either because of their personal beliefs or because of what a defeat would do to the men's belief. Chaplain Thomas Caskey of the 16th Mississippi Cavalry was one who had doubts that God would take sides in the war and was concerned about the results of a defeat if God were on their side. "It was expected that my preaching, prayers and exhortations would tend to make the soldiers hard fighters. It was difficult to find even texts from which to construct such sermons. . . . Some of my preaching brethren told the soldiers that our cause was just and that God would fight our battles for us. I never did feel authorized to make any such statements. I believed that our cause was just, of course, but I could see as clear as a sunbeam that the odds

---

6. Robert Dabney to S. I. Prime, Apr. 20, 1861, in *On the State of the Country*, 423–24, available at http://www.dabneyarchives.com/onthestateofthecountry.pdf.

were against us, and, to be plain, I gravely doubted whether God was taking any hand with us in that squabble" (quoted in Brinsfield 2003, 64–66).

Most of the Confederate chaplains focused their sermons on the importance of individual conversion and Christian behavior as outlined in the scriptures. Evangelism in the South was focused on "reforming the individual behavior rather than assuming a role as a critic of the social order" (Harvey 1998, 170). Most did not preach on states' rights and moral reasons for secession because such political sermons resulted in few conversions to Christ (Brinsfield 2003, 79). Chaplain John Granberry of the Virginia 11th wrote that eternal things and the claims of God through Jesus Christ were the "matter of preaching" (quoted in Brinsfield 2003, 79). However, some chaplains and preachers of both countries did use their vocation to tie Christianity to victory in the war. As late as the fall of 1864, the minutes of the Texas Baptist State Convention indicated a rejection of "lukewarmness" and "despondency" and the need to redouble energies for the deliverance of the country from "Yankee thralldom and oppression which we most solemnly regard as a direful curse–even worse than death" (quoted in Harvey 1998, 173).

Early in the war, the Confederate soldier had limited access to the Holy Bible. There were few publishing companies in the South, and a few northern "Christian" societies stopped sending their publications to the South because they thought the scriptures were contraband. To make matters more difficult, the Southerners associated with the American Bible Society severed their relationship and founded the Bible Society of the Confederate States. The American Bible Society, however, acted correctly and continued to make donations of Testaments, including one donation of 100,000 copies. The British and Foreign Bible Society also made large contributions and extended unlimited credit with no interest for Testament purchase. Early in the war the supply of Bibles was so lacking that after a battle the chaplains and interested soldiers would search the dead and collect Bibles and other religious literature (Wiley 1943, 176–77; Woodworth 2001, 165–66).

The leaders of the Protestant churches recognized the need for spiritual guidance for the soldiers and began to produce and distribute Bibles as well as the more numerous and influential publications such as periodicals and tracts. Will's continued concern for the family's spiritual welfare may indicate that he was exposed to and read religious periodicals supplied to the Union troops (see table 9.2). Similar publications were made available to the soldiers of the Confederacy in spite of the shortages of materials as the war continued into the fall of 1864.

For the Union soldiers, the US Christian Commission was formed through the support of the Young Men's Christian Association and the federal government. The commission's mission was to "persuade [the soldier] to become reconciled to God through the blood of His Son, if they had not already done so, and if they had, then to be strong in the Lord, resolute for duty, earnest and constant in prayer, and fervent in spirit, serving the Lord" (quoted in Woodworth 2001, 168). The organization was composed of men and women who lived near or in the army camps and whose functions were to pass out religious literature, stationery, and envelopes; to organize religious meetings, including visiting speakers; to act as nurses in hospitals; and to spread the Gospel.

TABLE 9.2
RELIGIOUS PERIODICALS PRODUCED DURING THE CIVIL WAR

North	South
The American Messenger	Army and Navy Messenger
Sunday School Times	The Soldier's Hymn Book (27 selections)
Presbyterian Standard	Soldier's Visitor
German Reformed Messenger	The Army Hymn Book (191 selections)
Christian Times	Soldier's Paper
Congregationalist	Army and Navy Herald
Independent	Soldier's Friend
Morning Star	

Sources: For the North, Wiley 1951, 272; for the South, Wiley 1943, 176–77.

Many of the letters written home were on stationery obtained from the US Christian Commission. During the war, the commission's more than 5,000 volunteer "delegates" used more than $6 million in distributing goods and supplies to the Union soldiers. In the later years of the war, the commission also furnished canvas roofing for churches if the army was willing to build the walls. Will, busy in the cookhouse in the camp on a rebel farm on October 30, 1864, could hear the dedication service for the chapel that had a canvas roof donated by the commission (letter 35). In this manner, more than one hundred chapels were constructed in 1864, with the commission also supplying stoves and hymnbooks (Wiley 1951, 271). One of the prized items distributed was the "housewife," a sewing kit that contained very useful things such as needles, thread, and buttons needed by soldiers who had to do their own sewing (Strong 1961, 77; Woodworth 2001, 172). If objections were made concerning the commission's dealing with the soldiers' physical needs and not just spiritual needs, the commission's president, George Stuart, reminded people that there is "a good deal of religion in a warm shirt and a good beefsteak" (quoted in Woodworth 2001, 168).

The Confederacy did not have anything equivalent to the Christian Commission. Spiritual guidance for the soldier in the field was by religious literature, missionaries, chaplains, and occasionally officers. Religious literature, including the scriptures, was not as available as in the Union camps, especially via an organization such as the Christian Commission. In the South, regiments and brigades formed Christian Associations for spiritual fellowship. The Christian Association became the local church away from home. These associations were multidenominational groups that often elected officers that led the group in tract distribution, sponsoring services, and the organization of prayer groups. A visiting minister reported, "We had a Presbyterian sermon, introduced by Baptist services, under the direction of a Methodist chaplain, in an Episcopal church" (quoted in Wiley 1943, 187). This multidenominational approach resulted in interesting cooperation when the number of deserters began to increase late in the war. Of the 104 deserters in McGowan's Brigade (South Carolina 14th), only 5 were ever captured. Within twenty-four hours, the deserters were tried, convicted, and sentenced to death. One of them turned out to be a boy and was released. The remaining four wanted "full baptism" before they were killed, so the brigade's couriers were sent to find a Baptist chaplain. "Our couriers could not find a Baptist chaplain," stated J. F. J. Caldwell, "and the Presbyterian ministers about us prayed to be excused. I could not blame them, for the rite could not be administered except by wading thirty yards or more into a pond of ice-cold water with a muddy, mirey bottom. But we secured, at last, the service of a Methodist chaplain: whereupon General McGowan exclaimed, 'Hurrah for the Methodists.' Then the men were shot" (Caldwell 1866, reported in Greene 2008, 93).

The Christian Association of the 14th South Carolina (Gregg's/McGowan's Brigade) was established in 1863 for the declared purpose of being "helpers of each other's joy in Christ, and laborers together with God. We covenant together with each other and with Christ to strive to grow in grace ourselves, to use all means in our power to promote the growth of grace in each other, and to be instrumental in bringing others to a saving knowledge of the truth as it is in Jesus" (quoted in Woodworth 2001, 221). This declaration appears to be a well-written and organized statement of faith that reflects the association's purpose: to be a church away from home that would focus on the soldier's spiritual, not political, welfare. The Union forces also developed a few regimental Christian Associations. The chaplain of the 13th Pennsylvania, Reverend Alexander Stewart, reported that the 13th's association mission statement required the members to pledge to live according to the rule of the Bible (Stewart 1865, 98; Wiley 1951, 272).

All of the attention brought to the soldiers on both sides of the war that there was a loving God who cared about them as persons and wanted them to have peace in their hearts through His Son began to exhibit fruit. In the Union and Confederate forces, religious meetings began and increased in frequency. In the fall of 1864, Will tells Lide that in the 188th New York it was possible to go to "church" twice a day. He reports that on Thanksgiving his general gave an excellent talk and was building a church. He also mentions that there might be several speakers during a meeting, including officers and privates. Perhaps Will included the chaplain of the 188th, Wayne Spicer (Scio, New York), as an officer because he did not mention Reverend Spicer by name. Perhaps he still considered Spicer a private because Spicer had been inducted into the infantry as a private.

The form of worship varied with the specific circumstances of the war and by denomination. The Sunday service was typically held in the afternoon, leaving the morning for the formal weekly inspection (Wiley 1951, 269). The nightly prayer meetings, which Will attended, usually consisted of singing, Bible reading, perhaps a short sermon, and testimonials from the men (Wiley 1951, 270). During 1864, many Union soldiers experienced renewal and salvation as the results of spreading the Gospel began to change lives. Charles LaForest Dunham, Company C, 129th Illinois, wrote to his mother, "Ma, I feal as iff God was on my side. . . . I have resolved to be a christon the rest of my life" (quoted in Woodworth 2001, 233).

The efforts of spreading the gospel to the Confederate army blossomed into great revivals experienced throughout the troops and with lifelong results that are still evident several generations later. The Confederate troops in the trenches around Petersburg and throughout the entire South increased their interest in the spiritual aspects of their lives, as evidenced by the frequency of religious meetings. In the spring of 1864, Kentuckian John Jackman of the Orphan Brigade went to church sometimes twice a day in Dalton, Georgia. He reported many baptisms, regardless of denomination, as the troops awaited General William T. Sherman's march toward Atlanta (Jackman 1990, 110–18). Although not every individual experienced a spiritual renewal, the Confederate army was never again like the horrible conditions feared by parents in 1861. In a review of Dr. James Jones's 1887 book *Christ in the Camp*, Bill Potter characterizes these revivals as follows: "Countless thousands of men confessed Christ as Savior, Christians were encouraged, and membership in churches expanded, all in the midst of the greatest slaughter of Americans that the nation would ever know" (2005).

In *The Life of Johnny Reb*, Bell Wiley lists four major causes of the revivals in the Confederate army. First, Southern churches and other Christian concerns were successful in supplying the army with tracts, the scriptures, and preachers. Second, most of the Confederate soldiers were affiliated with churches before being inducted and had experienced revivals back home. Third, although the South had been optimistic about the war in the early years, late in 1863 the Confederate army began to have setbacks. The army and the citizenry began to have doubts, and so sermons on humbling themselves and turning back to God were heard more frequently. And fourth, the soldiers had an increased prospect of death.

Across the trenches from Will in the winter of 1864, hungry, poorly clothed men of the Army of Northern Virginia were turning to God and building as many as sixty chapels along the trenches around Petersburg, one every six to eight hundred yards (Wiley 1943, 182; Woodworth 2001, 246). Dr. Jones believed that these revivals in the winter of 1864, under Lee's command, were as general and powerful as at any previous time in the war (Jones 1887, 353; see also Wiley 1943, 182).

One of the most solemn and touching sacraments of the Christian Church is communion or the Lord's Supper. The numerous meetings, both on Sunday and on weeknights, that Will attended in the fall and winter of 1864 must have provided him and his comrades the opportunity to come together and celebrate communion, bringing both the individual closer to God and the soldier closer to his Christian comrades in this corporate solemn ceremony. Private David Holt, in Company K of the Mississippi 16th, found this to be the case for him and his fellow soldiers in a huge communion service of the Army of Northern Virginia near the Rapidan River in April 1864. Private Holt was captured in the fall of 1864 at Petersburg and sent to prison at Point Lookout, Maryland. After the war, he became an Episcopal minister and later became archdeacon of the Sacramento Diocese in California ("16th Mississippi Infantry" 2010; Holt 1995, 232–33; Woodworth 2001, 234–36).

Private Holt reported that as many as fifteen chaplains were present at this meeting near the river with thousands of soldiers sitting on logs and stumps. The singing of hymns and preaching were accomplished by chaplains on the platform reading the words of a couple of verses of a hymn followed by singing and then two more verses "given out." To make sure that soldiers in all directions could hear the preaching, several chaplains repeated the phrases of the sermon. The chaplains blessed the bread, which was crumpled hardtack, and the wine in tin cups. As the men began to leave, an older chaplain stood up and asked them to wait.

> Men, before we part, let us sing *How Firm a Foundation Ye Saints of the Lord.* I know full well that this is the last communion for many of you. The next campaign will be the hardest fought and bloodiest of all. It will be the extreme test. Many of you in the pride and vigor of early manhood will be laid low in death, and all your fond ambitions for the future, expectancy of home, wife and children, will be blotted out in your blood. But, OH! This simple feast that we have just eaten is a token and a pledge of the undying love and power of our God. It is also an earnest of the feast and joy of the World to come. May the remembrance of it console you in your deepest distress, and comfort your hearts with a sense of the personal love and presence of your Lord.

Private Holt recorded that they sang with a will and quietly departed in small groups (Holt 1995, 232–33; see also Woodworth 2001, 234–36).

> How firm a foundation ye saints of the Lord,
> Is laid for your faith in his excellent word.
> The soul that on Jesus hath leaned for repose
> I will not, I will not, desert to his foes.
> That soul, though all hell should endeavor to shake,
> I'll never, no, never, no, never forsake. (Stanley [1787] 1977, 574)

IO

"We Will Probley Have to Go"

Battle of Hatcher's Run II (Dabney's Mills)

LETTER 39

In Camp Feb. 3rd . . . 1865

My Dear Wife

I have just reced yours of the 25th and hasten to ansur it. I reded one day befour yesterday dated the 23rd. I know well enough that I knot get all of your letters but I cant complain of you. I wrote one to you yesterday and now am writing another but when I get one form you I always ansur it if I have time rite away.

our compiny are all detaled to day to work on a fort repairing it and there is onley four or five left in camp. it seams quite lonesome. I am doing the cooking alone since Hughs went to the hospatle but will have a man detaled I guess tomorrow to help me. I should have had one to day but they wanted all that was able to work to go out on that detale. they are two or three miles from camp in the direction of paetersburg.

I dont hear eny thing about our moving since day befour yesterday. some say that the order is countermanded. I think they expected some kind of a movement among the rebles and was going to operate against them.

I heard last night that there was two corpse from the Shanenday coming over hear and we was going to extend our lines fifteen miles farther South acrst the Weldon road but it is all rumer and we cant tel whither eny thing is trew or not but I hope we shant have to brake camp agana til it is time of year that we shant have to bild winter quarters agane for I have got tired of bulding shantyes. but our corpse is the resurve corpse and liabel to be called on at eny time if they want to reinforce eny part of the armey. we will probley have to go. oh how I do hope they can manage to settle this war up so we can reenforse our homes instead of the armey. that would be a more pleasing task to do. if half of the talk we hear is true they are doing thear best but I dair not hope to strong for fear the disapointment will be worse. but we will hope for the best and if it dont come we will put up with the worst.

it is not quit as pleasant to day as it was ban for a week. I guess we are a going to have a cold rain storm.

Euzetta asks me what I do for a razor. I use a small pear of sisors. when the hair gets to long on my face I shear it off. that is all the shaving I do.

if you stay there where you are I hope it will be so you can send zetta to school down to Olean next spring. she tells me that she has got over half way through her Arithmatic. I think she has done well. how dos Stanley get along with his studys? dos Clary and Hankey learn very fast? tel Hankey pa will have to ansur his letter as soon as he gets a little time but I have no time now for it is such a long one. it will take me a good whild to write an ansur.

Well Lide I have cooked pork to day and have got my beans on to make a bean soup for the boys when they come in to night. I must get that don by four o clock so I can have thear coffe. I would have had the soup for dinner if they had ben in camp.

Well I cant think of anything more to write so I might as well close. Bob Wright told me today that he had a letter from Alegany and the report there that George Lowe is did. have you heard any thing about it?

Write often. my love to all. no more so good by.

yours truly
Will

In the fall and early winter of 1864, Will was involved in two offensives by the Union army to reduce the supplies to the CSA Army of Northern Virginia. The first of these offensives was the first Battle of Hatcher's Run on October 27–28, in which the Union forces managed to extend their entrenchments farther west–southwest from Petersburg both to solidify the siege fortifications and to shut down the supplies coming from the south to Lee's army (chapter 7). The second action was an expedition, December 7–12, 1864, down the Weldon Railroad to destroy the tracks to stop the transfer of goods to Lee's army from the open port of Wilmington, North Carolina (chapter 8). Rapid repair of the railroad north of the Meherrin River in Virginia allowed for some supplies to reach Lee's army overland from Stony Creek Station through Dinwiddie Court House (west of Petersburg) and then to Petersburg via the Boydton Plank Road.

Both of the armies then settled into their respective trenches south of Petersburg and awaited warmer weather. On January 13, 1865, Will was detailed to the job of cook, which reduced his hours as a picket in the trenches but kept him busy enough to inhibit his letter writing. He and George Hughes had acquired the job in the cookhouse perhaps because both men had health problems. Will had a bad cold that he was having difficulty recovering from as well as a shaking hand, and George was more seriously ill and visited the hospital frequently. Will had to stand guard in the cookhouse even when he was not cooking because soldiers attempted to steal rations. One of the major anxieties about the life of a soldier that occupied Will's mind during the month of January 1865 was receiving a gift box from home. The box, sent December 28, never did arrive. Although the box contained things other than food, such as the much desired gloves, some of the food items in the box would have helped to add a little diversity to his diet.

Across the trenches, Confederate forces were not concerned about diet diversity. They were suffering from malnutrition and worried about just having enough cornmeal to survive from day to day. During the winter, R. P. Scarborough of Alabama began to lose hope for a Confederate victory. In a letter to his cousin, he says that General Lee's men could hardly live on what they received from the government and that men were marrying women in and around Petersburg—"some for life some for the war and some for one winter only."[1] Troops often had to leave the trenches and look for wood at least a mile away because wood near the camp had already been cut for trenches and fires for cooking and warmth. While searching for wood, the soldiers were exposed to Yankee fire, including huge mortar rounds as large as eight- and twelve-inch shells (Glatthaar 2008, 443; Greene 2008, 74–78). In addition to food, the Confederates were not supplied with sufficient clothes. A law passed on October 8, 1862, implied that the Confederate government was to supply the major portion of clothes for the army. States rights, a major reason for the war, raised its sometimes ugly head where clothes were concerned, however. Instead of giving manufactured clothes to the Richmond authorities, Governor Zebulon Vance of North Carolina, with forty textile factories, held huge surpluses for his own troops and obtained wool and other raw materials from other Confederate states (Wiley 1943, 112–13). It was reported that North Carolina warehouses hoarded "92,000 uniforms, great stores of leather and blankets, and [that Vance's] troops in the field were all comfortably clad" (Owsley 1925, 126). In contrast, Captain Zimmerman Davis of the 5th South Carolina Cavalry wrote headquarters on November 17, 1864, that many of his men had no overcoats or blankets and that they were shivering on the picket lines.[2] After finally receiving a shipment of blankets, Lieutenant Luther Mills wrote to his brother that some men returned from duty on the picket line crying like children because of the cold.[3] As early as the spring of 1864, General Lee had written to Secretary of War James Seddon that he was greatly concerned about the lack of provisions for the army. He told the secretary

1. R. P. Scarborough to cousin, Jan. 31, 1865, Confederate Miscellany Collection, Special Collections, Emory Univ., Atlanta; see also Hess 2009, 222.

2. Zimmerman Davis to W. H. Taylor, Nov. 17, 1864, in *Orders, Company D, 5th South Carolina Cavalry*, South Carolina Department of Archives and History, Columbia; see also Power 1998, 221.

3. Luther Mills to brother, Nov. 26, 1864, quoted in Power 1998, 223; see Harmon 1927 for more letters by Mills.

that any derangement in the arrival of supplies such as a disaster to the railroad would prohibit him in "keeping the army together." When he wrote this letter to the secretary, the army had just two days' worth of supplies, and desertion was on the increase. A year later, in January 1865, General Lee asked for an increase in the food supply to the Army of Northern Virginia to help stem absenteeism, but no increase was seen, and the defections continued (Wiley 1943, 135).

Both the Confederacy and the Union had serious desertion problems through the entire war. Will Whitlock saw desertions and the associated punishment while still at Elmira. Although the actual number is difficult to determine, the records for just New York indicate approximately 45,000. Factors that contributed to this number were boredom between battles, heat, cold, disease, hunger, and delayed pay. In a letter to his wife, Esther, on December 6, 1864, Charles Biddlecom of the 147th New York describes a method of desertion among Union soldiers that he had observed at Petersburg. A Union soldier on picket duty would cross to the Rebel pickets and surrender, trade uniforms, and then go in front of another Union unit and surrender. He would then tell a "good story," get paroled, sign the Oath of Allegiance, and return to his home in the North. Biddlecom states that the Union's 2nd Corps reported at least 250 prisoners in Confederate uniforms claiming to be from Company B, 41st North Carolina. Yet, according to Confederate records, Company B consisted of 11 officers, 11 noncommissioned officers, and 118 privates, a total of 140 men (J. Moore 1882, 150–52). No wonder Biddlecom wrote, "[T]here must be a screw loose somewhere" (Aldridge 2012, 253).

By the winter of 1864, desertion had become an increasing problem for the hungry, underclothed Confederate soldiers (Donald, Baker, and Holt 2001, chap. 22; Greene 2008, 86–93). The Confederate desertion rate that was a trickle in 1864 became a flood in January and February 1865. In a March 14, 1865, letter written by a friend of Will's, Alanson Jones from Allegany (letter 40) to Morris, Will's brother, Mr. Jones reports that the Rebels were deserting more frequently and bringing their rifles with them. Because the location of the war was nearer to their homes, the pressure on the Confederate soldier to stay in the trenches may have been greater than for the Union troops. In addition, their homes were being invaded and destroyed by marauding Union troops. Because of the proximity of homes to battlefields, the Rebel deserters caused problems for Southern towns and counties. A well-documented example was the effect that deserters had in Floyd County in southwestern Virginia (Dotson 1997, 34–55). Although the majority of soldiers from the county served the Confederacy by fulfilling their commitment, nearly 23 percent deserted and went home to "lay out" in the mountains and woods of this county. This rate of desertion was twice that of the state of Virginia and three times that of the Confederacy (Dotson 1997, 34–55). They were welcomed and assisted by Unionists, who encouraged further desertions, provided food and protection, and even hired the deserters as day laborers. When Confederate troops were sent to hunt down the deserters, open warfare developed between the troops, on the one side, and a gang of deserters and supporters known as the "Sisson's Gang," on the other. This group was founded by Floyd County's David and James Sisson. The Sisson Gang even captured Captain Asa Booth and his men of the 54th Virginia when the soldiers came hunting deserters. The captured Confederate soldiers were turned loose to report their own capture in disgrace. The problems on the home front in Floyd County reached the attention not only of Governor William Smith in Richmond, but also of General Robert E. Lee. General Lee sent orders through Major General John Breckenridge to dispatch troops to Floyd County and arrest the runaway soldiers.[4] Virginians were now fighting Virginians instead of Yankees.[5]

4. John Breckenridge to Robert E. Lee, Apr. 9, 1864, *Official Records of the Union and Confederate Armies in the War of the Rebellion (OR)*, series I, chap. 33; see also Dotson 1997, 52.

5. A. Wilson Greene (2008) presents reasons for desertion, steps taken to prevent it, and the efforts made to apprehend offenders. For example, the North Carolina 5th, 20th, and 23rd were withdrawn from fighting in the Shenandoah Valley to hunt deserters along the Staunton and Roanoke rivers.

The situation was just as bad if not worse in North Carolina. North Carolina had lost more than 10,000 men in just two battles, Gettysburg and Chancellorsville. These great losses contributed to a rise in desertions (Glatthaar 2008, 413). Private John Futch, a holder of a few slaves and father of two, joined the 3rd North Carolina with three relatives. One of them was killed at the Seven Days' Campaign, and his brother was killed at Gettysburg. Private Futch wanted to go home because of the deaths, and he was so homesick that he did not know what to do. After hearing about his wife's financial problems at home, he told her that he wanted to come home even if he had to desert. He and his remaining relative, Hanson, left the camp and headed home. They were caught, tried, convicted of desertion, and sentenced to death by firing squad. Hanson died of smallpox at Castle Thunder Prison in Richmond, but John Futch was executed (Glatthaar 2008, 414).

Another tragedy involving human life also occurred within the greater tragedy of the war following the capture of deserters by Brigadier General Hoke's 54th North Carolina. On February 1, 1864, the 54th captured Union soldiers near the town of New Bern. Among the captured were twenty-two Confederate deserters who had taken the final step and became traitors by wearing the Yankee uniform and carrying muskets over their shoulders (Paris 1864). They were charged with treason, tried by court-martial, and hanged. Reverend John Paris, chaplain of the 54th, preached a sermon on February 28 to the troops concerning the evils of desertion, using the biblical account of Judas Iscariot and a reference to Benedict Arnold. Although he recognized the traitors' misdeeds, he leveled considerable blame on the citizens back home for holding so-called peace meetings in which people "emphasized their rights and not their duty and loyalty to their county." Chaplain Paris, unlike Reverend Thomas Caskey, chaplain of the 16th Mississippi Cavalry (see chapter 9), believed that God was on the side of the Confederacy. If Southerners surrendered to the "tyrant at Washington," the land would be sold to pay off the Yankee debt and would be purchased by Negroes. Negroes would be free and equal with whites, voting rights would be suspended, and ministers for southern churches would be approved and appointed by the Yankee military. "In addition to this, Gentlemen, we of course will have to endure the deep and untold mortification of having bands of negro soldiers stationed in almost every neighborhood to enforce these laws and regulations. These things would be some of the 'blessings' we would obtain by such a peace. Tell me today, sons of Carolina, would not such a peace bring ten-fold more horrors and distress to our country than this war, has yet produced? Can any people on the face of this earth, fit to be freemen, ever accept a peace that will place them in such a condition? Never! Never! Never!" The Reverend Paris closed by stating that if anyone wanted the union as it was, they should be scorned by good men and that they would bring disgrace for their children (Paris 1864, 5–14).

Numbers of Confederate soldiers remained with their troops to the very end of the war in spite of many hardships. W. E. Leak, 22nd South Carolina, was very concerned about his family at home as Sherman's army was marching across his state. His letters home describe the trenches as "hog pens" and hunger to the point of illness. As noted earlier, his daily rations were a tin cup of cornmeal and some beef. Even though he thought the Confederacy was at an end, he remained in the trenches. He unfortunately was captured and died a prisoner at Point Lookout Prison.[6]

Deserters also plagued Conway, South Carolina. Ellen Cooper Johnson was a young schoolteacher at Cool Spring (twelve miles north of Conway). She experienced the horrors of fighting off deserters who raided, burned, and stole from surrounding farms. To capture the deserters, Ellen's father enlisted three soldiers who were home on furlough: N. A. Dusenbury, Henry Innman, and James Singleton. They searched for two days but found none of the deserters. About that time, her future husband, C. L. Johnson, came home wounded from the war in Virginia. Expecting the raiders, Mr. Johnson, who could not walk,

---

6. W. Leak to wife and children, Jan. 30, 1865, Leak Letters, Petersburg National Battlefield Archives, Petersburg, VA; see also Hess 2009, 225.

positioned himself on the front porch with a rifle and cartridge box. His future bride, Ellen, and her sister, each armed with a pistol, waited near the door. A gun battle ensued in which they successfully defended the house but the next morning found that the smokehouse was missing barrels of pork and corn, fifty-eight hams, and two bushels of salt. Before these raids, they had noticed an elderly woman walking back and forth on the road. Captain Erwin, the local Methodist minister and captain of the Home Guard, captured the woman. She confessed that she knew the deserters were hiding in a nearby swamp. The Home Guard captured Abe Rabon, one of the raiders, and tied him to a tree in the Johnsons' yard. When told the penalty was death, he managed to get a jail term by helping the guard find the other deserters. When told that the Yankees were coming, Ellen said, "The Yankees on one side, and the raiders on the other—I did not know which was worse."[7]

The camps on both sides of the trenches outside Petersburg would empty out daily during the winter months because the soldiers were quite busy repairing the trench lines and fortifications. Frequent repairs included dilapidated parapets and broken and unconnected abates. Rainwater remaining in the trenches also had to be dealt with by more digging. Because of the fluctuating weather around Petersburg in the winter, both armies' living quarters were subject to very cold temperatures followed by warm spells, so that water would freeze in the structures that had been saturated by rain, then melt into mud puddles. These changes in weather resulted in the destruction and flooding of trenches, forts, and bomb proofs. If the troops were not digging, they were drilling. Because Will was busy in the cookhouse, he did not have to drill nearly as frequently as his comrades in the 188th New York. Some drills lasted for two hours and could be as frequent as two to three times per day depending on the commanders.

Several times late in the war, Will told Lide that he had heard rumors of peace talks. In the early days of 1865, a major attempt was

7. Ellen Johnson, "Memoirs of Ellen Cooper Johnson," 1920, unpublished manuscript no. 73972, Horry County Memorial Library, Conway, SC.

made to stop the war by bringing the leaders of the two countries together. The initiative to have a meeting started with Francis P. Blair Sr., who had been a longtime adviser to presidents all the way back to Andrew Jackson. He was a personal friend of Jefferson Davis even though he ended up siding with the North and supporting Lincoln (Foote 1974, 38; Strode 1964, 135). First Lady Varina Davis had rented the Blairs' Maryland home for a summer and urged her husband to let Blair visit (Strode 1964, 135). Blair arrived in Richmond on January 12, 1865, and saw the president that evening. The visit was unofficial, but Blair had President Lincoln's approval in making it. His "pass" to the South was written on a card he had received earlier on December 28, 1864, which read, "Allow the bearer, F. P. Blair, Senr. to pass our lines, go South and return, Signed, A. Lincoln" (Foote 1974, 38). The news of the visit leaked out even though Blair did not officially register at the Spotswood Hotel, where he stayed. President Davis's friend Judge James Lyons thought Blair was a spy. The *Richmond Examiner* carried an editorial that asked, "What right had Mr. Davis to allow the whispering old humbug to come here, spreading rumors and insinuating false suggestions?" (quoted in Strode 1964, 136). After a few messages back and forth, President Davis consulted with Vice President Alexander Stephens (the first conversation they had in four years), and the vice president suggested that they should pursue the possibilities of a conference. On January 25, after asking Stephens's opinion on who should represent the Confederacy, President Davis appointed as "commissioners" John A. Campbell, former Supreme Court justice and now assistant secretary of war; Robert Hunter, who was president pro tem of the Senate; and Stephens himself (Foote 1974, 40). President Davis gave the commissioners the following charge: "In conformity with the letter of Mr. Lincoln, of which the foregoing is a copy, you are requested to proceed to Washington City for an informal conference with him upon the issues involved in the existing war, and for the purpose of securing peace to the two countries" (quoted in Sandburg 1936, 4:34).

The last two words in the charge were important to both presidents because Davis knew that Lincoln would not recognize the

Confederacy as a separate nation (Sandburg 1936, 436, 37; Strode 1964, 137). With some delays, the three commissioners rode out onto the Jerusalem Plank Road on January 31 and headed for Washington. The road and path through the trenches were crowded with the gray and the blue shouting at the top of their voices as if to outdo each other, "Peace! Peace!" The commissioners stopped at General Grant's headquarters at City Point. Major Thomas Eckert arrived with orders from Lincoln to check the orders from Davis with respect to whether they referenced one nation or two. Eckert saw that the orders used the phrase "two countries" and therefore had not met President Lincoln's requirements, so he told the commissioners from the Confederacy that they could not proceed. It appeared that the peace conference was not to be, just as Vice President Stephens had experienced on July 3–6, 1863, when he had spent some days in the hot summer shipboard at Hampton Roads waiting for the Union to negotiate a prisoner exchange ("Alexander Stephens" 2010; Strode 1964, 138). President Lincoln was ready to call the conference off, but a long telegram from General Grant, who had talked with two of the Confederacy's representatives, asked the president to meet with them. Lincoln agreed and replied that he would meet with them at Fortress Monroe as soon as he could get there. He left immediately and by nightfall was resting aboard the *River Queen* under the protection of the guns at the fort (Foote 1974, 43). He also telegraphed General Grant and told him that nothing that was taking place should "change, hinder, or delay your military movements or plans" (quoted in Sandburg 1936, 4:35, 36).

The conference, which started after breakfast on February 3, lasted four hours and included some talk not on subject, some reminiscing about former days when they all were in Washington at one time or another, some attempts at humor, and some discussion of the possibilities of peace. Robert Hunter, who was taken aback by Lincoln's unwillingness to alter the terms of surrender, asked the president: "Mr. President, if we understand you correctly, you think that we of the Confederacy have committed treason; that we are traitors to your government; that we have forfeited our rights, and are proper subjects for the hangman. Is that not about what your words imply?" President

Lincoln replied, "Yes, you have stated the proposition better than I did. That is about the size of it" (quoted in Foote 1974, 45; Sandburg 1936, 443). The only good that came out of the conference was that President Lincoln promised the CSA vice president, Stephens, that he would help get Stephens's nephew, Lieutenant John Stephens—who had been captured at Vicksburg in 1863—out of the prison on Johnson's Island in Lake Erie. President Lincoln kept his word, had Stephens brought to the White House, and gave him a pass through the Union lines (Foote 1974, 45, 46; Sandburg 1936, 4:51). It is interesting to note that all three of the Confederate commissioners eventually blamed President Davis for the failure to obtain peace because of his "obstinacy" (Foote 1974, 48–51).

Thus, on the morning of February 4, 1865, there was no peace, and General Grant had planned an offensive for the next day.

A month earlier, on January 1, 1865, Major General Warren, having returned to the front after a furlough, had held a dinner party for Brevet Major General Ayres (2nd Division), Lieutenant Colonel Henry Bankhead (corps inspector general), Brevet Major General Samuel Crawford (3rd Division), Brevet Major General Charles Griffin (1st Division), Major General Andrew Humphreys (2nd Corps), and Brigadier General Charles Wainwright (artillery). A guest was also present, one of the Confederacy's peace "commissioners," John Campbell. It is assumed that battle plans for the next Union campaign were not discussed in the presence of the Rebel. The menu, which Warren reported to his wife, Emily, was certainly different from the Union soldiers' rations and especially from what was available to the Confederates across the trenches: oysters on the half shell, whiskey, soup, sherry, oyster patties and fish, roast beef and boiled mutton, macaroni au gratin, corn, beans, tomatoes, potatoes, and venison or prairie chicken. Dessert was fruit, coffee, and music by the band.[8] These leaders of the Union forces survived the dinner very nicely,

8. Gouverneur Warren to Emily Warren, Jan. 30 and 31, 1865, Warren Papers, New York State Library, State Univ. of New York; see also Jordan 2001, 204.

General Warren reported to his wife (Jordan 2001, 204). They were about to end the stay in winter quarters and take the offensive.

A much more public social event occurred two weeks later on January 19, 1865. All of Richmond high society was excited about a wedding at St. Paul's Church. The couple to be married was Brigadier General John Pegram and Hettie Cary. Hettie's mother, of Baltimore, Maryland, had obtained a pass from President Lincoln to visit her children in Richmond. The couple, who had been engaged for three years, decided that the visit was a good time to get married (Harrison 1911, 201–3). This was a marriage between a woman whom many thought to be the most beautiful woman in the South and a son of Richmond who was universally honored and beloved. Hettie had a strong record in support of the Confederacy. As a native of Baltimore, she was known to have waved the Confederate flag, which she and her sisters were the first to sew, out her window to passing Yankee soldiers. The three sisters had moved to Richmond to stay out of prison because people who sympathized with the Confederacy were being arrested in Baltimore (MacLean 2006; Walsh 2002, 406, 407). Although most weddings are accompanied by some mistakes, this wedding had more than its share. Two days before the wedding, while Hettie was showing her veil to relatives, a mirror fell and broke into many pieces (Harrison 1911, 201–3). President Davis had lent his horse-drawn carriage to carry the couple to the church, but the horses balked and became so unruly that the couple had to choose a shabby old hack that happened to be nearby on the street. Arriving late to the wedding, Hettie dropped her handkerchief on the way into the church and had to pick it up herself when no one noticed. In the process, she tore the tulle veil over her face almost to its full length (Walsh 2002, 406, 407). On February 2, Hettie visited her new husband in Petersburg. While there, Pegram's division passed in review, and General John Gordon moved back, leaving Hettie alone at the post of honor. With General Lee on her right and the other generals and their ladies close at hand, Hettie appeared to be a very happy new bride (Walsh 2002, 406, 407).

After the destruction of the Weldon Railroad down to the Meherrin River (chapter 8), Confederate supplies were reported to be reaching

Petersburg and Richmond from Wilmington, North Carolina, via the Meherrin River to the Boydton Plank Road and the Southside Railroad. General Grant wanted to go back to the area of Hatcher's Run and complete the offensive started at the end of October 1864 (Battle of Hatcher's Run I) by taking control of the Boydton Plank Road, but this time to leave the railroad out of the plan (Foote 1974, 52). General Humphreys had reported that the Confederate line of trenches and forts was nearly completed for some sixteen miles along the Petersburg line (W. Powell [1896] 2010, 389).

General Grant's plan involved a combined effort of Gregg's cavalry division, two divisions of Humphrey's 2nd Corps, and Warren's 5th Corps. Gregg was to outflank the Confederate line on its right by reaching the Boydton Plank Road at Dinwiddie Court House. At the same time, Humphreys was to move north of Hatcher's Run to shield Warren's forces south of the run that were supporting Gregg's cavalry (Jordan 2001, 205; Greene 2008, 99). Warren told his wife that they were going out to Dinwiddie Court House to see what was going on and to capture a wagon train of Confederate supplies and that he did not expect much fighting.[9] General Warren received specific orders from Brevet Major General Alexander Webb, who had replaced General Humphreys as General Meade's Chief of Staff on February 4,[10] to take four days of rations per person, fifty rounds of ammunition per person, and forty rounds per person in reserve wagons. No other wagons were to be taken except for those for trenching tools and hospitals and only half of the usual number of ambulances. Warren replied that the route he would take would be down Halifax Road to Rowanty Post Office, then on a road to the crossing of Rowanty Creek at West Perkins.[11]

9. Gouverneur Warren to Emily Warren, Jan. 30 and 31, 1865.

10. Alexander Webb to Gouverneur Warren, Feb. 4, 1865, *OR*, series 1, chap. 46, pp. 377–78.

11. Gouverneur Warren to General Alexander Webb, Feb. 4, 1865, *OR*, series I, chap. 46, part 2, pp. 377–78.

Sunday, February 5, 1865, began as a very cold, dark morning that threatened freezing rain and snow. General Gregg's cavalry moved out at 3:00 AM via Ream's Station toward Dinwiddie Court House and Boydton Plank Road. The men of the 188th New York were up most of the night looking for their company and preparing for the march (letter 40, chap. 11). Once assembled, Warren's 5th Corps moved out at 7:00 AM. The long train consisted of

> Front: Advanced Guard—3 squads from the 6th Ohio Cavalry, Captain Sexton
> Second Division—Bvt. Major General Ayres
> First Division—Bvt. Major General Griffin
> 12 field pieces (8 horses/piece and caisson)
> Third Division—Bvt. Major General Crawford
> One half of the corps ambulances
> 50 wagons of infantry ammunition
> Rear: 53 wagons for forage and ammunition of cavalry (compiled from W. Powell [1896] 2010, 390)

General Gregg's cavalry moved as planned into Dinwiddie Court House and captured a few wagons and prisoners on the Boydton Plank Road. Because of the small numbers of wagons seen, the cavalry was moved to Malone's Bridge over Rowanty Creek by the evening (Greene 2008, 100; W. Powell [1896] 2010, 390). Hatcher's Run became Rowanty Creek at its confluence with Gravelly Run.

General Warren's 5th Corps, moving west and north to meet the Vaughan Road where it crossed Hatcher's Run, had more difficulty not only because of the large number of men and wagons, but also because of the terrain. The crossing of Arthur's Swamp was accomplished by swimming, wading, and even walking on ice because of the falling temperature. The stream, which was sixty feet wide, could not be forded, so a bridge had to be built using available trees. Because of this delay, the wet and cold troops did not reach Vaughan Road until 3:45 PM (W. Powell [1896] 2010, 390). General Humphrey's 2nd Corps troops set up positions on the north side of Hatcher's Run at

Armstrong's Mill. He ordered Generals Gershom Mott and Thomas Smyth to build breastworks using wood from the nearby Tucker and Armstrong farms (Calkins 2003, 12). Smyth's division established these breastworks northward along the stream on the west side of the Duncan Road for one half mile. They were only about 1,000 yards from the new Confederate breastworks, with the Thompson Farm right between the two lines (Foote 1974, 53; W. Powell [1896] 2010, 391). Mott's division continued the line of breastworks southward on the east side of the stream. Owing to the proximity of the Confederate front, Confederate artillery began firing on Smyth's position at approximately 3:45 PM.

General Lee heard about the action while at church in Petersburg and headed for the Confederate lines near Hatcher's Run. He had placed General Heth's division of General Hill's Third Corps to hold the north side that faced General Humphreys' Yankees and protect the Boydton Plank Road. Farther north, in support of Heth was Mahone's Division under the command of General Joseph Finegan. General Lee had also brought the Confederate 2nd Corps from the Shenandoah Valley in December and placed them to the west and south of the run near Burgess' Mill. The Second Corps was made up of two divisions under the command of Brigadier General John Pegram (recently married to Hettie Cary) and General Clement Evans (Calkins 2003, 12–16). At about the time the Rebel Artillery opened up on Smyth's Yankees, two Confederate battle lines were formed. General Evans's division included (from west to east): Colonel John Lowe (Evans's Brigade, Georgia troops), Colonel William Peck (York's Brigade, troops from Louisiana), and Brigadier General William Terry (Terry's Brigade, Virginians). The battle line developed to the east of General Evans in General Pegram's division included (from west to east): Brigadier General John Cooke (Cooke's Brigade, North Carolinians), Brigadier General William MacRae (MacRae's Brigade, North Carolinians), and Brigadier General William McComb (mostly Tennesseans). Pegram's cavalry was assigned to protect Dabney's Mill (Calkins 2003, 12–16; Foote 1974, 53; Greene 2008, 102; W. Powell [1896] 2010, 391).

To press the battle, General Evan's division tried to outflank the Yankee troops facing them under the command of General Smyth. At the same time, another column appeared out of the woods on the Thompson Farm. These forces, under the command of General Heth, made three attacks that afternoon, led by a Confederate hero, Brigadier General John Cooke, who was wounded seven times during the war. The battle went back and forth, with Union general Gershom Mott's Third Brigade, under the command of Colonel Robert McAllister, taking most of the fight (W. Powell [1896] 2010, 391; Greene 2008, 102). The battle involved the 8th New Jersey, which was lined up on the left of the brigade and thus placed in the middle of the four-hour battle. The 8th suffered a loss of eleven enlisted men killed as well as two commissioned officers and thirty-five enlisted men wounded.[12] The fighting was so heavy that the next day four members of the 27th North Carolina, Company C, also in the middle of the fighting, deserted (Seymour 2010). The Confederate forces could not move the Union line, so they retreated to their trenches but kept up the artillery fire into the evening.

During the day, General Griffin's division had struggled at Rowanty Creek. Most of the infantry got across by swimming and wading in the icy stream. They were also involved in cutting trees and building a bridge so that by 4:00 PM the entire command was over the stream. Then they marched to within two miles of Dinwiddie Court House, their assigned position. With no sign of the enemy, they then built large fires to attempt to dry their clothes (Jordan 2001, 205). After setting up a picket line, the troops settled down to try and get some sleep. According to Major Evan Woodward of the 198th Pennsylvania, the strategic plan for February 5 was to have Griffin's 1st Division and Gregg's cavalry move close to Dinwiddie Court House to draw off a portion of enemy troops from the main body of the army

12. Henry Hartford to headquarters, Feb. 28, 1865, in *Hatcher's Run Movements and Activities of the 8th NJ Volunteers*, available at the website Old Newark, Military, http://www.oldnewark.com/infantry/civilwar/eighth/july1999.htm.

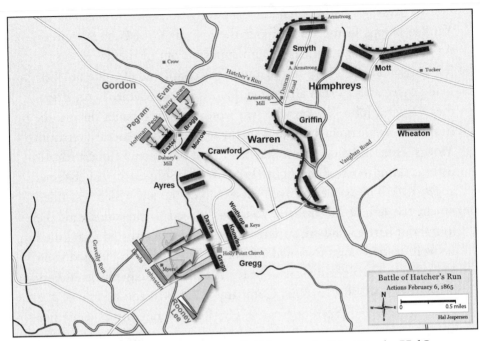

Map 4. The Battle of Hatcher's Run II, February 6, 1865. Map by Hal Jespersen, www.cwmaps.com.

(Woodward 1884, 17, 18). General Warren was given orders at 9:00 PM to move back to join Humphreys where Hatcher's Run crossed Vaughan Road. At 11:00 PM, the pickets were drawn in as rapidly and silently as possible and on the double-quick moved off to join the main body. At this point, it might be expected that older soldiers in the 188th New York, such as Will, were cold and exhausted—especially Will because he had not drilled very much since becoming a cook. Getting the pickets gathered up took longer than the high command wished, so it was nearly midnight before Will and his comrades were on their way (W. Powell [1896] 2010, 391). When the division ran into felled timber across the road, Griffin ordered a rest for the remainder of the night (Woodward 1884, 18).

At this point, it was becoming obvious that the major fighting on Monday, February 6, would be at Humphreys's front based on Confederate concentration of forces. General Meade ordered reinforcements in the form of Brigadier General John Hartranft's 3rd Division, 9th Corps, and General Frank Wheaton's 1st Division, 6th Corps, to join General Humphreys's troops. When they arrived during the night, General Humphreys placed them on the right of his forces (Calkins 2003, 16; W. Powell [1896] 2010, 391). Trouble arose because of miscommunication between Meade's headquarters and the generals at the front. According to General Meade's staff, communication was sent out at 12:15 AM on February 6 to General Warren that in the early morning his troops were to make a reconnaissance to the south and west of Hatcher's Run to find the Confederates (Calkins 2003, 16, 17; Jordan 2001, 206). General Alexander Webb, Meade's chief of staff, however, unfortunately thought that Humphreys outranked Warren so that the dispatch sent at 12:15 AM never reached Warren. By 8:00 AM, Warren did receive orders to do reconnaissance and fight the Confederates if the Rebels were outside their lines.

Major George Jones and Lieutenant Edward Fowler from the 150th Pennsylvania, 3rd Division, 1st Brigade (commanded by General Edward Bragg), had been enjoying a fifteen-day leave in Philadelphia. On the way back to the front, they found that the Potomac River was frozen over. When they asked the War Department what they should do, they were advised to wait until the river was thawed and that the "cause of the delay would be endorsed on their leaves" (Chamberlin 1905, 293). They decided not to wait, paid their own fares to Annapolis, arrived at the front via the Chesapeake Bay on February 5, and were ready to fight the next day. They were about to be involved in some of the heaviest fighting.

About noon on February 6, after a very cold morning, General Meade arrived at General Warren's headquarters and informed him that the orders of the early morning were for his troops and not just Humphreys's. So at about 1:15 PM, General Crawford's Third Division, including Major Jones and Lieutenant Fowler, were sent south along the Vaughan Road to Dabney's Mills Road. They then turned right and followed that road northwest toward the mill, which was about one mile away, to drive the Confederates back and to determine the location of their entrenched lines. General Ayres's division followed Crawford on his left, with Griffin's division (Will's comrades) in reserve (Calkins 2003, 16; Jordan 2001, 206; W. Powell [1896] 2010, 391). General Gregg's cavalry was sent down the Vaughan Road farther south to the crossing of Gravelly Run. General Lee, who had just heard from the capital that he had been appointed commander of all the armies of the Confederacy, separated General Pegram's division into two parts, sending part, along with the cavalry, to Vaughan Road, where they met Gregg's cavalry. The Confederates were stopped in the late afternoon with the assistance of the Union's General Frederick Winthrop's 1st Brigade, of General Ayres's 2nd Division (Jordan 2001, 206). The other part joined Generals Evans's and Mahone's divisions near the mill, where they faced Crawford's division. At about 11:00 AM, Confederate General John Gordon (2nd Corps) had called General Evans's Georgia Brigade into support of John Pegram's troops on Pegram's right.

The battle around Dabney's Mills began as Crawford's Division, with General Edward Bragg's 1st Brigade leading the way and the 150th Pennsylvania as skirmishers (Chamberlin 1905, 294). They were able to push the Confederate forces back to what appeared to be a Confederate fort. Lieutenant Edward Fowler, who had hurried back from Philadelphia to be at the front, was severely wounded and taken to a hospital at City Point that evening. He was thought to be a "gone gosling" by everyone except an unidentified "good old doctor" who refused to give up on him. Edward Fowler left the hospital for home on April 15 (Chamberlin 1905, 296).

This attack by the Union forces also involved the 2nd Brigade of Crawford's Division, commanded by General Henry Baxter. As Baxter's Brigade approached this supposed Confederate fort, the color bearers from the 16th Maine and the 97th New York got into a competition to see which flag could be placed in the fort first. The flag bearer for the 97th New York won the contest, only to find that what they thought was a fort was nothing but a huge pile of saw dust (Calkins 2003, 18; Walsh 2002, 407).

During this fighting near the mill, General John Pegram, just recently married to Hettie Cary, was shot near his heart and died as he was being assisted from his horse (Calkins 2003, 24). The young Mrs. Pegram received her dead husband's body in Petersburg, where she was staying with her mother. Another tragedy occurred about this time to "man's best friend. Sallie, a brindle bull Terrier mix, had been the mascot for the 11th Pennsylvania since the Battle of Gettysburg. After the battle on the first day, she was found lying with the dead and wounded and almost dead herself. The 11th nursed her back to health, and she accompanied them into every battle" ("Gettysburg National Military Park" 2002). On February 6, 1865, near Dabney's Mills, the commander of the 24th Michigan, General Edward Bragg, noticed that at a certain location in his lines, the men had stopped shooting. Sallie had been killed, and the men of the 11th had paused to bury her (Calkins 2003, 26).

The battle around Dabney's Mills was characterized by charges and countercharges most of the afternoon of February 6. Some of the fiercest fighting occurred with the advancing of General Bragg's (1st Brigade) and General Baxter's (2nd Brigade) troops under General Crawford against Confederate troops under the commands of Colonel John Lowe of Gordon's Division (General Clement Evans in command) and General Joseph Finegan of Mahone's Division (Jordan 2001, 206; W. Powell [1896], 382). Colonel Lowe's troops from Georgia were especially hit hard in the battle. The 60th Georgia lost eleven out of thirteen of their commissioned officers, and the 61st Georgia lost all of its officers, leaving sergeants in command (G. Nichols 1898, 212). In a major counterattack by General Finegan with Mahone's Division, Private William Wellmaker of General Moxley Sorrel's Brigade from Georgia (22nd, Company F) was wounded below his knee while on horseback. Without stopping and looking at his wound, he rode his horse for several miles to get assistance. By then, blood had filled his boot to overflowing. Later in February, a piece of bone was removed from his leg, and his mother kept it. He died on furlough two months later. Mrs. Wellmaker buried five sons in this war ("Notes on Wellmaker" 2010). General Sorrel was also wounded during this battle.

About the time that General Pegram was killed, the Confederate forces also sent troops around the left flank, which ran into General

Gregg's cavalry protecting General Crawford's left flank. The Confederates pushed Gregg's forces back to Hatcher's Run and closer to Will's position under the command of General Griffin (Woodward 1884, 18). General Ayres's 2nd Division, which had advanced to support Crawford's troops, was also repulsed and retreated in confusion under attack by General Finegan. The 1st Division under General Griffin was posted behind breastworks in support. The 1st Brigade, under the command of General Horatio Sickel, immediately charged out of the breastworks, with the 198th Pennsylvania leading the way (Woodward 1884, 18). The brigade turned sharply into an open field and met Finegan's troops. The 1st Brigade was successful in splitting the advancing Confederate troops in half and sending them into some confusion. General Sickel received a painful flesh wound in his left thigh from a rifle bullet (Woodward 1884, 19).

At this point, it is assumed that the 2nd Brigade, under the command of Colonel Allen Burr, was ordered to support the 1st Brigade. This brigade—composed of the New York 187th, 188th (Will's regiment), and 189th—had not fired a shot at the enemy since the first Battle of Hatcher's Run at the end of October 1864. The 188th marched to form a line of battle, and about the time they were lined up, troops from the 6th Corps came running out of the woods and broke up the line. The 188th got back into line, faced left, marched back about fifty yards, and then charged into the woods (letter 40, March 14, 1865, chap. 11).

Somewhere in the woods of Virginia in the late afternoon of this cold and rainy February 6, 1865, a Confederate bullet ended the war for Private William Whitlock of Allegany, New York (letter 40).

II

Epilogue
Fires and Rainbows

Mor I have came in from service tonight. We have got marching
orders and hav 60 rounds of cartidg. Thair is something up now.
Mor, let Drate see this and the folks.

Army of the Potomac
Hatcher's Run
March the 14, 1865

Far distant friend this plesant morning I take pen in hand to write
to you. I am well and enjoying good health and hoping this will
find you the same.

    Morris I recieved your letter last night and will try to answer
it this morning. Morris you wanted I should write the particku-
lars about William. O Mor it seems like a dream to me. Mor he
went into battle on Monday afternoon Feburary the 6. He was in
a file just ahead of me. I think he looked rather sober that day. He
did not say much all day but I thought it was on the account of
being up all night before we started on the march looking for the
company. Mor when we marched down to form line of battel we
had hardly got into line before the 6 corps came running out of
the woods through our lines and broke us all up. We got into line
again and left faced and martch back 8 or ten rods and charged

into the woods. I did not see Will after that til he was brought out dead. This was on Monday and his body was found Wednesday morning. He was shot through the head. His watch and the rest of his things wer with him. He did not have much money with him. I think 50 or 60 cts. Mor he let Harrison Newel have 10 dollars and he has paid 2 of it and I think his wife will get the rest. Mor Lieutenant [blank space] has not [got] the watch, memorandum, and pocket book. He said he was going to send them home. Will let Samuel Row have 2 dollars I think but he says it Isnt but 50 cents and has paid it to Solomon and he will send it in. This Charles Smith ose him 1.00 dollar. I just saw him, he says he will pay it this afternoon. If he will I will send it in this. That is all I know of his pay. Proply will be sent to his wife. Mor concerning Williams burial: we dug his grave and wraped his blanket around him and then laid him down to reste and then spread his rubber blanket over him and buried him as decently as we could. His body is on the inside of our picket line. Mor what clothes Will had I do not know what was done with them. Thair wass one shirt one pair of drawers and the rest of his clothes was left on him. Mor when the Lieutenant sends his memorandum book home that will be a great comfort to his wife. Morris I cant think of mutch more to write only that the rebs come over conciderable fast and some of them bring thair guns. They say they have got tiard of this war.

Mor it is pleasent and warm here and I think we shall make another move before long and if we do Grant well take the railroad before he stops and the Rebs says they hav got 3 lines of breastworks and three lines of stockades. I think we shall hav some hard fighting before we get the road.

Mor tell Drate that I am sorry to think he is going weste before I get home. Tell Drate to write whether he has sold his place or not and if I can get my likeness taken I will send it to him. Tell our folks I have not had a letter from them since the 27 of last month and it seems like a long time. I have to send them some money by express, it is time it was thair. Tell them to write often and you must do the same. I must close for I have to go out on review. Mor please excuse my poor scrabings for I have to hold my paper on my lap.

> Yours truly Morris Whitlock,
> Alanson Jones

Letter 40, written by Alanson Jones to Will's brother Morris, describes how Will was killed. Alanson Jones, two years older than Will, was mustered into the army at Allegany the same day as Will. He survived the war and was mustered out as a corporal. Mark Whitney was fortunate to find this letter because it was not in the box with the letters that Will wrote home to Lide, but rather loose and on its own in the rafters of the attic in the Whitlock/Whitney house. Will's original burial site, as indicated by this letter, was within the picket lines back at the camp the 188th had left on February 5. The burial site was quite simple, as explained in the letter. Will's body was later identified, so the burial site must have been marked in some manner, probably with a headboard across a stake in the ground. A soldier's body was usually not transported back to his home because of the cost, which would have to be met by either the soldier's relatives or his comrades in arms (Dunkelman 2004, 159–60).

As early as 1862, a federal program was established to develop national burial grounds for the war dead. This program was still in its initial stages when the war ended. In 1866, Lieutenant Colonel James Moore was appointed to select a location in the area around Petersburg. He located a farm south of Petersburg where the 50th New York Engineers had their camp and had built a pine log church called "Poplar Grove." Unfortunately, the church no longer stands at the site. The one hundred men assigned to the "burial corps" used ten army wagons, forty mules, and twelve saddle horses in the search and recovery over a three-year period. They covered nine Virginia counties from Petersburg to Lynchburg and more than one hundred separate burial sites in the area. A total of 6,718 remains were reinterred, but only 2,139 were positively identified (US National Park Service 2010c). William Whitlock's final resting place is Grave Number 2702 in Poplar Grove National Cemetery. In the 1930s, the upright head-stones were sawed off and placed flush with the ground to facilitate maintenance.[1] The flat stone on Will's grave is quite worn, and only part of his name remains legible. But a memorial monument for him is also located in the Five Mile Cemetery, Allegany, New York, as a marker for the Whitlock family. In addition, there is a smaller marker for Will next to Lide's grave.

The remains of nearly 30,000 Confederate soldiers were found in and around the battlefields of Petersburg and reinterred in Blankford Church Cemetery in Petersburg. Unfortunately, only about 2,000 individual names are known (US National Park Service 2010c).

Another member of the Whitlock family was killed the same afternoon at Hatcher's Run. Theodore Whitlock, Will's cousin, was born on January 24, 1835, in Ithaca, the son of Benajah Whitlock (Will's younger brother) and Catherine "Katie A" Apgar (see appendix A).[2] Theodore enlisted in Humphrey, New York, for three years in the 147th Regiment, Company K, on August 31, 1863 (*Annual Report* 1904). Thus, by the time Will joined up, Theodore was a veteran and had survived the Battles of the Wilderness, Spotsylvania, and Globe Tavern. At the second Battle of Hatcher's Run on February 6, the 147th, commanded by Brevet Brigadier General Henry Morrow, was involved in some of the heaviest fighting at Dabney's Mills (Calkins 2003, 20–22; Jordan 2001, 206; W. Powell [1896] 2010, 392).When Theodore Whitlock—whom Will does not mention in any of his let-ters to Lide—was killed, he left a wife, Amanda, and three children, Emily, Caty Ann, and Almond. They moved into her brother Sidney Newell's house in Humphrey in 1865 (US Census 1865).

In the overall history of America's Civil War, the Battle of Hatch-er's Run II (Dabney's Mills) resulted in a continuation of Northern

---

1. Wallace Elms to Howard Mark Whitney, Jan. 9, 1978, in Mark Whitney's collection, Allegany, New York.

2. Theodore Whitlock, descendant #29, 2010, genealogy available at http://familytreemaker.genealogy.com/users/r/o/c//charles-w-rockett/gene19-003.html.c.

17. The William and Mary Eliza Whitlock Memorial at the Five Mile Cemetery, Allegany, New York, 2010. William was in actuality buried at Poplar Grove National Cemetery in Virginia. Photograph by the author.

lines to the west of Petersburg, making Confederate control of the Boydton Plank Road and the Southside Railroad even more tenuous. During February 5–7, 1865, the Union reported 1,539 casualties, and the Confederacy lost approximately 1,000 soldiers. As a consequence, more than 2,500 men were lost for the extension of an entrenchment just three additional miles (Greene 2008, 105).

The loss of William Whitlock in General Grant's push to obtain control of Boydton Plank Road and the Southside Railroad was felt by his comrades in arms as well as by his family and friends back home in western New York. With the exception of George Strohuber, who had his left leg amputated below the knee, all of the friends Will mentions in his letters (chapter 3) survived Hatcher's Run on February 5–7, 1865 ("Special Schedule" 1890, 3). Ten enlisted men of the 188th were killed in the battle, the bloodiest battle the regiment experienced in the war.

The war had to go on, however, and once back in the trenches the 188th New York Volunteers suffered from illnesses, the stress of previous battles, and the exceptional cold weather of February and early March ("Special Schedule" 1890, 3). Even though the Union soldiers knew that Confederate desertions were increasing and that Rebel supplies were very limited or nonexistent, they also knew that the Rebels were very active in strengthening their fortifications (letter 40; Greene 2008, 75–77, 83, 84). With the victory of General Philip Sheridan's troops in the Shenandoah Valley, General Grant could now bring those troops to support the front at Petersburg and the drive westward to outflank the Confederate lines.

On March 25, in an attempt to force the Union troops eastward to relieve his right flank, General Lee ordered Major General John B. Gordon to attack Union forces at Fort Stedman, east of Petersburg. If successful, the Confederate lines that were being dangerously stretched westward would be relieved. The 188th New York was ordered, along with the rest of General Griffin's division, out of the camps along Hatcher's Run to support the Union's attempts to hold Fort Stedman. After a day of missed communications and heavy fighting, especially along picket lines, the Union forces prevailed. Watching the battle from nearby Fort Wadsworth were President and Mrs. Lincoln, General and Mrs. Grant, and General Meade. The soldiers took time to give the spectators cheers, and some of them saw President Lincoln for the first time. On the same day, Union forces were also successful to the southwest at the Battle of Jones's Farm near Fort Fisher in the Union's trench system. Although the 188th New York saw no fighting in their support role, they were about to see heavy fighting in the Appomattox Campaign, which would last from March 28 to April 9.

Now that General Grant had General Sheridan's additional forces at the Petersburg front, a major push was made on to the west to outflank the Confederate right, block the Boydton Plank Road, and cut the Southside Railroad. Will's comrades in the 188th would spend the rest of the war outside of the cold, muddy trenches around Petersburg, marching and fighting every day until the end of the war.

About this time, the leadership of the 188th changed. At the second Bull Run, Captain John McMahon (Company G, 105th New York) had been severely wounded and returned home to Rochester for healing. Because of so many losses, the 105th was consolidated into the 94th New York on March 17, 1863. McMahon returned as captain of Company G. He went back to battle and was captured on July 1 at Gettysburg. Before submitting his sword, Captain McMahon broke the blade over a stump in defiance. A Confederate lieutenant saved McMahon from being shot and sent him to Libby Prison in Richmond (McNamera 2012, 3–5). While in prison, he was promoted to major on February 17, 1864. On October 20, New York governor Horatio Seymour commissioned McMahon as head of the 188th, which he led under General Warren and then General Charles Griffin.

The Appomattox Campaign began on March 29 with General Grant ordering the 5th Corps under General Warren to move to the junction of Quaker and Vaughan roads. When the 2nd Corps under General Andrew Humphreys arrived, it was to be in position with Quaker Road on his left and Hatcher's Run on his right. Then Warren would move 5th Corps up the Quaker Road and on to the Boydton Plank Road. General Sheridan was to attack the Confederates at Dinwiddie Court House in attempt to force the Rebels to leave their breastworks and fight in the open. The cavalry had a difficult day as the roads turned to mud. General Fitz Lee was verbally placed in command of the cavalry of the Army of Northern Virginia and moved to attack Sheridan's troops at Dinwiddie Court House. Forces were now confronting each other in what is now known as the Battle of Lewis's Farm (or Gravelly Road or Quaker Road).

Led by General Joshua Chamberlain's brigade (198th Pennsylvania; 185th New York), the Union forces stopped at Lewis's Farm and waited for Colonel Edgar Gregory's brigade to come into line on his left. Fierce fighting developed and the CSA forces under General Henry Wise, with support from General William Wallace's South Carolinians, began to drive the Union forces back from the farm. General Griffin then sent support to Chamberlain's and Gregory's men in the form of the 198th Pennsylvania and the 188th New York.

With the help of the 188th New York, the Federal troops finally had control of Boydton Plank Road. General Chamberlain, Union hero at Little Round Top during the Battle of Gettysburg, was once again wounded. He was hit in the left arm by a minie ball that then traveled to his elbow and glanced off a leather case of field orders and a brass mirror in a left pocket near his heart. General Griffin was very concerned when he saw Chamberlain covered with blood, from both Chamberlain's own and his horse's wounds. General Chamberlain stayed at the front in spite of the pain and was almost captured. When approached by Confederate soldiers, he was so covered in blood and mud that he was left alone when he claimed to be a Confederate officer (Calkins 2003, 38; Maes 2010, 17). The 188th New York lost a total of four enlisted men: two were killed, and two died of their wounds.

A steady rain had begun the night of March 29 and continued all the next day. At first, General Grant wanted to cancel any plans for fighting, but General Sheridan, who rode in the rain all the way to Grant's headquarters, persuaded him to continue to push the Confederates. As Sheridan had promised Grant, he had General George Custer's entire division corduroying the Dinwiddie supply roads. Sufficient progress allowed General Grant to order Sheridan to move up the road leading northwest to Five Forks (Grant 1885, 601).

In spite of the mud and high water, General Grant moved the Ayres and Crawford divisions of the 5th Corps toward Confederate lines on White Oak Road. General Warren had three-day rations given to the men of the 5th Corps. Griffin's division solidified control of the Boydton Plank Road by moving up the road as far as Burgess' Mill (Foote 1974, 134).

March 31, 1865, was a day of two battles: 5th Corps (188th New York) was involved in the Battle of White Oak Road, and General Sheridan's forces in the Battle of Dinwiddie Court House. White Oak Road was a very important road that connected Boydton Plank Road, now under the control of 5th Corps, with Five Forks, an intersection of five roads held by CSA forces.

When the rain slowed about midmorning, General Warren was ordered to have the 5th Corps occupy White Oak Road, and he sent General Romeyn Ayres's 2nd Division forward at 11:00 AM. Out of the woods stepped a line of Confederate soldiers that immediately drove Ayres's division backward through a swamp in a ravine to General Samuel Crawford's 3rd Division, which was backing up the attack by Ayres. There was mass confusion all the way back to Griffin's reserve division in the rear. The Confederates were able to defend against three separate attacks by General Chamberlain's and General Griffin's forces. Four Confederate brigades had forced more than 5,000 Union troops hurrying in retreat through the swamps and over Gravelly Run. By 2:30 PM, Ayres and Crawford had returned order to their divisions, and Warren gave an order for a second major advance. This time, however, General Charles Griffin took command of the advancement (Calkins 2003, 42–44; Greene 2008, 170–74; Lowe 2010). Although wounded on March 29, General Chamberlain agreed to mount an attack with Griffin's Division (188th New York) in support. With Griffin's support, the Union forces forced the Confederates back, captured most of the 56th Virginia, and took possession of the White Oak Road. The fierce-fighting McGowan's South Carolinians were cut off and retreated by a roundabout road so that they could fight the Yankees one more day (Evans 1899, 353).

General Grant's army lost 1,865 troops at the Battle of White Oak Road: 177 killed, 1,134 wounded, and 554 missing. The 188th New York, over the three-day period March 29–31, lost 6: 4 enlisted men killed and 2 wounded who later died. General Bushrod Johnson listed Confederate losses (killed, wounded, and missing) at 800, with the capture of 470 Union troops (Calkins 2003, 54; Phisterer 1890, 514).

White Oak Road extends westward through a junction—Five Forks with three other roads, Courthouse (from the southeast), Scott's (from the south), and Ford (from the junction north). By April 1, 1865, troops available to General Lee—the infantry division of General Pickett and the cavalry divisions of Rooney Lee, Fitz Lee, and Thomas Rosser (total of 9,000–10,000 troops)—were located at or near the junction and were facing Sheridan's cavalry (13,000) and Warren's infantry (54,500).

Trouble developed quickly because of muddy roads, swollen streams, and thick vegetation (Calkins 2003, 88–92; Greene 2008, 184; Jordan 2001, 230). Under these conditions, the Union attack, to be led by General Warren, did not occur until 4:15 PM. General Sheridan, who did not know about the conditions, blamed Warren for the delay and, with Grant's agreement, later had General Warren relieved of command and replaced by Will's former commander, General Griffin. General Crawford's troops got lost in the thick underbrush and trees and proceeded too far north of the Confederate line in attempting to outflank the Rebels. Warren caught up with Crawford and directed his troops south to the Confederate rear. Fortunately for the Union army, this directive placed Crawford's men in the path of any possible Confederate escape along Ford Road from the Five Forks intersection. The delay only made matters worse between Generals Sheridan and Warren.

Meanwhile, the Confederate generals Pickett, Rosser, and Fitz Lee were enjoying a fish dinner (Shad Bake) just across Hatcher's Run on Ford Road. They did not tell their staffs where they were, however, and when the Yankees attacked, there was little coordination (Calkins 2003, 80, 81; 2011, 28; Greene 2008, 186). By 7:00 PM, Sheridan's troops from the south and Griffin's troops from the east had routed the Confederate troops. Griffin's troops, including the 188th New York, pushed the Rebels all the way to Ford Road. Total Union losses numbered about 830.

Will's former general, Gouverneur Warren, took his dismissal to military court after the war ended. Because of court and administrative delays, he died at age fifty-three on August 8, 1882, before the "not guilty" verdict was announced to the public (Jordan 2001, 307). Warren had been very unhappy with the military and had directed that he be buried as a private citizen (Foote 1974, 142).

During the Battle of Five Forks, from the 188th New York one enlisted man was killed, and one officer and two enlisted men died of their wounds. General Sheridan reported the capture of 2,400 soldiers and 600 killed or wounded (Foote 1974, 186).

By nightfall on April 1, the Confederates were scattered north along Ford Road, and the 5th Corps followed in pursuit. On the next day, the 5th Corps encamped along the Namozine Road in reserve (north of the Southside Railroad). By this time, the entrenchments around Petersburg had been flanked, and Petersburg and Richmond fell on April 2. On April 3, General Custer attacked the fleeing Confederates at Namozine Church and captured 1,200 solders under the command of General A. P. Hill (Calkins 2003, 119). The 5th Corps under General Griffin encamped near the crossing of Deep Creek.

While peace messages were being sent back and forth between Generals Lee and Grant, the Union army continued to pursue the hungry, battered Confederate forces. On Saturday, April 6, the 5th Corps marched all day south of the Appomattox River in support of Sheridan's cavalry (Calkins 2011, 100). During this march, General Edward Ord's men of the Army of the James became tired, but in the spirit of competition Griffin and the 5th Corps marched five miles farther before resting. Two days later General Sheridan was still pursuing isolated Confederate units and called for the 5th Corps to advance to Appomattox Station.

While the 5th Corps was involved in the all-day march on April 6, the Confederate army was falling apart at the Battle of Sailor's Creek. The battle was a collection of three different major confrontations around Big Sailor's Creek and Little Sailor's Creek and resulted in the loss of six Confederate generals and the capture of thousands of soldiers. General Lee, on seeing the confusion in one of the confrontations at Big Sailor's Creek, said, "My God! Has the army been dissolved?" (quoted in Calkins 2011, 114–15).

On April 9, Palm Sunday morning, General John Gordon, leading the Confederate 2nd Army Corps, was contemplating a continuation of the fighting near the village of Appomattox Court House. Through his field glasses, he must have been able to see the entire Union 5th Corps, along with General Ord's Army of the James, General John Gibbon's 24th Army Corps, and General William Birney's Negro Division (Calkins 2011, 160–64). General Gordon knew that his forces would probably be officially surrendered by General Lee. That same day General Edward Alexander, brigadier general of artillery, had a conversation with General Robert E. Lee in which General Lee said, "I can tell you for your comfort that General Grant will not demand unconditional surrender. He will give us as honorable terms as we have right to ask or expect. The men can go to their homes and will only be bound not to fight again until exchanged" (quoted in Gallagher 1989, 533).

General Grant sent most of his armies on missions to capture any isolated groups of Confederate soldiers and the army under General Joseph Johnston. Only the 5th Corps remained at Appomattox to accept the Confederate surrender. Fifteen days later, on April 21, 1865, General Johnston surrendered his forces to General Sherman near Durham Station, North Carolina.

Will was not there to share in the surrender or in a display of honor for the displaced General Warren as the 5th Corps passed through Petersburg on the way to Washington. General Griffin arranged the display, and General Warren and his wife, Emily, watched from the balcony of the Bolingbroke Hotel (Jordan 2001, 238). General Joshua Chamberlain wrote that the 5th Corps could not hold to the formal march but stopped, took off their caps, and cheered for their former general (Chamberlain [1915] 1991, 228–29). Will also missed the Grand Review of the Armies on May 23, 1865, in Washington, DC. On this first day of the Grand Review, General George Meade led the Army of the Potomac, approximately 80,000 men marching twelve across, followed by hundreds of artillery and a seven-mile-long group of cavalry (Chisholm 1989, 91, 92). General Meade stopped in front of the review stand and joined President Andrew Johnson, General in Chief Ulysses S. Grant, and other government officials to review the parade ("Grand Review" 2011). Will certainly would have been proud to join his comrades of the 5th Corps as they led the parade.

In addition, Will missed a reunion of his friends and comrades held at Allegany Cemetery in Allegany, New York, thirty-nine years later in 1904. A picture taken by N. J. Turano shows twenty-one Civil War veterans who came from the area. Four of the identified men were in the 188th Regiment, and two, George Strohuber and Ashebel Buzzard, are mentioned in Will's letters to Lide.

18. Reunion of Civil War veterans from the Allegany, New York, area in 1904. *Standing (left to right):* M. O. McLure, Company I, 64th New York; Frederick Forness, Company A, 188th New York; George Strohuber, Company A, 188th New York; John D. Smith, Company I, 64th New York; Ashebel Buzzard, Company C, 154th New York; John Fries, Company A, 188th New York; John Presack, Company E, 16th New York Cavalry; Francis J. Waters, Company H, 37th New York. *Sitting (left to right):* Joseph Nolte, Company I, 64th New York; Henry Altenburg, Company K, 64th New York; John Boats, Company C, 105th New York; George Bascom, Company I, 64th New York; Matthew Mosman, Company A, 188th New York; Michael Collins, Company F, 85th New York; Eliah Barber, Company F, 85th New York; A. C. Wing, Company G, 154th New York; William Spacker Jr., Company I, 64th New York; unidentified; unidentified; unidentified; John Moscript, Company I, 64th New York. Photograph by N. J. Turano. Courtesy of Mark Whitney, Allegany, New York.

Will left three major legacies in the context of the fires of war and tragedy and the rainbows of blessing. The fires of war had created two new Whitlock widows and seven fatherless children back in western New York. Lide now faced life alone with her four children—Euzetta, Stanley, Clara, and Henry, ages fourteen, twelve, nine, and five. Near the end of his last letter home to Lide, Will expresses his concern for all four of his children by name (letter 39, chap. 10). In all four cases, he is concerned for their education. He hopes that his eldest daughter, Euzetta, will be able to go to Olean, New York, to school and inquires about the success of the other three children. Lide and her children passed on the first of Will's legacies, the rainbow of education, to the succeeding generations. Because of this support of education and the increasing need for an educated society, eight out of eleven of Will's great-great-grandchildren hold at least a master's degree in their selected area of study. Will's descendants continue to receive rainbows of opportunity and success through education.

The second lasting legacy Will left, involving both fires and rainbows, was his family. Mary Eliza (Lide) did everything possible to make sure the federal government fulfilled its responsibilities in financial matters related to Will's death. One of the first forms she completed was the basic form for a widow's pension from the federal government. She inserted the name of a local attorney in place of the law firm in Washington, DC. Additional forms included a statement from the Whitlock's family physician, Dr. John Palmer, that verified the children's date of birth so that Mary could apply for additional compensation for children under the age of sixteen.[3] Her success in seeking out these funds made life a little easier for this family of five.

Initial family rainbow connections had been made between the Whitlocks and the Trowbridges, with three marriages between the families: the double-ring ceremony in which Will and Mary Eliza were married along with Will's sister Elizabeth and Mary Eliza's brother Marshall as well as an earlier marriage between Will's younger

---

3. Dr. Palmer's statement is included in Mark Whitney's collection.

sister Christina and Reuben Trowbridge (see chapter 1 and appendix A). Although the supply of potential marriage partners became less restricted as family members moved out of the area and the society became more mobile, many of Will's descendants found marriage partners within the area, forming connections between the Whitlock and the Linderman and Whitney families.

Stanley Whitlock, Will and Lide's oldest son, moved his family from Humphrey to the Elmwood Farm located at the corner of Five Mile Road and Morgan Hollow Road in Allegany in 1897. Stanley and Medora Linderman Whitlock had three children: Ray (1882–1943), Clare (1890–1943), and Bessie (1893–1970). Both Clare and Bessie married members of the Whitney family. This rainbow of blessing included the marriage of Clare Whitlock to Grace Whitney (1891–1970) and Bessie Whitlock to Howard B. Whitney (1895–1959). These unions became even closer when Howard and Bessie Whitney moved to Five Mile Road and became partners on the farm with Clare and

19. Four generations of Whitlock women, 1886–88. *Left to right:* Mary Eliza "Lide" Trowbridge Whitlock (William Whitlock's wife, tentatively identified); Margarette Malby; Clara Whitlock Linderman (Will and Lide's youngest daughter); and Mable Linderman Malby. Courtesy of Mark Whitney, Allegany, New York.

Grace Whitlock. Together, the families built a large, profitable dairy farm. When Clare Whitlock died in 1943, Howard Whitney took over operation of the farm. Howard and Bessie Whitney had one son, Walter L. Whitney (1923–2003). Walter married Rita Button (b. 1928), and the couple parented three children: Howard (b. 1947), John (b. 1948), and Lynne (b. 1955). The oldest, Howard Mark Whitney, made this book possible.

The third legacy Will passed is a rainbow of faith. Although faith in God must be a personal decision, the atmosphere necessary to influence that decision has certainly been present in the Whitlock family. Church attendance had been emphasized as early as Will's grandparents, John and Mary Whitlock, who with their thirteen children joined the First Presbyterian Church in Ithaca, New York, in 1812 (chapter 1). Numerous conversations by letter between Will and Lide indicated that the Whitlock family was very much involved in the church. They prayed for each other, their children, and other relatives.

The fires of tragedy, of course, happen even to people who have placed their trust in God. A son of Ray Whitlock and Ellen Linderman (1884–1962), Paul Whitlock (1909–45), believed that he and his wife, Helen Magnin Whitlock, were called to be missionaries in Africa. On

20. Whitlock/Whitney barn in flames, 1970. Courtesy of the Whitney Collection, Mark Whitney, Allegany, New York.

a trip to the mission field, he, his wife, and three of their five boys (Robert, five; Richard, three; and Stanley, two) boarded the *China Clipper* in Miami to fly to their destination. In 1945, the *China Clipper*, registration number NC-14716, was still the state of the art in passenger aircraft (Cartwright 2002), yet the plane crashed into the water, and fourteen of the eighteen passengers, including all of the Whitlock family on board, were killed. The two older Whitlock boys—Paul, thirteen, and Kenneth, nine—were spared because they were enrolled in school and did not make the trip ("Hinsdale Man" 1945).

Everyone recognizes that both fires of tragedy and rainbows of blessing happen regardless of religious belief and family ties. Perhaps for the extended Whitlock family, photographs taken by Mark Whitney may illustrate the relationship between the two. In 1970, tragedy resulted from an accident that burned all of the barns on the Whitlock/ Whitney Farm. Yet after a period of time during which the family was greatly concerned about the farm's future because of the fire, they spotted a rainbow after a rainstorm. A photograph taken from across Five Mile Road seems to place the rainbow where the barns had burned.

21. Rainbow at the Whitlock/Whitney Farm, c. 1980. Courtesy of the Whitney Collection, Mark Whitney, Allegany, New York.

Perhaps these pictures speak to the extended Whitlock family, as do the words sung by the Confederate Army of Northern Virginia in April 1864 as they prepared to go back into battle following a communion service (chapter 9):

When through fiery trials thy pathway shall lie,
My grace all-sufficient shall be thy supply;
The flame shall not hurt thee; I only design
Thy dross to consume, and thy gold to refine. (Stanley [1787] 1977,
574)

Appendixes

References

Index

Selected Descendants of Reuben Whitlock

Reuben Whitlock, b. 1767 (NJ), married Christina (NJ, maiden name unknown), d. 1858

Children

1. **John,** b. Nov. 11, 1767, NJ; d. Mar. 9, 1858, NJ
2. William, b. Jan. 17, 1778, NJ; d. Jan. 26, 1864, NJ
3. George, b. Aug. 27, 1781, NJ; d. Oct. 24, 1837, PA

John Whitlock married Mary Morris Dec. 26, 1793, NJ, b. 1772, NJ, d. Jan. 25, 1858, NY

Children

1. Sarah, b. Dec. 11, 1794, NJ
2. Eleanor, (Nelly), b. Mar 15, 1797, NJ
3. Reuben, b. May 8, 1799, NJ; d. March 4, 1862, Ithaca, NY
4. Morris, b. Apr. 24, 1801, NJ; d. Mar. 1, 1870, Ithaca, NY
5. Thomas, b. Apr. 24, 1801, NJ; d. c. 1870–75(?), Ischua, NY
6. Elizabeth, b. Feb. 25, 1803, NY
7. Mary, b. Feb. 14, 1805, NY
8. Rebecca, b. May 11, 1807, Ithaca, NY; d. Mar 10, 1849, Ischua, NY
9. Benajah, b. May 28, 1809, Ithaca, NY; d. Mar. 2, 1893, Souix City, IA
10. Jesse, b. May 18, 1812, Ithaca, NY; d. June 6, 1901, Ithaca, NY
11. Uzetta, b. May 18, 1812, Ithaca, NY; d. May 5, 1890?
12. John, b. May 18, 1812, Ithaca, NY; d. after 1880, NY?

1.5. Thomas Whitlock married Jane Norton (b. 1803, NY; d. Sept. 26, 1872, Allegany, NY) c. 1820, NY

Children

1. Freeman, b. July 23, 1821, Ithaca, NY

2. Amanda, b. Jan. 19, 1823, Ithaca, NY
3. Phoebe, b. June 23, 1824, Ithaca, NY
4. Marie, b. Oct. 12, 1825, Ithaca, NY
5. Morris, b. Jan. 2, 1828, Ithaca, NY
6. William, b. May 3, 1829, Ithaca, NY; d. Feb. 6, 1865, VA
7. Christana, b. Aug. 3, 1830, Ischua, NY
8. Elizabeth, b. Sept. 6, 1832, Ischua, NY
9. Malvina, b. Jan. 29, 1834, Ischua, NY
10. James, b. Feb. 16, 1835, Ischua, NY
11. Anna, b. Oct. 27, 1836, Ischua, NY
12. John, b. Sept. 7, 1838, Ischua, NY
13. Rachel, b. Feb. 1, 1840, Ischua, NY
14. Jane, b. Jan. 30, 1842, Ischua, NY; d. Nov. 10, 1915

1.5.5 Morris Whitlock married Elizabeth, lived in Humphrey in 1880 and then in Almer, Tuscola County, MI

Children

1. Jessie, b. Dec. 24, 1863; d. Aug. 31, 1882
2. Nellie, b. Oct. 1865
3. Giles, b. Apr. 1868
4. Dora, b. c. 1876

1.5.8 Elizabeth Whitlock, d. July 15, 1890, married Alpheus Marshall Trowbridge, Sept. 9, 1850; Elizabeth buried in Fitch Cemetery in Ischua, NY, with her husband, siblings, and children

Children

1. Francinella Jane, b. Mar. 12, 1853
2. Alice Evangeline, b. July 15, 1854; d. Apr. 13, 1923
3. Edwin James, b. July 5, 1855; d. 1925
4. Charles Frederick, b. May 27, 1859; d. Feb. 13, 1885
5. Albert Alpheus, b. Dec. 9, 1861; d. 1939
6. Dora, b. 1872; d. 1955
7. Ora, b. 1873

1.8. Rebecca Whitlock married Nicholas Linderman (b. Nov. 22, 1803, NY; d. 1887, Humphrey, NY), Jan. 6, 1831, Ithaca, NY

Children

1. John, b. Oct. 4, 1831, NY
2. Ezekiel, b. ?
3. Orson, b. Mar. 23, 1836, NY
4. Alonzo, b. 1838, NY
5. Mary, b. 1840
6. Lester, b. 1842, NY
7. Emeline, b. Aug 25, 1844
8. Adeline, b. Aug 25, 1844
9. Edgar, b. March 17, 1847, NY; d. Sept. 11, 1850, NY

1.9. Benajah Whitlock married Catherine Apgar (b. Dec. 13, 1812, NY; d. Feb. 23, 1882, Humphrey, NY) before 1830, NY

Children

1. William, b. 1829
2. Mary, b. Sept. 6, 1833, NY; d. Feb. 11, 1906, Jamestown, NY
3. Theodore, Jan. 24, 1835, Ithaca, NY; d. Feb. 6, 1865, VA
4. Ann, b. Dec. 25, 1836, NY; d. Nov. 19, 1912, NY
5. Spencer, b. Mar. 31, 1841, NY; d. Feb. 14, 1865, NY
6. Phoebe, b. Apr. 10, 1843, NY
7. Helen, b. Aug. 16, 1848, NY
8. John, b. Apr. 26, 1850, NY; d. June 12, 1924, NY

1.5.6. William Whitlock married Mary Eliza Trowbridge (b. Oct. 30, 1831, Hinsdale, NY; d. 1889, Allegany, NY), Sept. 9, 1850, Ischua, NY

Children

1. Francis Euzetta, b. July 18, 1851, married Ernest Hollister
2. Stanley Meade, b. Dec. 13, 1853; d. 1935
3. Clara Hulda, b. Aug. 10, 1856, married Lester Linderman
4. Henry C., b. July 6, 1860

1.5.6.2 Stanley M. Whitlock married Medora Linderman (b. 1859, d. 1943) in 1877

Children

1. Ray, b. 1882, d. 1943

2. Clare E., b. 1890, d. 1970, married Grace O. Whitney (b. 1891, d. 1970)
3. Bessie, b. 1893, d. 1970

1.5.6.2.1 Ray Whitlock married Ellen Linderman (b. 1884, d. 1962)

Children
1. Paul, b. 1909, d. 1945
2. Lenna
3. Mable, married Carl Hoeldtke
4. Stanley

1.5.6.2.1.1 Paul Whitlock married Helen Magnin (d. 1945)

Children
1. Paul Jr., b. 1932
2. Kenneth, b. 1936
3. Robert, b. 1940, d. 1945
4. Richard, b. 1942, d. 1945
5. Stanley, b. 1943, d. 1945

1.5.6.2.2 Clare E. Whitlock married Grace O. Whitney (b. 1890, d. 1970)

Children
1. Viola F., b. 1914, d. 2005
2. Alma M., b. 1917, d. 2008
3. Medora F., b. 1922, d. 1961

1.5.6.2.2.1 Viola F. Whitlock married Verne L. Dunham (b. 1909, d. 1972)

Children
1. Vaughn, b. 1937, married Frank Estep (b. 1935, d. 2005)
2. Valgene, b. 1940, married Elizabeth Mills (b. 1940)
3. Virgil, b. 1944, married Sheila Hitchcock (b. 1940)
4. Verlee, b. 1944, married Andrea Gagino (b. 1953)

1.5.6.2.2.2 Alma M. Whitlock married Kenneth B. Chesebro (b. 1915, d. 1961)

Children
1. Esther, b. 1936, d. 2008
2. Harlan, b. 1939, d. 1992

3. Donavan, b. 1946, d. 1993
4. Stephen, b. 1949

1.5.6.2.2.3 Medora F. Whitlock married Wesley Potter (b. 1923, d. 2010)

Children

1. David, b. 1949
2. Vernon, b. 1951, d. 1954
3. Grace, b. 1953
4. Faith, b. 1954

1.5.6.2.3. Bessie Whitlock married Howard B. Whitney (b. 1895, d. 1959)

Children

1. Walter, b. 1923, d. 2003

1.5.6.2.3.1 Walter Whitney married Rita Button (b. 1928)

Children

1. Howard M., b. 1947
2. John, b. 1948
3. Lynne, b. 1955

Order of Battle
Battle of Hatcher's Run II (February 6, 1865)

UNION ARMY

2nd Corps, Major General Andrew A. Humphreys
    2nd Division, Brigadier General Thomas A. Smyth
        1st Brigade, Colonel William A. Olmstead
            19th Maine
            19th, 20th Massachusetts
            7th Michigan
            1st Minnesota (two companies)
            59th, 152nd New York
            184th Pennsylvania
            36th Wisconsin
        2nd Brigade, Colonel Mathew Murphy (mortally wounded Feb. 5,
            1865, Colonel James P. McIvor)
            8th New York Heavy Artillery
            155th, 164th, 170th, 182nd New York
        3rd Brigade, Lieutenant Colonel Francis E. Pierce
            14th Connecticut
            1st Delaware
            12th New Jersey
            10th New York (battalion)
            108th New York
            4th Ohio (four companies)
            69th Pennsylvania
            106th Pennsylvania (three companies)
            7th West Virginia (four companies)

3rd Division, Brevet Brigadier General Gershom Mott
   1st Brigade, Brigadier General Regis De Trobriand
      20th Indiana
      1st Maine Heavy Artillery
      17th Maine
      40th, 73rd, 86th, 124th New York
      99th, 110th Pennsylvania
      2nd US Sharpshooters
   2nd Brigade, Brevet Brigadier General George W. West
      1st Massachusetts Heavy Artillery
      5th Michigan
      93rd New York
      57th, 105th, 141st Pennsylvania
   3rd Brigade, Brevet Brigadier General Robert McAllister
      11th Massachusetts
      7th, 8th, 11th New Jersey
      120th New York
   Artillery: Brevet Lieutenant Colonel John G. Hazard
      10th Massachusetts Light Artillery
      4th United States, Battery K

5th Corps, Major General Gouverneur K. Warren
   1st Division, Brevet Major General Charles Griffin
      1st Brigade, Brevet Brigadier General Horatio G. Sickel (wounded
         Feb. 6, 1865)
         185th New York
         198th Pennsylvania
      2nd Brigade, Colonel Allen L. Burr
         187th, 188th (battalion), 189th New York
      3rd Brigade, Brevet Brigadier General Alfred L. Pearson
         20th Maine
         32nd Massachusetts
         1st, 16th Michigan
         83rd (six companies), 91st, 118th, 155th Pennsylvania
   2nd Division, Brevett Major General Romeyn B. Ayres
      1st Brigade, Brevet Brigadier General Frederick Winthrop
         5th, 140th, 146th New York

15th New York Heavy Artillery
2nd Brigade, Colonel Richard N. Bowerman
 1st, 4th, 7th, 8th Maryland
3rd Brigade, Brevet Brigadier General James Gwyn
 3rd, 4th Delaware
 157th (four companies), 190th, 191st, 210th Pennsylvania
3rd Division, Brevet Major General Samuel W. Crawford
 1st Brigade, Brigadier General Edward Bragg
  24th Michigan
  143rd, 149th, 150th Pennsylvania
  6th, 7th Wisconsin
 2nd Brigade, Brigadier General Henry Baxter
  16th Maine
  39th Massachusetts
  97th New York
  11th, 88th Pennsylvania
 3rd Brigade, Brevet Brigadier General Henry A. Morrow
  94th, 95th, 147th New York
  56th, 107th, 121st, 142nd Pennsylvania
 Artillery, Major Robert H. Fitzhugh
  1st New York Light Batteries D, L
  9th Massachusetts Light Artillery

6th Corps
 1st Division, Brevet Major General Frank Wheaton
  1st Brigade, Lieutenant Colonel Edward L. Campbell
  2nd Brigade, Colonel James Hubbard
  3rd Brigade, Brevet Brigadier General Joseph E. Hamblin

9th Corps
 3rd Division, Brigadier General John F. Hartranft
  1st Brigade, Colonel Charles W. Diven
  2nd Brigade, Colonel Joseph A. Mathews
 Cavalry, Brevet Major General David McM. Gregg
  1st Brigade, Henry E. Davies Jr. (wounded Feb. 6, 1865)
  2nd Brigade, Brevet Brigadier General J. Irvin Gregg (wounded Feb. 6, 1865)
  3rd Brigade, Colonel Oliver B. Knowles

CONFEDERATE ARMY

2nd Corps, Major General John B. Gordon
   Ramseur's Brigade, Brigadier General John Pegram (killed Feb. 6, 1865),
      replaced by Brigadier General Robert D. Johnston
   Pegram's Brigade, Colonel John S. Hoffman (wounded Feb. 5, 1865),
      replaced by Lieutenant Colonel John G. Kasey
   Lewis's Brigade, Brigadier General William G. Lewis
   Johnston's Brigade, Colonel John W. Lea, replaced by Brigadier General
      Robert D. Johnston
   Gordon's Brigade, Brigadier General Clement A. Evans
   Evans' Brigade, Colonel John H. Lowe
   Terry's Brigade, Brigadier General William Terry
   York's Brigade, Colonel William R. Peck
   Heth's Division, Major General Henry Heth, replaced by Brigadier
      General Joseph R. Davis
      Davis's Brigade, Colonel Andrew Mc. Nelson (captured), replaced
         by Colonel Reuben O. Reynolds
      Cooke's Brigade, Brigadier General John R. Cooke
      MacRae's Brigade, Brigadier General William MacRae
      McComb's Brigade, Brigadier General William McComb
   Mahone's Division, Brigadier General Joseph Finegan
      Weisiger's Brigade, Brigadier General David A. Weisiger
      Harris's Brigade, Brigadier General Nathaniel H. Harris
      Sorrel's Brigade, Brigadier General Moxley Sorrel (wounded)
      Finegan's Brigade, Colonel David Lang
      Forney's Brigade, Colonel William H. Forney
   Wilcox's Division, Major General Cadmus M. Wilcox
      McGowan's Brigade, Major General Samuel McGowan
         1st South Carolina Provisional Army
         1st South Carolina Rifles
         12th, 13th, 14th South Carolina
      Scales's Brigade, Colonel Joseph H. Hyman
   Cavalry
   W. H. F. Lee's Division, Major General William H. F. "Rooney" Lee
      Barringer's Brigade, Brigadier General Rufus Barringer
      Beale's Brigade, Brigadier General Richard L. T. Beale

Dearing's Brigade, Brigadier General James Dearing
Artillery
    Chew's Artillery Battalion
        Virginia (MacGregor's) Battery
    Pegram's Artillery Battalion
        Virginia (Ellett's) Battery

Source: Compiled and modified from Calkins 2003.

Additional Whitlock Letters

Letters 1–11, 16, 24, 26, 39,and 40 are found at the beginning of chapters 3–8, 10, and 11. Portions of letters 17, 20, 33, and 35 are found at the beginning of chapter 9. Letters 12, 14, 15, 18, 25, 28, and 31 are not directly referred to in the text. Other letters frequently referred to in the text (13, 19, 21, 22, 22A, 23, 27, 29, 30, 32, 34, 36, 37, and 38) are included here.

LETTER 13

Camp Near the yellow house, Nov. 4th . . . 64

Well Lide
    I received a letter from you today and hasten to ansur it. I have not had one befour in three or four days. we have ben moving agane and it keeps us in an uprore all the time. I think we have written two letters this week befour this.
    I am getting some better of my cold. the boys are fixing our tent to day. they wont let me do much onley sit in the shanty and watch things. I have a good lot of boys to tent with. thear names are Moyer, Jones, Buzzard, Newil, and C. Colvin—bully fellows all of them. Lide I think if they would let us lay stil about a week I would be all right. they all seem to think we wont move very soon but we cant tell. they dont move us but a little at a time but it makes so much work. our tents has to be put up just so every time if we don't stay in them two days. it has rained some for two days and if it should come on much rain we may stay hear all winter. I hope it will for I hate this moving after we get all fixt up comfortable.
    I was glad to hear that you have got yourself and the children cloathed so you can go to church and other doings down to town. was glad to hear you attended those political meetings. I hope you will attend every place

you can enjoy yourself and have time fly as fast as possible. I cant say time flyes slow with me but rather fast for which I am very thankful.

I tel you Lide some time when I have more time and my hand dont tremble so bad I will give you a little better detale of our battel we had the other day. But I cant today for I must help the boys some. we could not call it a regular battel whare we was; it was just a strong skirmish line sent out. it was a thick woods whare we was. the Johnies breastwork was just in the edge of the field. we drove them out of the woods back in thear breastwork and it seems that was all our officers wanted.

Nov.5th . . . Well Lide I will try and finish this letter this morning. I have no news to write but will try and fil up with sompthing. we are getting our tent fixed up quite comfortable agan but dont know how long we can occupy it. we hope we shant have to leav rite away but we cant tel.

Lide I wish you would write the prices in Olean. are they eny loer than they was when I left home? write all the news. it seems as though you might have lots of news to tel me but here it is every day alike and it has got to be an old thing with me and I dont think it very interesting. if I live to come home I will tel you lots.

I must close now for this time. my love to you and all the children and neighbors. write often

From
Will to Lide

LETTER 19

Old Camp, Novmb. 23 . . . 64

Dear Wife

I have rec'd a letter every night for three nights and I hope they will keep coming just so all the time. I am well and hope you are all the same. Well Lide I am going to try and ansur some of your questions. allthe maggoty bread we have had was one box of hard tack that was when we was down to City Point. the rest of our provision has all ben good. if our officers had mine thear own bisness as well as they do now they would have sent them back. Sam Roe did have his money taken befourwe had ben in Washingto-none hour. we donated eleven and a half for him that night. I lent him two dollars and a half in Elmira he has not pade me yet. he said he would pay day. he was dtaled the next day, after we come to this camp, for teamster and I have not seen him since he is to City Point. I did not make a pocket in my shirt. I bought me a belt that I put my money in and wear it next to me. I have lent what money I havnt used to the boys. I lent H.Newil ten dollars. he sayed if we did not get our pay he would send home for some. I have about six dollars yet so I can get along myself if we don't get our pay. (unless you want some). if you do just say so and Newell will get that ten dollars any time. it seems I didnt buy much but it takes money fast. we buy tea sometimes and a little cheas and butter and appels and my tobacco is by and it all takes the change off. in the corse of a month it amounts to quite a sum. if you want some money just let me know when you write.

I think it will be so I can get my likeness in a few days. they say there is a man takes them about a mile from hear. they talk about having Coulars taken if we get our pay. I think I will get one of them and send it to you. it will cost twelve shillings. If you want one of them I will try and get it. I will get you mine the first chance I get. to leave camp.

Lide you wanted to know who I write to so much. I have written two to Hank, two to Jim, two to Marsh, one to George, one to your Mother, and all the rest I have writen has ben to you.

we are about one and a half miles beyond the Weldon Railroad towards the Dansvile Road. we are about six miles west of Petersburg. we left the James River when . . . [rest of letter missing].

LETTER 21

Old Camp, Sunday, Nov. 27th . . . 64

Dear Wife

I rec'd a letter from you yesterday while on gard and now hasten to ansur it. I am well and hope this will find you all the same. I was sorry to hear you was trubled with Newralgia. I do hope you are better now.

that telegraph Dispatch was a mistake for Grant has had no battel that eny of us knows off and I hope he wont have this fall. I do wish this thing would be fixed up this winter for I would like to come home but I think that that is hard teling when it will be closed but we will have to trust too providence and hope for the best.

Lide you say that you feal glad to get a letter from me. I think I know how you feel for I know ther is no one more rejoiced to hear from friends than I am to hear from my dear family and I hope you will continue to write as often as you have lately. I cant complain of you for I think I get all of your letters now. I got yours of the 14, 16 and 18th and I guess all the rest you send me.

Lide I have now news to tel so I hardly know what to fill up with but say something if it isnt so funy.

Oh Lide I liked to forgot to tel you that our thanksgiving got along hear yesterday and it was a big thing I tel you and I had one appel and a half and littel peace of a turkeys boan. there was about two lbs. of cheas for our compiny of about 75 men. we had one littel cucky in our tent for six men. I tel you Lide I dont believe much in sending provisions that is donated to the soldiers for it all goes through the hands of the officers and but very little of it gets to the privit. the officers and thear niggar waters has plenty. there was one negro in our compiny told me that he had a whole duck and ten or twelve appels; as much as he could eat at two meals. I think if the soldiers has eny thing sent them it had better be boxed up by ther friends and sent to them. each one send ther own friends a box and then they got what is sent to them.

Now Lide I hope this will find you better than you was when you rote your last. you must take cair of yourself or I am afraid you will soon get clear down sick and then I dont know what you would do.

Lide write often and so will I. give my respecs to all. No more from your loving husband.

Will

LETTER 22

November 29 . . . 64

Dear wife and children

I rec'd two letters from you last night and was glad to hear from you but am sorry you are having such a time with your teath. I am well and hope by the time this reaches you will be better.

we are having very plesant wether here agane but I hope it will rain befour we have orders to march agane but we are expecting it every day but it is warm and looks like rane every day.

Lide those letters I got all at once was not maled in one day. I got two last night. one was maled the 23rd the other the 25 so you se they lay over on the way some whare.

Lide just as soon as the slaying will ansur you must call on George for that wood. I think Stanley has done prety well and if I live to come home I will get him something that will pay him for being a good boy. tel Hankey he must be a good boy to and bring in the wood and then I will remember him to.

Lide you asked me in one of your letters who don my washing? now you ask if I get wimon to do it? I have not seen over a half dosin wimon since we left Washington. there is once in a while one pases through but they are ladyes ascorted by officers ridingthrough to se the armey. I tel you Lide there is a perfect rush of soldiers moving today. there has ben probely eight or ten thousand passed our camp this four noon. they are going both ways. the Ninth Corps lay on our left and the second Corps lay on our right and they are changing places and they all pass through our camp so looks like quite and army. I can look out of our tent as I am writing and as far as I can se boath ways it is one soled body of men. I am afrade that if the wether keeps good we shal have to move but I do hope we shant.

Lide I think Docter Eddy has got in more than he can have the face to charge for doctoring you last winter.

Well Lide I have just ben eating a harty dinner and will try now and finish my letter. I write so much that I hardly know what to write for I dont get much news but I must fill the sheet with something if it aint very interesting to you.

Ned got a letter from his wife and Mrs. Lowe the other night and when he ansured it he had one page that was not fild so I wrote a few lines to Mr. Low and I shal expect a letter from her. she wrote that she did not here anything from George yet. I tel you Lide I would not want to be taken prisner but I suppose we all comevery near it when we had fight for the rebs was flanking us when we left the woods.

Well Lide I thought I could not think of enough to fil the other sheet but I did and am going to scratch a littel on this.

they dont call us to dril so I will keep writing until they do.

Oh! Thear I have braged to quick for I hear the order now to fall in for dril.

Well Lide I have got through drilling and will try and write a few lines more. that is the way it goes, we write a few lines at a time liabel to be called at eny moment. but we have to put up with it and there is no use complaining for we are not considered as good as the negro.

well Lide I will close and write a few to the children. write often Lide. No more—good by

From
Will

LETTER 22A

Dear Children

I rec'd your letter last night and was glad to hear from you. I am well and hope you are all the same. your ma wrote that she was trubled with that old complaint in her teath and face. now Euzetta you must be kind to her and have her keep still and be careful and dont let her go out in the cold nor work eny more than is nessary. I want you all to learn those versis I send home so you can sing them for me if I am ever permited to come home.

I want you to write me as often as you can this winter. I must close, tel the yong folks to write to me.

good by from
Pa

LETTER 23

Dec. 5th . . . 64

Dear Lide

I recied two letters from you to night and hasten to ansur. I was vary glad to hear that you are getting better. I hope you will be careful of your helth this winter. I am well and hope this finds you all the same.

I am on gard to night and while my reliefs was off I thought I would ansur your letter.

Lide we are under march orders agane. we have ben for two days but we expect now to move to morrow morning but maybe we wont. we don't know whare or which way we shal go nor we shant until we get there. we may not go at all but I think we will.

Lide I cantget my likeness now for the man that took them belonged to the ninth corps and befour I could get away to have it taken they moved away. they lay in front of peetersburg now but if we move maybe we will go whare I can get it taken. if we do I get it the first posable chance. Lide I guess I look about as I did when I left home. it saems to me as though I had ben gon frome home a long time; about long enough to come home. I have surved only one fourth of my time. the weeks seam to pas off fast but the months fly slow. when you write Charley send him my best respacs. tel Cinda I am going to write to her just as soon as we get over this panic about moving. give my best respecs to all of Mr. Kratts folks and tel them to write to me and all the rest of the old neighbors.

Lide I shal have to close for to night for it is time for me to go on gard agane. if we dont go in the morning I will finish this sheet and if we do so I cant have time. I will write just as soon as we get in camp agane. you must get some money of some of the boys on the hil. I must close. Write.

Yours truly
Will

LETTER 27

Saterday Dec. 17 . . . 64

Well Lide

I will try and write a few more lines becose I have plenty of time if I only had a good place to write I would be glad. but I will do the best I can. it is not hard to stand on picket for it is one hour on and two off for twelve hours and then we go back a peace from the lines and are held in reserve for twelve hours so the last twelve hours we have nothing to do at all.

Lide there is not a copperhead in my tent. It is just what I have seen that makes me think and talk as I do. if I am rong I hope I may se it but I know it is to much of a speculation [?] war to be all right. the jenral impression amongst the soldiars hear is that we will have plenty of fighting to do for four years yet. I hope they are mistaken but it looks to me as though they are right for the rebs seam to fight through this part of the country with corage. I have not yet seen Old Abe speech but I heard he gave them no other terms than he always had—lay down thear arms, free thear slaves and come back and I dont believe they will do that during his administration.

I tel you Lide if you had ben whare I have and se the cornfields you would not think they was starved. yet I saw fields with from thirty to two hundred acors of corn and it was good to but Lide no one wants them to give up eny worse than I do for I tel you I want to come home and enjoy peace and quiet once more. but I shal have to wate and se what time will bring forth. if I had no family I could get along very well but Lide there is no place like home. as long as I am permitted to enjoy as good helth as I do now ans can hear frome you often I am very thankful and shal ever try and be so.

Well I think I have done pretty well considering the place I have to write so I guess you will have to excuse me for this time. write often for I do like to get letters frome you. it is reviving to me. Lide if it is going to cost you to much and you are bothered to get money you ned not send me a box but send me a pear of gloves for they cost so much hear and I nead them very much. I can get along without the other things. if Marsh was near to help you fix it up and se to sending it would be a little different. do as you think best.

now write often and so will I as I can. my respecs to all. tel the children to write to me agane. tel the Little One I will ansur her letter as soon as I can and thank her very much for writing to me. tel her to write agane. no more. good by from your loving husband;

Will

Letter 29

Dec. 26th . . . 64

Dear Lide

I think that I feel as well this morning as you did when you got my letter for I have just recieved two letters from you one dated the 13th the other

Dec. 20th. I am well and hope all of you are the same. I was glad to hear from you and to hear that you were well. it had been the longest since I had a letter than it has ben in a long time. last night when I came to camp from the picket lines the boys told me I had a letter I flew and got it but as soon as I saw it I told them it was not from the one I wanted to hear from. I opened it and it was from Mrs. Low. I was disapointed for I had been expecting one from you for two or three days. I red a littel of it just enough to know she had not herd from George and then I told the boys I had red enough and was redy for supper but dont tel her I did not think enough of her letter to read it. the same night she said she was going up to see you in a few days. dont let her se this letter.

Lide the news came last night that Sherman had taken 500 bales of cotton and 150 pecies of theheaviest canon and small arms without number but said nothing about prisners. I hope that there will be enough don this winter to stop the war by spring for I would like to come home just as well as you would like to have me. if I dair to I would get homesick but that wont do for there have been some in our compiny got that disese. they was sicker than I want to be. I suppose it is the worst sickness a man can have.

Lide I would liked to have been thare when you got that letter; to have seen the children felt happy too but I cant come yet but I hope the Lord will spair my life so I can se my family once more. we shall have to wate his time and see I dont dair what the hard ships are. I can stand that if my life is spaired to go home to my family and enjoy a quiet life once more.

Lide how did you enjoy yourself yesterday Christmas? did you have a mary one. I took mine out on the picket line. I had to go out Saturday and stay twenty four hours. it was not very mary I tel you. I think I thought of home some but it done no good; I was not there. I would very much like to have a box of something that come from home if it dont bother you to much but if you are plaged for money you need not bother about it. the most I cair is to have something from home. I guess you will think I am getting a littel old maidish. The gloves I need very much. I wish if you send eny thing it could get through by New years but never mind it will be very exciting eny time.

Lide is the going so bad that Marsh dont come down to se you oftener or dont they want to come and se you. I have never had a letter from him since I left.home. I have written him two and would write mor if he would write to me but it seems to me as if he wanted to hear from me he would ansur some of my letters. I have not recieved a letter from your Mother yet. Perhaps I ought to write to her agane and I will as soon as I can. I would very much like to get a letter from her.

Well Lide I think they are having strange time on the five mile. I think if I was in George Wilburs place I would shoot him and kick her face. I think if she had been very much opposed to it she would have exhorted hime on the start but I hope it will never be our lot to have such trubleso let er rip. I wish Hank could get rid of old Jack. if he cant sel him I wish he would trade him for something for itwill cost more to winter him than he will sel for in the spring. if he could se Frank Townson I think he could trade with him for something. get a bugy or eny thing that dont eat.

I am sorry I cant get muy likeness for you now. Jesst as soon as I can find out whare there is an artist you shal have it.

I dont hed my letters at eny place for I dont know whare we are. We lay south east of Peetersburg near what they call the Jerusalem Plank road. I think we are stationed here to do picket duty this winter and I hope they will let us stay here all winter and I guess they will for we are puting up winter quarters and they are very petickluar. they have to all be bilt just so and all alike. standing on picket is not hard only it is rather uncomfortable in stormay wether but we have plenty of cloths, rubber blankets and woolen blankets so we can stank it very well.

You write that you want to take a paper. I dont know what you had better take. you must be your own jug and take the one that will suet you the best.

I hope we will get our pay next month so I can send you some money for I know you must be short and I know I am but if I can get my pay nex month we will be alright agane.

Well Lide I think it is a bout time for me to close for I think I have done pretty well for me. Now write often. give my respecs

this from your ever loving husband
Will

Letter 30

Jan. 1 . . . 65

Well Lide and Children

I will commence my letter this morning by wishing you all a happy new year. I was in hopes I should get a letter from you last night but was disappointed but maybe it will come to night. the last one I got was dated the 22nd. I hope this will find you all enjoying as good helth as I do myself.

Jones and Moyer are out on picket and Hughs and myself are all a lone today. cinder lonesome so I thought I could write a few lines to you to pass away time. I tel you Lide I would like to be at home with you today if it was a fesable thing but it is not so I must be contented to stay whare I am. it seames the most like winter this morning than it has since last winter. it rained and snowed together yesterday but this morning it had cleared off but the grond is white with snow. it is plesent to day but the wind blowes very cold but we have a good shanty and a bully good fire and nothing to do today. George and I are trying to enjoy our selves by writing home and I hope you are writing to me today.

Lide I declair I dont know what you will do with that old horse. I am sorry Hank did not sel or give him away. if he had took him when he was in good flesh as he was when I left him and went down to Frank Townsons he mite have traded him off for something to a pretty good advantage but perhaps that would be to much trouble. if you cant get rid of him may be you had better get some one to kill him.

Lide I do hope by another New Years day that this war will be over and peace and quiet rain once more through our land so that solders can spend there holedays at home. we will have to trust to providence for that. do you know Lide that my year is almost one third gone. time flyes midling fast with one considering but 8 months looks like a good while to stay yet but it will pass off after a while I suppose. some think we will not have to stay our year. others think the war will last four years yet. I dont pertend to know anything about it all. I want it for my slef and famaley to have our helth and live until I can come home. I think we will know how to enjoy each others compiny if that time ever comes dont you Lide? Well Lide George and I have just been to dinner. we had some coffee and boiled beef and hard tack. It relished bully for my appitite is first rate. George is not very well nor has not been since he has been in the armey.

I dont think he can stand soldiering. Lide write often for you dont know how I wanted a letter last night so I could have one to ansur but I thought I would write one eny way. I dont want to complane for you do first rate. Lide this ink is so miserbel I don't know as you can read what I have wrote. I must close. I want the children to write agane. tel all the neighbors I wish them a happy new year.

no more this time so good by all

LETTER 32

Jan. 10th . . . 65

My Dear Wife

I have just rece'd a letter from you. it is the one you sent the day you sent the box dated the 28th. it has been detaned some whare for I have had two dated since this one was. I am well and hope you are all the same. I am glad the children enjoyed them selves so well Christmas. those boys you spoke of was to Elmira when I was there. I saw them train every day. while I was there they was pretty well driled.

Lide I hope that box will come through for it cost you to much to have it lost. I did not think it would cost so much to send one. it must have been a large one. Lont has had one on the road three weeks and it has not got here yet. I hope mine wont be so long.

Lide the wether is real warm. It rained very hard amost all night and all the morning. so far I expect I shal have to go on picket agane to night. oh you don't know how mudy it is. this sandy grond gets soft very quick. Lide I am glad you done as well as you have with old Jack for if he lives through til spring he will get up so you can get something for him and that will be better than to kill him. how do you get along for wood? has George brught you any yet? I hope he has so you can keep warm for I know that it is a cold place on that hil in the winter. nothing to brake the wind. I suppose it loks about as usual around there. I wish I was at home. I think if I live to get home I will know how to enjoy it dont you?

tel Mr. Kratts if he thinks you think to much of me that every one knot feal towards thear comanions as he does towards his. I hope we have got more affection for each other than he has for his famley. Lide I hope I shal get my pay this month so I can send you some money for I se you had to sel potatoes to get money to send that box. I could sel my watch but would have to wate til pay day. So you se that would not help us eny now. I can get 30 dollrs for it cost me 25 dollars but I cinder hate to let it go for it is more compiny to me than all the men in the armey but if I could get the money for it I would let it go. I traded when I was in washington the one I got of Jones and gave 10 dollars to boot. it is a hunter case watch and good one to. it cost the fellow I had it of 35 dollars in Dunkirk. it is a new one but anought of the watch. are they getting the men for this call? is there much excitement about it? I am glad I come when I did for one third of my time is about out now and If God spairs my life I shall come home a thankful man dont you think. now Lide write often for some how if I dont get a letter as often as every other day, I get real lonesome. get along the best you can. take good care of your selves all of you and I trust I shal meet a gane in about eight months. no more this time but remane as ever your loving and affectinate Husband and Father.

From Will to Lide and children

Letter 34

Camp Near the Jeruslem Plank, Jan. 18th . . . 65

My Dear Wife

I reced yours of the 11th and will try this evening to ansur it. I was very glad to hear from you and to hear that you are well. I am will my self and do hope this will find you all the same. I have ben quite bisy to day with our cooking so I have to write this evening. George is not very well so I have to bring the water and tend to things. it is not hard work only I have to stay rite hear in the cook house for the bouys would steal all the rations but I dont have to stay on eny gard nor eny other duty so you se I am well suted. I would a grate deal rather do cooking than other duty.

You say I never have sed eny thing about George Hughs being with us. I thought I had. he did not get to our regment until a few days after Newel left so he came rite in with us and has ben with us ever since. he has not ben will since he has ben in the armey. I don't know what I would do if my helth was not better than his.

Lide don't let things you hear truble you. what do we cair for what folks say. we know whether you drove me off or not and that is enough so let er rip.

You say Mrs. Low is going to write to me about your being jealous of her and me. I would like to know what she has to say to me about it. does she think I will say you was?

You say Dolly lost her calf. dos she give much milk now. it must have hade her poor. You must give her a littel grain this winter.

Lide they saythere is more hopes of peace now than there has ever ben befour. they say Georgey and one other state has come back in the union. I do hope all the news we hear is trew. a dispatch come in yesterday that fort fisher has fel and fort Sumter. ther was one hundred Canon fired hear as a selute and all the regments have three rousing chears on dres perade last night. if half we hear is trew the prospecs is faverable and I do hope it is don't you? they say that Grant says thar wont be an other sampane. if that is so wont it be glories? but I dair not hope to strong. we will trust the Lord to bring peace around in his own good time.

Lide I am afraid we wont get our pay this month forit is time we had it now. some think we wont get paid til March. If we don't you must get what money you want to us of Mar. I will have Newel send home get some for me.

Lide that box has not come yet. was it a very hevy one and was it put together strong? there is a good meny large boxes broke open by handling them rough on the way. a lite one comes safer than a hevy one but may be it will come yet. Joneses was four weeks on the way. some has come that has ben fine.

now Lide take cair of yourself and childran and let us hope we shal come out all right yet. it is getting late and I must close for this time.

I thought you was going to send me Euzettas likeness. George Hugh got his wife and girls likeness the other day. I have yours and would like to have Zets and all the rest if I could.

> Write often, give my love to all
> Good night, yours in love
> Will

LETTER 36

Wednsday Evening. Jan. the 25th . . . 65

Well Lide

I will have to say with you that I feel pretty well for I got two letters from you last night. I was very glad to hear from you. I dreamed last night after reading your letters of going home and shaking hads with and kissing you. I dreamed of shaking hands with a number of people that I knot know am I ever saw befour. I thought I was home on a furlough but I awoke and it was a dream. I am well and good. grant that this will find you all the same.

Lide you need not worry about danger on the picket line for the rebs has no pickets in front of our lines but I dont have to stand gard now nor shant as long as I cook. if I dont write very often dont worry for all the time I can get is evenings but will try and write as often as twice a week and oftener if I can get time.

night befour last we heard hevy canonading all night in the direction of the James river and a part of last night. to day we herd that the rebs come down Dutch Gap with three boats and our fleet took one and sunk one and the other got away. they tried it agane last night but we did not hear the result. there has been no firing today.

Lide it dont seam hardly possable that the snow is two and a half feet deep up there. I have not seen a half an inch of snow this winter. we have some cold winds and rain and it is freezing some tonight but nothing like winter. I wish I was at home doing chores or teaming. I think I could enjoy myself better than I do hear but there is no use of complaining—time will tel whither I ever be permitted to come home or not. we must wate and se.

Lide is the oats all thrashed? if they are how meny did we have? cant Stanley help Zety milk so you wont have to go out in the cold and snow yourself? I am glad you have plenty of milk this winter. I wish I was there to help you use it but never mind.

Lide I despair of getting that box. it has ben four weeks to day since you started it. there was four loads come to our brigade to day but none for me. they say there is about one hundred and fifty more to corpse hedquarters for this brigade. if it is not with them I shal give it up. I am sorry for you was to so much on my account but never mind; if it comes I will let you know right off.

Lide it is getting late and I will have to try and finish this tomorrow. the bugal has sounded for lights out so good night.

Jan. 26th Well Lide I have got my beans on cooking and will try and finish my letter. [not complete]

LETTER 37

In Camp Jan. 29th . . . 65

Dear Lide

I am some what disapointed this morning for I expected a letter but the male come and no letter for me but I will write for I have promised you that I would write as often as twice a week. perhaps I shal get one the next male.

I am well and hope you are the same. I dontknow as I have eny news to tel you. we have not had eny papers in camp for a number of days. the journal of opinion hear is that we will not have another campain. I hope and pray we may not for I do want this war stoped so I can come home dont you? I tel you Lide I think it would be the hapeist part of my life to be shiped for home once more.

our Captin come up hear last friday to make us a visit. he looks pretty slim but better than we ever expected he could be. I wish he was abel to stay with us but he is not nor will be abel to take the field agane. he is a going to start for home tomorrow.

the wether has ben quite cold for a few days but no snow. I suppose you are having tip top sleighing up in old Cataraugus now. I wish I was there; wouldnt we have a sleigh ride. I rather think we would.

Lide I think I might as well give up looking for that box for it has ben over a month since you started it. I think it has got destroyed or it would have ben hear befour this time. George Hughs got one last thursday that was started the 13th. since his come I have give mine up as lost. I feel wors about it on your accont than I do on mine for I know you worked hard and the expence it was to you and I know you need the money for your own comfort but it cant be helped. we are not to blame.

Lide has George brot you all of that wood yet? if not hury him up a littel so he will get it all there while it is good sleighing.

Lide I feel quite lonesome to day. it is sunday but it dont seme like sabith hear in the armey. every day is very much a like, there is meting to be shuer but one can hardly tel when sunday comes. I cant leav the cook room long enough to go to church eny how but I am in hopes this kind of life wont last always. we will put up with it while we are obliged to with out complaining.

how do you get along this cold wether with your choers. Can the children learn very fast? this winter have them go to school as stidy as they can.

I am very sorry we dont get our pay so I could send you some money. you must try and get along some way. we will have the more when we do get it.

Now Lide take good care of your self and keep good corage. what do they think up there about peace? do they think it will last a year longer or not?

I must close. write soon. I am in hopes I shal get a letter the next male then I will write agane.

good bye yours truly
Will

LETTER 38

In Camp Feb. 2nd . . . 65

My Dear family

I read yours of the 23rd and was glad to hear from you and to hear that you are well. I am well as usual and hope this will find you stil in good health. there has ben a good deal of excitement in camp for two days consurning a move. just as I was reding your letter yesterday the drums beat a sick call and all the men that thought they was not abel to march was ordered to the Doctors for examintion. he has sent four out of our compiny to the hospital. George Hughs was one of them. they sent all that the doctor thought was not abel to march. we all had orders to have our guns in good order but to day it is more quiet. the rumer is to day that they thought the rebs wer leaving Richmond and peetersburg and our armey was a going to follow them up. but to day every thing is quiet. there is so many camp rumors agoing around that it is a hard matter to find out the truth of eny thing. we cant believe eny thing we hear. we may have to move yet but the most of them think we wont. I hope we shant but if we do then it is no use of finding falt. we must obay our orders without a murmur.

Well Lide you say that wind is blowing and it looks wintery. it is not so hear it is warm and plesant, the birds are singing like spring.

it seams odd to me to hear the birds sing in the midel of winter. but I have not sean eny winter yet and probly we shant se much Cattaraugus winter.

You ask if we got much corn when we was on that rade. we got eight loads mostly corn a few bags of potatoes.

I should think that Capt. Rice that man that was killed was about my age. he was a smart man and a good officer. I dont know how much of a famely he had but they said that when he fel from his horse he told some of the boys that was near him to tel his Wife and Children that he was shot through the body and was dying but when we got to the body he had ben shot through the head and through the brest so they must have got to him befour he died and shot him twice more. I think if I had had the command of the train I would have tried and get him at the time he first fel for it is posable he might have got well. the doctor sad that the shot that went through his body would not have kild him.

Lide it must be that I dont get all of your letters for I know I have not had twelve letters within three weeks. you say in this one that you wrote one the night befour that one. I have not got [it] yet. I dont believe that mine goes through as regular as they did for I guess I write about as often as I ever did. I average as often as twice a week and some times oftener but never mind we will keep writing whether they get through or not. they don't all get lost for which I am very thankful for if I did not get eny I dont know what I should do. but thank God I get a goodley shair of letters and I write a good meny but I always have a better part to write when I have a letter to ansur dont you? but I must close for my sheat is about fild but never mind. I guess I have time to write a pert of another sheet so I will write nonsense.

You sed Hankey was not very well when you wrote. what is the matter of him and is he eny better yet? I dont like to hear of eny of you being sick for what would you do if eny of you should be clear down sick and no one to help you or do eny thing for you.

What is the reson you think of leving thare next spring? do you think you would enjoy your self eny better on the hil? whare do you think you can get a house? may be it would be as well for you. if you dont want [to] stay whare you are I want you to live whare you can take the most comfort but if you do move get as near a school as you can so we can give the children all the chance we can while they are young for perhaps when they get a littel larger they will have to work and cant go to school.

Well Lide it is getting abut time for me to get on my coffy so I must close. I have to do the cooking a lone now. George has gone but if we don't move there will be some one detaled to help me.

now Lide keep up good corage and dont despair for peace rumers are very chearing through the camp. if we only new them to be a fact.

write often and so will I as often as I can. you may depend on that.

I will write to the children befour long. give my love to all but resurve the largest shair for your self. I must get on my coffe do good by all. wtite al the news what they say about peace.

yours truly
Will

References

For online references, if the original date of publication was not available, the access date is given instead.

"$100 for a Barrel of Flour." 2010. In *Inflation in the South*. Available at http:// civilwar.bluegrass.net/HomeFront/inflationinthesouth.html.

"The 16th Mississippi Infantry (Army of Northern Virginia, 1861–1865)." 2010. Available at http://www.norfield-publishing.com/16ms/16thhome .html.

Alcott, Louisa May. 1860. "With a Rose, That Bloomed on the Day of John Brown's Martyrdom." *The Liberator* 30 (Jan. 20): 3. Available at https:// trans-video.net~rwillisa/jbpoems.htm.

Aldridge, Katherine, ed. 2012. *No Freedom Shrieker: The Civil War Letters of Union Soldier Charles Biddlecom, 147th Regiment New York State Volunteer Infantry*. Ithaca, NY: Paramount Market.

"Alexander Stephens." 2010. In *Georgia's Blue and Gray Trail Presents America's Civil War*. Available at http://blueandgraytrail.com/event/Alexander _Stephens.

Anderson, John. 2010. *New York Volunteers 188th Regiment*. Available at http:// home.swbell.net/jcanders/index.html.

Annual Report of the Adjutant-General of the State of New York. 147th Infantry. 1904. Albany, NY: Brandow. Available at http://dmna.state.ny/us/reghist /civil/rosters/infantry/147th_infantry.CW_roster.pdf.

Baggett, James. 2003. *The Scalawags: Southern Dissenters in the Civil War and Reconstruction*. Baton Rouge: Louisiana State Univ. Press.

Baker, Ida. 2010. "At Christmas People Did Not Have Luxuries." Interview at Spartanberg, SC, Jan. 12, 1938, for the Federal Writers' Project, *American Life Histories, 1936–1940*. Washington, DC: Library of Congress. Available at http://memory.loc.gov/learn///features/timeline/civilwar /southwar/hawkes.html.

Barringer, Sheridan. 2010. *Brig. Gen. Rufus Barringer: Rantings of a Civil War Historian.* Edited by Eric Wittenberg. Available at http://civilwarcavalry.com/?cat+3.

Bartlett, Irving. 1993. *John C. Calhoun, a Biography.* New York: W. W. Norton.

Bernstein, Iver. 1990. *The New York City Draft Riots: Their Significance for American Society and Politics in the Age of the Civil War.* New York: Oxford Univ. Press.

Billings, John. 1888. *Hardtack and Coffee, or the Unwritten Story of Army Life.* Boston: George M. Smith.

Boyd, Joseph. 2012. *Shohola Train Wreck: Civil War Disaster.* At http://www.angelfire.com/ny5/elmiraprison/boydarticle.htm.

Brinsfield, John W. 2003. "The Chaplains of the Confederacy." In *Faith in the Fight: Civil War Chaplains,* by John W. Brinsfield, William Davis, Benedict Maryniak, and James Robertson Jr., 51–96. Mechanicsburg, PA: Stackpole Books.

Brooks, Ulysses. 1994. *Butler and His Cavalry in the War of Secession, 1861–1865.* Germantown, TN: Guild History.

Browder, George. 1987. *The Heavens Are Weeping: The Diaries of George Richard Browder, 1852–1886.* Edited by Richard Troutman. Grand Rapids, MI: Zondervan.

"Burgess Mill." 2010. In *The Civil War Siege of Petersburg.* Available at http://www.craterroad.com/burgessmill.html.

Caldwell, J. F. J. 1866. *The History of a Brigade of South Carolinians, Known First as "Gregg's" and Subsequently as "McGownan's Brigade."* Philadelphia: King and Baird Printers.

Calkins, Chris. 2003. *History and Tour Guide of Five Forks, Hatcher's Run, and Namozine Church.* Sailor's Creek Research Library. Columbus, OH: Blue & Gray Magazine.

———. 2005a. "The Apple Jack Raid." Tour Guide, Sailor's Creek Research Library. *Blue & Gray Magazine* 22, no. 3: 58–65.

———. 2005b. "The Apple Jack Raid, December 7–12, 1864." Sailor's Creek Research Library. *Blue & Gray Magazine* 22, no. 3: 18–25.

———. 2010. "Cutting the Supply Lines: The Battles of Weldon Railroad and Reams Station." In Civil War Preservation Trust, *Saving America's Civil War Battlefields.* Available at http://www.civilwar.org/battlefields/reamsstation/reams-station-history-articles/weldonreamscalkins.html.

————. 2011. *The Appomattox Campaign: March 29–April 9, 1865.* Lynchburg, VA: Schroeder.

Cartwright, Steve. 2002. "Martin M-130." In *The Romance of the Pan-American Clippers.* Available at http://www.avisim.com/pages/0502/clipper_history _feature/flyingboats.html.

Casey, Silas. 1862. *Schools of the Soldier and Company: Instruction for Skirmishers and Music.* Vol. 1 of *Infantry Tactics for the Instruction, Exercise, and Manoeuvres of the Soldier, a Company, Line of Skirmishers, Battalion, Brigade, or Corps d'Armee.* New York: D. Van Nostrand.

Census Office. 1810. *United States Census of 1810.* Washington, DC: US Government Printing Office.

————. 1830. *United States Census of 1830.* Washington, DC: US Government Printing Office.

————. 1835. *United States Census of 1835.* Washington, DC: US Government Printing Office.

————. 1840. *United States Census of 1840.* Washington, DC: US Government Printing Office.

————. 1850. *United States Census of 1850.* Washington, DC: US Government Printing Office.

————. 1855. *United States Census of 1855.* Washington, DC: US Government Printing Office.

————. 1865. *United States Census of 1865.* Washington, DC: US Government Printing Office.

Chamberlain, Joshua. [1915] 1991. *The Passing of the Armies: An Account of the Final Campaign of the Army of the Potomac.* Reprint. Dayton, OH: Morningside Bookshop.

Chamberlin, Thomas. 1905. *History of the One Hundredth and Fiftieth Regiment, Pennsylvania Volunteers, Second Regiment, Bucktail Brigade.* Philadelphia: F. McManus Jr. . Available at http://books.goggle.com/booksabout /reminiscences_of_a_Confederate_soldier_0.html?

Channing, Steven. 1974. *Crisis of Fear: Secession in South Carolina.* New York: W. W. Norton.

Charles, Henry. 1969. *The Civil War Diary of Henry Fitzgerald Charles, 1862–1865.* Compiled by Edwin Charles and John Charles. Edited by John Neitz. Middleburg, VA: Middleburg Post. Available at http://www .dm.net/~neitz/charles/hfcharles.pdf.

Chisholm, Daniel. 1989. *The Civil War Notebook of Daniel Chisholm: A Chronicle of Daily Life in the Union Army, 1864–1865.* Edited by W. Springer Menge and J. August Shimrak. New York: Orion Books.

Clark, James. [1863] 1977. "The Children of the Battle Field." In *The Civil War Songbook*, selections by Richard Crawford, 73–77. New York: Dover.

Clinton, Catherine. 1999. *Public Women and the Confederacy.* Milwaukee: Marquette Univ. Press.

Coddington, Ronald. 2008. *Faces of the Confederacy: An Album of Southern Soldiers and Their Stories.* Baltimore: Johns Hopkins Univ. Press.

"Commander for the 112th." 1862. *Jamestown Post Journal,* Aug. 14.

"Cost of the American Civil War." 2002. In *Historical Times Encyclopedia of the Civil War,* edited by Patricia Faust. Available at http://civilwarhome .com/warcosts.htm.

Dangerfield, George. 1952. *The Era of Good Feelings.* New York: Harcourt.

Dauchy, George. 1890. "The Battle of Ream's Station." In *Military Essays and Recollections: Papers Read before the Commandery of the State of Illinois, Military Order of the Loyal Legion of the United States.* Chicago: Dial. Available at http://www.beyondthecrater.com/resources/mollus/illinois-mollus/the -battle-of-reams-station.

DeCredico, Mary. 1996. *Mary Boykin Chesnut, a Confederate Woman's Life.* Madison, WI: Madison House.

DeFontaine, Felix. 1864. *Margin-Alia; or Gleanings from an Army Note-Book.* Columbia, SC: Steam Power Press.

DeForest, John. [1946] 1996. *A Volunteer's Adventure: A Union Captain's Record of the Civil War.* Edited by James Croushore. New Haven, CT: Yale Univ. Press. Reprint. Baton Rouge: Louisiana Univ. Press.

Delo, David. 1998. *Peddlers and Post Traders: The Army Sutler on the Frontier.* London: Kingfisher.

Detzer, David. 2001. *Allegiance: Fort Sumter, Charleston, and the Beginning of the Civil War.* New York: Harcourt.

Deutsch, Charles. 2010. "Murder and Mayhem Ride the Rails: Union Soldiers Rampage in Virginia." Available at http://www.historynet.com/murder -and-mayhem-ride-the-rails-union-soldiers-rampage-in-virginia.htm/2.

Dieckmann, Jane M. 2004. "City of Ithaca." In *Place Names of Tompkins County,* edited by Carol Kammen. Ithaca, NY: Office of the Tompkins County Historian. Available at http://www.tompkins-co.org/historian /PlaceNames/PlaceNamesofTC.pdf.

Dilts, James. 1993. *The Great Road: The Building of the Baltimore and Ohio, the Nation's First Railroad, 1823–1853.* Palo Alto, CA: Stanford Univ. Press.

Donald, David, Jean Baker, and Michael Holt. 2001. *The Civil War and Reconstruction.* New York: W. W. Norton. Excerpts in "Desertion in the Civil War." Available at http://www.civilwarhome.com/desertion.htm.

Dotson, Paul, Jr. 1997. "Sisson's Kingdom: Loyalty Divisions in Floyd County, Virginia, 1861–1865." Master's thesis, Virginia Polytechnic Institute and State Univ. Available at http://scholar.lib.vt.edu/theses /available/etd-401912204972139.

Dunkelman, Mark H. 2004. *Brothers One and All: Esprit de Corps in a Civil War Regiment.* Baton Rouge: Louisiana State Univ. Press.

Ellis, Edward R. 1966. *The Epic of New York City.* New York: Kodansha International.

Ellis, Franklin. [1879] 2004. "Town of Ischua." Transcribed by Joanne Donk. In *The History of Cattaraugus County, New York.* USGenWeb Project. Available at http://www.rootsweb.ancestry.com/~nycattar/1879history /ischua.htm.

Ethier, Eric, and Rebecca Pawlowski. 2008. *Insiders' Guide: Civil War Sites in the Eastern Theater.* Guilford, CT: Globe Pequot Press.

Evans, Clement, ed. 1899. *Confederate Military History: A Library of Confederate States History.* Vol. 5. Atlanta: Confederate Publishing.

Field, Ron. 2009. *Petersburg 1864–65: The Longest Siege.* Oxford, UK: Osprey.

"First Hatcher's Run, October 27, 1864." 2010. In *Siege of Petersburg.* Available at http://www.petersburgsiege.org/hatch.1.htm.

Foote, Shelby. 1974. *The Civil War, a Narrative: Five Forks to Appomattox, Victory and Defeat.* New York: Random House.

Foreman, Amanda. 2010. *A World on Fire: Britain's Crucial Role in the American Civil War.* New York: Random House.

"Fort Sumter." 2012. In *Confederate Military History,* vol. 5, chap. 1. Available at http://civilwarhome.com/CMHsumter.htm.

Fox, William. 1889. *Regimental Losses in the American Civil War 1861–1865.* Albany, NY: Albany Publishing. Available at http://www.civilwarhome .com/foxspref.htm.

Freeman, Douglas. 1934. *R. E. Lee.* Vols. 3–4. New York: Scribner's.

Gallagher, Gary, ed. 1989. *Fighting for the Confederacy: The Personal Recollections of General Edward Porter Alexander.* Chapel Hill: Univ. of North Carolina Press.

Garvey, John. 2005. "Reverend Daniel Foster: The Fighting Chaplain of the Massachusetts 33rd." *Chester Historical Society* 4, no. 2 (Oct.). Available at http://www.chestermass.com/chester_historical-society/newsletter /2005_october.pdf.

General Griffin's Report of the Battle of Hatcher's Run. 2010. Available at http:// home.swbell.net/jcanders/eyewitness.htm.

"Gettysburg National Military Park." 2002. Available at http://www.bitsof blueandgray.com/july2002.htm.

Glatthaar, Joseph. 2008. *General Lee's Army: From Victory to Collapse.* New York: Free Press.

Goellnitz, Jennifer. 2010a. *Biography of A. P. Hill: A. P. Hill's Antebellum Years.* Available at http://www.aphillcsa.com/n3.html.

———. 2010b. *And Then A. P. Hill Came Up: Biography of General John Caldwell Calhoun Sanders.* Available at http://www.aphillcsa.com/sanders.html.

Golay, Michael. 1999. *A Ruined Land: The End of the Civil War.* New York: Wiley.

"Grand Review of the Armies, May 23–24, 1865." 1865. Available at http:// www.civilwarhome.com/grandreview.htm.

Grant, Ulysses. 1885. *The Personal Memoirs of Ulysses S. Grant.* Old Saybrook, CT: Konecky and Konecky.

Greene, A. Wilson. 2008. *The Final Battles of the Petersburg Campaign: Breaking the Backbone of the Rebellion.* 2nd ed. Knoxville: Univ. of Tennessee Press.

Griffin, John. 2004. *A Pictorial History of the Confederacy.* London: McFarland.

Hagadorn, Henry. 1930. "On the March with Sibley in 1863: The Diary of Private Henry J. Hagadorn." *North Dakota Historical Quarterly* 5: 103–29.

Hall, Yancey. 2010. "U.S. Civil War Prison Camps Claimed Thousands." Available at http://www.news.nationalgeographic.com/news/2003/07/07 01_030701_civilwarprisons.html.

Harmon, George, ed. 1927. "Letters of Luther Rice Mills—a Confederate Soldier." *North Carolina Historical Review* 4, no. 3 (July): 1–30.

Harris, Leslie. 2003. "The New York City Draft Riots." In *In the Shadow of Slavery: African Americans in New York City, 1626–1863,* 279–88. Chicago: Univ. of Chicago Press.

Harrison, Mrs. Burton. 1911. *Recollections Grave and Gay.* New York: Scribner's.

Harvey, Paul. 1998. "'Yankee Faith' and Southern Redemption: White Southern Baptist Ministers, 1850–1890." In *Religion and the American Civil War,* edited by Randall Miller, Harry Stout, and Charles Wilson, 187–207. New York: Oxford Press.

Heidler, David, and Jeanne Heidler. 2010. *Henry Clay: The Essential American.* New York: Random House.

Hershey Medical Center. 2010. "Neuralgia." In *Health and Disease Information.* Available at http://www.hmc.psu.edu/healthinfo/no/neuralgia .htm.

Hess, Earl. 2009. *In the Trenches at Petersburg: Field Fortifications and Confederate Defeat.* Chapel Hill: Univ. of North Carolina Press.

"Hinsdale Man, Family Lost in Clipper Crash." 1945. *Olean Times Herald,* Jan. 10.

"History of the Town of Allegany." 1893. In *Historical Gazetteer and Biographical Memorial of Cattaraugus Co., N.Y.,* edited by William Adams. Syracuse, NY: Lyman, Horton. Available at http://archive.org/details /historicalgazettooadam#page/n3/mode/2up.

Holt, David. 1995. *A Mississippi Rebel in the Army of Northern Virginia: The Civil War Memoirs of Private David Holt.* Edited by Thomas Cockrell and Michael Ballard. With editorial comments. Baton Rouge: Louisiana State Univ. Press.

Horigan, Michael. 2002. *Elmira: Death Camp of the North.* Mechanicsburg, PA: Stackpole Books.

Hyde, James. 1857. *The Chinese Sugar-cane: Its History, Mode of Culture.* Boston: John P. Jewett.

Hyde, W. L. 1866. *History of the One Hundred and Twelfth Regiment N. Y. Volunteers.* Fredonia, NY: W. McKinstry.

Jackman, John S. 1990. *Diary of a Confederate Soldier: John S. Jackman of the Orphan Brigade.* Edited by William C. Davis. Columbia: Univ. of South Carolina Press.

Jameson, J. Franklin, ed. 1900. *Calhoun Correspondence.* Vol. 2, part 1, of *Annual Report of the American Historical Association for the Year 1899.* Washington, DC: US Government Printing Office.

Jensen, Todd, John Underwood, and David Lewes. 2003. "Bone, Bottles, and Buttons, Oh My! Archaeological Analysis of a Civil War Feature from City Point, Virginia." Paper presented at the Middle Atlantic Archaeological Conference, Virginia Beach, VA, Mar. 15. Available at http://web .wm.edu/wmcar/hopewellarch/more.htm.

Johnson, Larry. 2006. "Baltimore & Ohio Railroad: The Union's Most Important Supply Line." *America's Civil War* (Mar.). Available at http:// www. historynet.com.

"Johnson's Island." 2011. Available at http://www.johnsonsisland.org/history/war.hta.

Jones, James. 1887. *Christ in the Camp or Religion in Lee's Army.* Richmond, VA: B. F. Johnson.

Jordan, David. 2001. *Happiness Is Not My Companion: The Life of General G. K. Warren.* Bloomington: Indiana Univ. Press.

Jortner, Adam. 2012. *The Gods of Prophetstown: The Battle of Tippecanoe and the Holy War for the American Frontier.* New York: Oxford Univ. Press.

Judson, Amos. [1865] 1986. *History of the Eighty-Third Regiment Pennsylvania Volunteers.* Erie, PA: B. F. H. Lynn. Reprint. Dayton, OH: Morningside Books.

Kammen, Carol. 2004. "The Many Names of Tompkins County." In *Place Names of Tompkins County,* edited by Carol Kammen, 8. Ithaca, NY: Office of the Tompkins County Historian. Available at http://www.tompkins-co.org/historian/PlaceNames/PlaceNamesofTC.pdf.

Karnes, Cynthia. 1999. "How to Make Iron-Gall Ink." In *Paper Conservation.* Rotterdam: Paper Conservation Department. Available at http://www.knaw.nl/ecpa/ink/make_ink_html.

Keegan, John. 2009. *The American Civil War: A Military History.* New York: Knopf.

King, Janet. 2010. "Civil War Medicine." In *Vermont in the Civil War.* Available at http://vermontcivilwar.org./medic/medicine2.php.

"The Kings Proclamation of October 7th 1763." [1892] 2012. In *American History Leaflets, Colonial and Constitutional,* edited by Albert B. Hart and Edward Channing, no. 5, Sept. New York: A. Lovell. Available at http://www.ushistory.org/declaration/related/proc63.htm.

Klein, Maury. 1997. *Days of Defiance: Sumter, Secession, and the Coming of the Civil War.* New York: Knopf.

Kleman, Marie. 2001. "Dr. James Trowbridge/Olive Sackett." In *Trowbridge/Sachett.* Available at http://genforum.genealogy.com/trowbridge/messages/525.htm.

Kreth, Melinda. 2010. *Silas Weir Mitchell (1829–1914) on His Rest Cure.* Available at http://www.chsbs.cmich.edu/Melinda_Kreth/Silas%20Weir%20Mitchell.pdf.

Lane, David. 1905. *A Soldier's Diary: The Story of a Volunteer.* Ann Arbor: Bentley Historical Library, Univ. of Michigan.

LeConte, Joseph. 1903. *The Autobiography of Joseph LeConte*. Edited by William Armes. New York: D. Appleton.

"Life in a Civil War Army Camp." 2010. In Civil War Society, *Encyclopedia of the Civil War*. Available at http://www.civilwarhome.com/camplife.htm.

Lincoln, Abraham. 1860. "Cooper Union Address." Feb. 27. Available at Abraham Lincoln Online, http://www.showcase.netins.net/creative/lincoln/speeches/cooper.htm.

———. [1861] 1939. "First Inaugural Address." Mar. 4, 1861. In *Abraham Lincoln: The War Years*, by Carl Sandburg, 1:125–35. New York: Harcourt, Brace and World.

Lockwood, Jeffrey. 2009. *Six-Legged Soldiers: Using Insects as Weapons of War*. New York: Oxford Univ. Press.

Lowe, David. 2010. *White Oak Road*. Available at http://www.american militaryhistorymsw.com/blog/529753-white-oak-road.

Lumbard, J. A., ed. 1868. "On the March." In *The History of Company G, 147th Pennsylvania Volunteer Infantry*, 30–32. Selinsgrove, PA: Synder County Tribune. Available at http://josephlumbard.tripod.com/jalumdiary.htr.

MacLean, Maggie. 2006. "Hetty Cary Pegram." On the Civil War Women Blog at http://www.civilwarwomenblog.com/2006/10/hetty-cary.html.

Maes, Christopher. 2010. *Lewis's Farm (Quaker Road)*. Available at http://www.beyondthecrater.com.

Manning, Chandra. 2007. *What This Cruel War Was Over*. New York: Knopf.

Marshall, Jesse, ed. 1917. *Private and Official Correspondence of General Benjamin Butler*. Vol. 5. Norwood, MA: Plimpton Press.

Martin, Samuel. 2001. *Southern Hero: Matthew Calbraith Butler*. Mechanicsburg, PA: Stackpole Books.

Maryniak, Benedict. 2003. "Union Military Chaplains." In *Faith in the Fight: Civil War Chaplains*, by John W. Brinsfield, William C. Davis, Benedict Maryniak, and James I. Robertson Jr., 3–50. Mechanicsburg, PA: Stackpole Books.

McCarthy, Carlton. 1882. *Detailed Minutiae of Soldier Life in the Army of Northern Virginia, 1861–1865*. Richmond, VA: Carlton McCarthy.

McGinley, Daniel. 1897. "Life in the Trenches." Transcribed from the *Port Washington Star*, Nov. 20, in *Ozaukee County's War History*. Available at http://rootsweb.ancentry.com/~wiozauke/warhistory/LifeinTrenches2html.

McKay, Cyrus. [1879] 2004. "Town of Allegany." Transcribed by Samantha Eastman. In *The History of Cattaraugus County, New York*. Available at http://www.paintedhills.org/CATTARAGUS/allegany1879Bios/Allegany1879Hist.htm.

McNamera, Robert. 2012. *History of the One Hundred and Eighty-Eight Regiment of New York Volunteer Infantry*. Available at http://www.caltim.com/188th.

McPherson, James. 1988. *Battle Cry of Freedom: The Civil War Era*. New York: Ballantine Books.

Mewborn, Horace. 2005. "Herding Yankee Cattle: The Beefsteak Raid, September 14–17, 1864." *Blue & Gray Magazine* 12, no. 3: 6–17, 44–50.

"The Military Tract of Central New York for the Area within Tompkins County." 2012. In *Revolutionary War Bounty Land*, coordinated by Janet Nash. Available at http://www.nytompki.org/bounty.htm.

Miller, Francis, and Robert Lanier. 1911. "Forts and Artillery." In *The Photographic History of the Civil War*, vol. 5, edited by O. E. Hunt, 103–218. New York: Patriot.

Mize, W. W. 2010. "Life during Confederate Days (Georgia)." Interview at Athens, GA, Oct. 3, 1939, for the Federal Writers' Project, *American Life Histories, 1936–1940*. Washington, DC: Library of Congress. Available at http://memory.loc.gov/learn///features/timeline/civilwar/southwar/hawkes.html.NYSA2012.

Moore, Albert. 1924. *Conscription and Conflict in the Confederacy*. New York: MacMillan.

Moore, John W. 1882. "Forty-First Regiment-Cavalry, Company B." In *Roster of North Carolina Troops in the War Between the States during the Years 1861–1865*, 3:150–53. Raleigh: Ashe and Gatling for the North Carolina General Assembly.

Nichols, G. W. 1898. *A Soldier's Story of His Regiment (61st Georgia) and Incidentally of the Lawton-Gordon-Evans Brigade, Army of Northern Virginia*. Jesup, GA: G. W. Nichols. Available through the Cornell Univ. Library at http://www.archives.org/details/cu31924030922383.

Nichols, James. 1886. *Perry's Saints or the Fighting Parson's Regiment in the War of the Rebellion*. Boston: D. Lothrop.

Noblin, Stuart. 1949. "Leonidas Lafayette Polk, Agrarian Crusader." PhD diss., Univ. of North Carolina, Chapel Hill.

Norris, David. 2009. *Life during the Civil War*. Niagara Falls, NY: Moorshead Magazines.

"Notes on Wellmaker, William Washington." 2010. Available at http://gen forum.geneology.com/wellmaker/messsages/53.html.

"Organization of the Confederate States of America." 1904. *Journal of the Congress of the Confederate States of America* 1 (1861–1865). First Session, Feb. 4, Mar. 16, 1861. Reprint. Washington, DC: US Government Printing Office.

Owsley, Frank. 1925. *States Rights in the Confederacy.* Chicago: Univ. of Chicago Press.

Paris, John. 1864. "A Sermon: Preached before Brig. Gen. Hoke's Brigade, at Kinston, N.C., on the 28th of February, 1864, by Rev. John Paris, Chaplain Fifty Fourth Regiment N.C. Troops, upon the Death of Twenty Two Men, Who Had Been Executed in the Presence of the Brigade for the Crime of Desertion." Academic Affairs Library, Univ. of North Carolina, Chapel Hill. Available at http://thomaslegion.net/54thnorthcarolina infantryregiment.html.

Peck, Rufus H. 1913. *Reminiscences of a Confederate Soldier of Company C, 2nd Virginia Cavalry.* Fincastle, VA: n.p. Available through the New York Public Library Archives at http://www.archive.org/details/reminiscences ofcoopeck.

Pember, Phoebe Y. [1879] 2002. *A Southern Woman's Story.* Reprint. Columbia: Univ. of South Carolina Press.

Pennington, James. 2010. "The Position and Duties of the Colored People." In *Preaching with Sacred Fire: An Anthology of African American Sermons, 1750 to Present*, edited by Martha Simmons and Frank Thomas, 189–92. New York: W. W. Norton.

Phisterer, Frederick. 1890. *New York in the War of the Rebellion.* Vol. 1. 2nd ed. Albany, NY: Weed, Parsons.

Porter, G. W. D. [1878] 2009. "Nine Months in a Northern Prison." Edited by Edwin Drake. *Annals of the Army of Tennessee* (July). Available at http://www.tennessee-scv.org/4455/index/htm.

"The Potomac Flotilla: Farwell Order of Commander Parker." 1864. *New York Times*, Aug. 2. Available at http://www.nytimes.com/1865/08/06 /news/the-flotilla-farewell-order-of-commander-parker.html.

Potter, William. 2005. "*Christ in the Camp.*" Book review, Book Blog, the Vision Forum, Inc. Posted Nov. 8 at http://www.visionforum.com/hot topics/blogs/books/2005/11/2385.aspx.

Powell, Kimberly. 2012. "Bounty Land Warrants." at http://genealogy.about .com/od/records/p/bounty_land.htm.

Powell, William. [1896] 2010. *The Fifth Army Corps (Army of the Potomac): A Record of Operations during the Civil War in the United States of America, 1861–1865.* New York: G. P. Putnam's Sons. Reprint. Memphis: General Books.

Power, J. Tracy. 1998. *Lee's Miserables: Life in the Army of Northern Virginia from the Wilderness to Appomattox.* Chapel Hill: Univ. of North Carolina Press.

"Proclamation of 1763—October 7, 1763." 2012. In *Revolutionary War and Beyond.* Available at http://www.revolutionary-war-and-beyond.com /proclamation-of-1763.html.

"The Proposed Dinner to General Lee's Army Postponed to New Year's Day." 1864. *Richmond Examiner,* Dec. 22.

Pyne, Henry. 1871. *The History of the First New Jersey Cavalry (Sixteenth Regiment, New Jersey Volunteers).* Trenton, NJ: J. A. Beecher.

Reese, Deborah. 2010. "James Reese, Elmira Prison." In *American Civil War.* Available at http://www.factasy.com/civil_war/2009/06/20/james _reese_elmira_prison.

"The Removal of General McClellan." 1864. *Harper's Weekly,* Nov. 19.

"Reported Bread Riot at Richmond." 1863. *Harper's Weekly,* Apr. 18.

Revised Statutes of the United States (passed 43rd Cong., 1st sess.). 1875. Washington, DC: US Government Printing Office.

Rhea, Gordon. 1994. *The Battle of the Wilderness, May 5–6, 1864.* Baton Rouge: Louisiana State Univ. Press.

Rhodes, John. 1894. *The History of Battery B, First Regiment Rhode Island Light Artillery in the War to Preserve the Union, 1861–1865.* Providence, RI: Snow and Farnham.

———. 1917. *History of the Civil War.* New York: MacMillan.

Roberts, Giselle. 2003. *The Confederate Belle.* Columbia: Univ. of Missouri Press.

Robertson, James, Jr. 1962. "The Scourge of Elmira." In *Civil War Prisons: A Study in War Psychology,* edited by William Hesseltine, 80–98. Kent, Ohio: Kent State Univ. Press.

Rogers, William. 1865. "189th Regiment of the Civil War Company C." Available at NYGenWeb, http://www.rootsweb.ancestry.com/~nysteube /189/189-c.html.

Roth, David, ed. 1989. "Andersonville: The Story of an American Tragedy," *Blue & Gray* 3, no. 3: 22–37.

Rutkow, Ira. 2005. *Bleeding Blue and Gray: Civil War Surgery and the Evolution of American Medicine*. New York: Random House.

Selkreg, J. H. [1927] 2012. "Landmarks of Tompkins County." In *The History of New York State*, edited by James Sullivan, book 7, chap. 7. New York: Lewis Historical.

Sandburg, Carl. 1939. *Abraham Lincoln: The War Years*. 4 vols. New York: Harcourt, Brace and World.

Seymour, Kevin. 2010. "North Carolina Guards, 27th North Carolina, Company C." Available at http://www.angelfire.com/nc/twsj/page4.html.

Simmons, Martha, and Frank Thomas. 2010. Introduction to James William Charles Pennington, "The Position and Duties of the Colored People." In *Preaching with Sacred Fire: An Anthology of African American Sermons, 1750 to the Present*, edited by Martha Simmons and Frank Thomas, 189–92. New York: W. W. Norton.

"Special Schedule: Surviving Soldiers, Sailors, and Marines, and Widows, etc." 1890. In "Allegany, N.Y.," *Eleventh Census (1890) of the United States*, 3. Washington, DC: US Government Printing Office.

Spencer, Cornelia. [1866] 1993. *The Last Ninety Days of the War in North Carolina*. New York: Watchman. Reprint. Wilmington, NC: Broadfoot.

Stanley, John. [1787] 1977. "How Firm a Foundation." In *Christian Hymns, Evangelical Movement of Wales*, 574. Oxford, UK: Oxford Univ. Press.

Stewart, Alexander. 1865. *Camp, March, and Battle-field; or, Three Years and a Half with the Army of the Potomac*. Philadelphia: Jas. B. Rogers.

Stover, John. 1999. *History of the Baltimore and Ohio Railroad*. West Lafayette, IN: Purdue Univ. Press.

Strode, Hudson. 1964. *Jefferson Davis, Tragic Hero: The Last Twenty-Five Years, 1864–1889*. New York: Harcourt, Brace and World.

Strong, Robert. 1961. *A Yankee Private's Civil War*. Edited by Ashley Halsey. Chicago: Regnery.

Stuckenberg, John. 1995. *I'm Surrounded by Methodists: Diary of John H. W. Stuckenberg, Chaplain of the 145th Pennsylvania Volunteer Infantry*. Edited by David Hedrick and Gordon Davis Jr. Gettysburg, PA: Thomas.

Swanton, John. 2003. *The Indian Tribes of North America*. Washington Bulletin. Washington, DC: Bureau of American Ethnology, Smithsonian Institute.

Tax History Project, Tax History Museum. 2010. *1861–1865: The Civil War*. Available at http://www. taxhistory.org.

Taylor, Raleigh. 1939. "Twelve Thousand in for a Sixty-Mile Railroad: The Capture of the Petersburg and Weldon Line in 1864." *Regional Review* 3, no. 3 (Sept.). Available at http://www.nps.gov/history/online_books /regional_review/vol13-3e.htm.

Theaker, James. 1974. *Through One Man's Eyes: The Civil War Experiences of a Belmont County Volunteer.* Edited by Paul Rieger. Mt. Vernon: Ohio Printing Arts Press.

Thompson, Holland. 1912. "Exchange of Prisoners." In *Prisons and Hospitals,* vol. 7 of *The Photographic History of the Civil War in 10 Volumes,* edited by Francis Miller and Robert Lanier. Available at http://localhistory .morrisville.edu/sites/miller.html.

Titone, Nora. 2010. *My Thoughts Be Bloody: The Bitter Rivalry Between Edwin and John Wilkes Booth That Led to an American Tragedy.* New York: Free Press.

Trinque, Bruce. 2010. *Battle of Boydton Plank Road: Major General Winfield Scott Hancock Strikes the Southside Railroad.* Available at http://www .historynet.com/battle-of-Boydton-plank-road-major-general-winfield -scott-hancock-strikes-the-southside-railroad.htm.

Trulock, Alice Rains. 1992. *In the Hands of Providence: Joshua L. Chamberlain & the Civil War.* Chapel Hill: Univ. of North Carolina Press.

"Two Inaugurations—Two Republics—Two Presidents." 1861. *Philadelphia Morning Pennsylvanian,* Feb. 18.

Under the Maltese Cross, Antietam to Appomattox: The Loyal Uprising in Western Pennsylvania, 1861–1865. 1910. Pittsburgh: 155th Regimental Association.

US National Park Service. 2010a. "Appomattox Plantation." At http://www .nps.gov/pete/historyculture/appomattox-plantation.htm.

———. 2010b. "Fort Foote Park, History and Culture." At http://www.nps .gov/fofo/historyculture/index.htr.

———. 2010c. "Poplar Grove National Cemetery." Available at http://www .nps.gov/archive/pete/mahan/eduhistory.html.

US Surgeon-General's Office. 1870. *Medical and Surgical History of the War of the Rebellion, 1861–1865.* Vols. 1 and 3. Washington, DC: US Government Printing Office.

"The Virginia Campaign" 1864. *Harper's Weekly,* Nov. 19.

Wainwright, Charles. 1962. *A Diary of Battle: The Personal Journals of Colonel Charles S. Wainwright, 1861–1865.* Edited by Allan Nevins. New York: Harcourt.

Walker, Francis. 1884. "Reams' Station." *Papers of the Military Historical Society of Massachusetts* 5: 267–305. Available at http://www.beyondthecrater .com/siegeofpetersburg-resources/mhsm-papers/mhsm-vol-05/reams -station-walker.

———. 1887. *A History of the Second Army Corps in the Army of the Potomac.* New York: Scribner's.

Walsh, George. 2002. *"Damage Them All You Can": Robert E. Lee's Army of Northern Virginia.* New York: Tom Doherty Associates.

Walther, Eric. 1992. *The Fire-Eaters.* Baton Rouge: Louisiana State Univ. Press.

Ward, Geoffrey. 1990. *The Civil War: An Illustrated History.* New York: Knopf.

"The War for Southern Independence in South Carolina." 2010. In *26th Infantry Regiment.* Available at http://www.researchonline.net/sccw/unit 159.htm.

"Warren's Great Raid." 1864. *New York Times,* Dec. 25.

Wiley, Bell. 1943. *The Life of Johnny Reb.* Indianapolis, IN: Bobbs-Merrill.

———. 1951. *The Life of Billy Yank.* Indianapolis, IN: Bobbs-Merrill.

Williams, Michael. 2011. "Bullets vs. Bricks in Baltimore." *Civil War Times* 49, no. 5: 34–41.

Woodward, Evan. 1884. *History of the One Hundred and Ninety-Eighth Pennsylvania Volunteers.* Trenton, NJ: MacCrellish & Quigley. Available at http://www.family2remember.com/198th/198history.htm.

Woodworth, Steven. 2001. *While God Is Marching On: The Religious World of Civil War Soldiers.* Lawrence: Univ. Press of Kansas.

Wray-Welsh, Teresa. 2012. "Organizers Prepare for Civil War Living History Event in Emporia, April 6–7." *VaNcNews,* Feb. 7. Available at http://www .vancnews.com/independent_messenger_d9506902-51ae-11e1-81fa-00 19bb2963f4.htm.

Writer's Project. 2010. *Sussex County: A Tale of Three Centuries, Part I, 1607–1864.* American Guide Series. Available at http://www.natanielturner.com /sussexcountyataleofthreecenturies.htm.

Zinnen, Robert, Jr. 1991. "City Point: The Tool That Gave General Grant Victory." *Quartermaster Professional Bulletin* (Spring). Available at http:// www.qmfound.com/citypt.htm.

Index

Italic page numbers denote illustrations and tables.